Clive Phillipps-Wolley

Sport in the Crimea and Caucasus

Clive Phillipps-Wolley

Sport in the Crimea and Caucasus

ISBN/EAN: 9783742899156

Manufactured in Europe, USA, Canada, Australia, Japa

Cover: Foto ©ninafisch / pixelio.de

Manufactured and distributed by brebook publishing software
(www.brebook.com)

Clive Phillipps-Wolley

Sport in the Crimea and Caucasus

SPORT

IN THE

CRIMEA AND CAUCASUS

SPORT

IN

THE CRIMEA AND CAUCASUS

BY

CLIVE PHILLIPPS-WOLLEY, F.R.G.S.

LATE BRITISH VICE-CONSUL AT KERTCH

LONDON

RICHARD BENTLEY & SON, NEW BURLINGTON STREET

Publishers in Ordinary to Her Majesty the Queen

1881

CONTENTS.

CHAPTER I.

SPORT IN THE CRIMEA.

CHAPTER II.

CRASNOI LAIS.

CHAPTER III.

ODESSA AND MISKITCHEE.

CHAPTER IV.

THE RED FOREST AND BLACK SEA COAST.

CHAPTER V.

REIMAN'S DATCH.

CHAPTER VI.

GOLOVINSKY.

CHAPTER VII.

DENSE COVERTS.

CHAPTER VIII.

HUNTING WITH DOGS.

CHAPTER IX.

RETURN TO KERTCH.

CHAPTER X.

TIFLIS.

CHAPTER XI.

EN ROUTE FOR DAGHESTAN.

CHAPTER XII.

THE LESGHIAN MOUNTAINS.

CHAPTER XIII.

FROM GOKTCHAI TO LENKORAN.

CHAPTER XIV.

SHORES OF THE CASPIAN.—RETURN TO TIFLIS.

CHAPTER XV.

THE RAINS.

A verst is equal to three-quarters of an English mile.

SPORT IN THE CRIMEA AND THE CAUCASUS.

CHAPTER I.

SPORT IN THE CRIMEA.

Outfit — The droshky—A merry party — The Straits of Kertch— The steppe—Wild-fowl—Crops—The Malos—The 'Starrie Metchat '—Game— Tscherkess greyhounds — Stalking bustards—A picnic—Night on the steppe.

SCARCELY a week's journey from London, with delicious climates and any quantity of game, it always seemed a marvel to me how few English sportsmen ever found their way to the Crimea or Caucasus. It is now something more than five years ago since I first made myself acquainted with the breezy rosemary-clad steppes of the former, or the low wooded hills on the Black Sea coast of the latter. For nearly three years resident at Kertch, I had ample opportunity of testing all the pleasures of the steppe, and a better shooting-ground for the wildfowler or man who likes a lot of hard work, with a plentiful and varied bag at the end of his day, could nowhere be found. Of course the sportsman in the Crimea must rough it to a certain extent, but his roughing it, if he only has a civil tongue and cheery manner, will be a good deal of the 'beer and beefsteak' order. The Russians are hospitable to all men, especially to the sportsman; and the peasants, even the Tartars, are cordial good fellows if taken the right way.

On the steppes you need rarely want for a roof overhead, if you prefer stuffiness, smoke, and domestic insects to wild ones, with dew and the night air. If you can put up with sour cream (very good food when you are used to it), black bread, an arboose, fresh or half-pickled, with a bumper of fearful unsweetened gin (vodka) to digest the foregoing, you need never suffer hunger long. But for the most part sportsmen take their food with them. Perhaps if my readers will let me, it would be better to take them at once on to the steppe, and tell them all this *en route*.

Imagine then that for the last two days you have been hard at work out of office hours loading cartridges with every variety of shot, from the small bullets used for the bustard down to the dust-shot for the quail. Here, in Kertch, take a victim's advice: make your own cartridges, don't buy them. The month is July; the first of July, with an intensely blue sky, far away above you, giving you an idea of distance and immensity that you could never conceive in England, where the clouds always look as if they would knock your hat off. I should have said the sky will be blue by-and-by, for at present it is too dark to see, and we are carefully tucked away in bed; the impedimenta of the coming journey—cold meats, flasks of shooting powder, and jumping powder; bread, guns, and a huge string of unsavoury onions—all on the floor beside us. Ding, ding, ding! as if the door-bell were in a fit, then a crash and silence. No one ever rang a door-bell as a Russian droshky-driver rings it. He likes the muscular exertion, he loves the noise, and doesn't in the least mind being sworn at if, as in the present instance, he breaks the bell-wire. A year in Russia has hardened us to all this, so merely speculating as to whether our landlord will pay more for broken bell-wires this half than last, we bundle out of bed and submit meekly to the reproaches of our friends outside on the cart. They, poor fellows, have had half an hour's less sleep than we have, and it's only 4 A.M. now, so any little hastiness of speech may be forgiven them.

But on such a morning as this, and on such a conveyance as our droshky, no one could remain sleepy or sulky long. The brisk bright air makes the blood race through your veins, and the terrible bumpings of the droshky on the uneven track, or half-paved streets, keep you fully employed in striving to avoid a spill or a fractured limb. Anything more frightful to a novice in Russia than the droshky I cannot conceive. This instrument of torture is a combination of untrimmed logs and ropes and wheels, with cruelly insinuating iron bands, merciless knots, and ubiquitous splinters. Manage your seat how you will, you are bound to keep bumping up and down, and at each descent you land on something more painful than that you have encountered before.

In spite of all this, as the droshky leaves the town, the old German jäger breaks out into a hunting ditty, and, truth to tell, until the wind is fairly jogged out of us we are a very noisy party. Then we try to light our cigarettes and pipes, and if we are lucky, only have the hot ashes jerked on to our next neighbour's knee. Gradually the dawning light increases, the clouds of pearly grey are reddening, and the long undulating swell of the steppeland slowly unfolds itself around us. On our left are the Straits of Kertch, the sea looking still and hazy, with some half-dozen English steamers lording it amongst the mosquito fleet of fruiterers and lighters which fills the bay. All round us are chains of those small hills, whose dome-like tops proclaim them tumuli of kings and chiefs who went to rest ages ago, when the town behind us was still a mighty city, rejoicing in the name of Panticapæum.

Once clear of the ranges of tumuli or kourgans, as they call them here, there is nothing but steppe. On all points, except the seaside of the view, a treeless prairie; no hills, no houses, scarcely even a bush to break the monotony of bare or weed-grown waste. On the right of the post-road by which we are travelling (a mere beaten track and really no road at all) run the lines of the Indo-European Telegraph Company, their neat slim posts of iron contrasting not unfavourably with the crooked, misshapen posts which support the Russian lines on our left. Unimportant as these might appear elsewhere, they are important objects here, where they are the only landmarks to man, and the only substitute for trees to the fowl of the air.

All along the road on either side of us the wires are now becoming lined with kestrels, just up evidently, and looking as though they were giving themselves a shake, and rubbing their eyes preparatory to a day's sport amongst the beetles and field-mice that swarm on the steppe. The number of kestrels round Kertch is something astonishing, and I almost think that with the other hawks, the blue hen harrier, kites and crows, they would almost outnumber the sparrows of the town. Now, too, our lovely summer visitants, the golden-throated bee-eaters, begin to shoot and poise swallow-like over the heads of the tall yellow hollyhock growing in wild profusion over the plain; hoopoes, with broad crests erect, peck and strut bantam-like by the roadside, while every now and again the magnificent azure wings of the 'roller' glitter in the morning sun among the flowers.

The 'bleak steppeland' is what you always hear of, and shudder as you hear, dread Siberian visions being conjured up at the mere name. But who that has seen the steppes in the later days of spring, or in the glow of midsummer, would apply such an epithet to lands that in their season are as richly clad in flowers as any prairie of the West? Long strips of wild tulip, Nature's cloth of gold, blue cornflower, crow's-foot and bird's-eye, the canary-coloured hollyhock and crimson wild pea, all vie in compensating the steppeland for her chill snow-shroud in the months that are gone and to come.

Rich as the land is, the crops by the roadside are few and paltry, the chief being rye, maize, millet, and sunflowers. The sunflowers are cultivated for their seed, which is either used for making oil, or more generally is sold in a dry state as 'cernitchkies.' 'Cernitchkies' furnish the Malo Russ, male and female, with one of their most favourite means of wasting time. Go where you will, at any time, in Kertch, you will find people cracking these sunflower seeds, and trying to make two bites of the kernel. At every street corner you find a stall where they are sold, and you rarely come in without finding one of the little grey shards clinging to your dress, spat upon you by some careless passer-by, or sent adrift from some balcony overhead.

Beside these crops, you come across long strips of water melons, the principal food of the Malo Russ in the summer, and one of the chief sources of the Asiatic cholera sometimes so prevalent here. But for the most part the land is untilled—left to its wild-flowers and weeds.

The peasant of the Crimea makes but a sorry agriculturist. The Malo Russ is a lazy, good-natured ne'er-do-weel ; his days being more than half 'prasniks' (saints' days), he devotes the holy half to getting drunk on vodka, the other half to recovering from the effects of the day before. One day you may see him in long boots and a red shirt, with his arms round another big-bearded moujik's neck in the drinking den, or husband and wife, on the broad of their backs, dead drunk, on the highway. The day after you'll find him in a moralizing mood, seated on his doorstep, smoking the eternal papiros, or nibbling sunflower seeds.

Russians have told me that there are more holy days than calendar days in the year. To be holy a day need not be a saint's day—a birthday in the Emperor's family is quite enough to make a 'prasnik.' Of the actual Church fêtes there are 128.

The best agriculturists here are the German colonists, whose neat homesteads remind one for the moment of lands nearer home. Even the Tartars are better than the Malo Russ, but they have lately been leaving the Crimea in large numbers to escape the compulsory military service which Russia seeks to impose upon them. Everywhere the army seems to be the worst enemy of the State.

At last our ride comes to an end, and there is a general stretching of limbs and buckling on of shot-belts and powder-flasks, for with many muzzle-loaders are still the fashion here. The place at which we have stopped is the ' Starrie Metchat,' or old church, a Tartar ruin near a well, embosomed in rosemary-covered hills. Near this well we pitch our tents, and then we each go off on a beat of our own. Here there is room enough for all, and as some excellent Russian sportsmen have a careless way of shooting through their friends' legs at a bolting hare, perhaps solitude has its peculiar advantages.

As you breast the first hill the sweet-scented covert comes nearly up to your waist, and right and left of you huge grasshoppers jump away or into your face with a vicious snap that is at first enough to upset the best regulated nerves. But see, your dog is pointing, and as you near him a large covey of grey birds, larger than our grouse, get up with whistling wings, and with smooth undulating flight skim round the corner of the next hill. You get one long shot and bag your bird perhaps. The dog moves uncertainly forward, and then stands again. Go up to him; wherever strepita (lesser bustard) have been you are sure to find a hare or two close by. Time after time have I found this, although I cannot account for the fact in any way. The hares here are larger than our English hares, and in winter turn almost white, the skins in autumn having sometimes most beautiful shades of silver and rose upon them. The largest hare I ever remember to have seen weighed nearly thirteen pounds—it was an old buck—while in England a hare of eight pounds is exceptionally large.

The dogs used in the Crimea for coursing are called Tscherkess greyhounds; they stand considerably higher at the shoulder than our own dogs, are broken-haired, with a much longer coat than our staghound, and a feathered stern. I am told that on the flat the English greyhound beats them for a short distance; but that in the hills, or with a strong old hare well on her legs before them, the Crimean dogs have it all their own way. I never had the good fortune to see the two breeds tried together. In fact, what coursing I did see was utterly spoilt by the Russian habit of cutting off the hare, and shooting her under the dog's nose. This is, of course, utterly alien to our notions of sport—but so are most of their sporting habits. They never shoot flying if they can get a chance sitting. Bears and boars and such large game they shoot from platforms in trees at night ; and I never saw a horse jump in all my three years in Southern Russia. Of course, what applies to the Crimea and the Caucasus may not apply to other parts of Russia.

As long as we keep in the rosemary, hares, quails, and strepita are all we are likely to meet with, except that in the valley and on the less sunny hillsides the dogs ever and anon flush large owls, that sail away hardly as bewildered as they are generally supposed to be by the sunlight. Overhead kites and harriers swim about in the clear sky, keeping a keen look-out for winged quails or wounded hares. But as we get to the top of the next rising ground we see in the plain far away at our feet a long line of what might well be grey-coated infantry. A closer inspection, or a previous acquaintance with the objects before us, will enable us to make them out to be bustards feeding line upon line in a flock—or herd, to speak correctly —of several hundreds. Most of them are busy with their heads on the ground, gleaning what they can from an old maize field ; but here and there, at a slight distance from the rest, stands a sentry that the most wary stalker cannot baffle, or the most alluring grain tempt from his ceaseless watch.

Knowing that we are already seen, and being perfectly well aware that by ordinary stalking on these open plains we could never get nearer than three hundred yards from the herd before the old sentinel sets them all in motion with his shrill call, we retrace our steps, and get our comrades together. Then the horses are put to, and all with our guns in readiness we drive towards the point at which the bustards were seen. When within sight of them we make arrangements among ourselves, and then the drosky is driven quietly past the bustards some five hundred yards from them. All their heads are up, and the whole of the herd of two hundred is watching us intently; but they know something of the range of a gun, and feel safe enough to stay yet awhile. Watch hard as you may, grey birds, you didn't notice that one of the occupants of the droshky has just rolled off, gun in hand, and is now lying flat buried in a deliciously fragrant bed of rosemary. One by one, as the droshky circles round the watchful birds, the occupants drop off and lie still, until at last we have a cordon of sportsmen drawn right round the herd, and only the yemstchik remains on the droshky. Slowly, so as not to frighten them, he narrows his circle, while each hidden gunner keeps his eye anxiously on his movements.

At last, having stretched their necks to the very utmost limit and twisted them into gyrations that would surprise a corkscrew, the bustards think they have had enough of it, and there is a slow flapping of wings, and hoisting of the heavy bodies into air. Slowly, with a grand solemn flight, wonderfully in keeping with the wild majesty of the boundless plains on which they live, they sail away towards the hills. Suddenly the leaders stop with a jerk, and try too late to change their direction. From the covert beneath the sportsman starts to his feet, two bright flashes are seen, two reports follow, one huge bird collapses at once and another lowers for a moment, and then goes feebly on to fall at the first discharge of the next hidden gun. Right and left the remainder fly, rising somewhat as they do so, but still not high enough to take them out of danger, and when at last they have passed the fatal circle, five fine birds reward our stratagem.

One of us has to face a storm of chaff hard for a disappointed sportsman to bear, for in his excitement he had neglected to change his cartridges ; and although standing within short pistol-shot of a passing monster, the quail-shot produces nothing more than a shower of feathers, enough almost to stuff a bolster with.

By thus surrounding them, and by shooting them occasionally from a cart, a few of these magnificent birds (larger than a turkey and finer eating) are killed from time to time throughout summer and autumn. A few too are sometimes picked up by the gunner in the early summer whilst still young, as they hide separately or in small coveys in the deep undergrowth. But the only time when any quantity are exposed in the bazaar for sale is in the depths of winter. Then when a snowstorm has caught the birds hiding in the valleys, and clogged their wings with snow, which a bitter wind still more surely binds about them, these poor denizens of the desert are surrounded and driven like a flock of sheep into the Tartar villages, where they are butchered, and thence sent in cartloads into Kertch, to be sold at a rouble and a half (3s. 6d.) apiece.

After slaying the bustards, having done enough for glory, we have time to remember a thirst that would empty a samovar and an appetite that would astonish a negro. Gladly we hurry back to our little tent in a cleft at the foot of the hills, and while one unpacks the cold meats, dried sturgeon and caviare, another gets water for that tea without which our repast would be poor indeed to a Russian. Being born and bred Englishmen, two of us might well have been expected to prefer our native beer to tea, but it is wonderful how fond men get of the delicious tea brewed in Russia, with its slip of lemon in it to add piquancy to the flavour. For my own part, after really severe exertion I am most thoroughly convinced it is by far the best restorative you can take, and one which I should prefer to any other liquid whatever. Try as you will you can neither get nor make such tea in England, and once away from Russia, you must be content to leave the blessings of tea, ' swejie ikra ' (fresh caviare), and the soothing papiros (cigarette) behind you ; for numerous as tobacconists are in England, I know none where really good cigarette tobacco can be bought, such as you smoke in the Crimea.

Meanwhile, as we are still here, let us lie on our backs and enjoy the delicious weed, watching the yemstchik arrange that wonderful puzzle of old cord which constitutes the harness of a troika. At last the horses are ready, and depositing ourselves and game on the jolting vehicle, we let our legs swing over the side, and if used to the motion manage to get a great deal of pleasure out of the drive home.

As the evening closes in over these wild waste lands, a stillness and peace seem to come with it of which one has no knowledge in the towns. The piping of the quails, the long soft wail of the coolik (curlew), and even the notes of the German hunting horn on the other droshky far in front, all seem to make fitting music for the hour and scene ; and as the stars begin to shine out from a sky of infinite depth and metallic blueness, the oojai domoi (home already) is spoken not without an accent of regret, though limbs are tired and steppe roads rough.

CHAPTER II.

CRASNOI LAIS.

A frozen sea—Swarms of wild-fowl—The Indo-European telegraph—
Sledging on the Azov—A desolate scene—Taman—Journey in-
land — Tumerūk—Hotels—A dangerous sleep—Foxes—Wolves
—A hasty retreat—Ekaterinodar—Supper in the forest of Crasnoi
Lais—An exciting night's sport—Driving the forest — Cossack
beaters—Wild deer—Other game—The bag—Rations of vodka—
A Cossack orgy—Vulpine sagacity —Wolf stories—Return to
Kertch.

It was in February of 1876 that I first made
acquaintance with the Caucasus. Once or twice
before then it is true that I had crossed over to
Taman and had a day's pheasant-shooting on the
reedy shores of the Kuban. As we poled our flat-
bottomed boat along its sluggish waters, I had a
glimpse every now and again of the track of boar
or cazeole (roe), that made me long for a chance of
a longer stay on its banks. But it was not until
the February of 1876 that my wish was granted.
For weeks we had had all business stopped by the
frost. The whole of the Azov was frozen as hard
as the high-road, and it was only beyond the forts
and well into the Black Sea that any open water
could be found. Here the wild-fowl swarmed.

Along the edge of the ice, where the open water began, lines of cormorants stood solemn and patient, fringing the ice with a black border of upright forms for miles. Beyond these in the open water were myriads of crested duck (anas fuligula), golden-eye pochards, scaups, and whistlers. Here and there in bevies, with hoods extended, the great grebes sailed about, while great northern divers and rosy-breasted mergansers all added their quota to the beauty of the scene. More beautiful than all others, groups of smews, with their plumage of delicately pencilled snow, ducked and curtsied on the swelling wave, while overhead the pintail whistled by, the large fish-hawks poised in air, and the gulls laughed and chattered perpetually.

For the last few weeks most of my time had been spent among the wild-fowl or skating with the fair ladies of Kertch on the rink by the jetty. But one fine morning the lines of the Indo-European Telegraph Company between Taman and Ekaterinodar were good enough to break down, and my friend the chief of the Kertch station was ordered to make an inspection of them along their whole length from one point to another. It seemed to him a long and wearisome journey to make by himself, so that like a good man and considerate, he asked me to share his sledge with him. Always glad to give me a chance of enjoying myself in my own way, my kind old chief readily agreed to the arrangement, and within an hour from the time when K. first proposed the trip, he and I were hard at work in the bazaar purchasing stores for the journey. There is of course a post-road from Taman to Ekaterinodar, but badly indeed will those fare who trust to the resources of a Russian post station for their bodily comfort. This we well knew, and in consequence a large stock of German sausages, caviare, vodki, and other portable eatables and drinkables were stowed away in the body of our sledge.

For many days previous to the time of which I write, the over-sea route from Yenikale to Taman had been open to carts and sledges, while vans, laden with corn, had been continually crossing with only an aggregate of two accidents in the last four days. It was then with but few misgivings that we embarked in our sledge with a really good 'troika' (team of three) in front, coached by the noisiest rascal of a yemstchik that ever swore at horses. Our road for the first twenty-two versts lay over the bosom of the Azov, and as we passed through regular streets of mosquito shipping, and now and then under the hull of some big steamer caught in the ice, the sensation was strangely novel. For the first ten versts the road was good, the pace exhilarating, and buried in our warm rugs we hugged to ourselves the conviction that we were in for a really good thing.

After this, however, we got to piled and broken ice, where the accidents of the last four days had occurred, and where our driver averred a current existed. Here my friend got nervous, and insisted on walking at a fair distance from the sledge, which proceeded meanwhile at a foot's pace. This in the increasing frost mist was not so cheerful, but the current was soon cleared, and in another half hour we landed safe and sound at that miserable little town of Taman.

The only living things we had passed on our way were several wretched assemblies of pale-looking gulls, literally frozen out, poor fellows, and a few huge eagles, squatting on the ice, their plumes all ruffled up, suffering probably as much from a surfeit of wounded ducks as from cold. The whole scene as we crossed was as desolate as the mind can well imagine ; Kertch behind us, white with snow, clustering round the hill of Mithridates, a mere skeleton of her former glory in the days of Greek and Persian ; Taman, once too a prosperous city, now a few hovels buried in a snowdrift ; Yenikale perhaps more dead than either ; and all round the long low hills, the rounded tumuli of dead kings ; the tall bare masts of the belated ships ; a frozen sea beneath and a freezing sky above.

Once in Taman we gave our driver a good tip (' na tchai ') for the tea as they call it, and betook ourselves to a friend's house for a few minutes' rest before our next start. Why a yemstchik's fee, which is invariably spent in nips of vodka (unsweetened gin) should be called tea-money, has always appeared to me an unanswerable enigma. Taman hardly deserves a description, even from so humble a pen as mine. It has a jetty and a telegraph station ; is the post from which a few cattle are shipped to Kertch, and to which a few travellers to the Caucasus come from the same place. Once it was a large and flourishing city, twin sister to Panticapæum (Kertch) on the other side of the straits ; now it is a collection of miserable hovels, surrounded by mud knee-deep in winter and storms of dust in summer, with an odour of fish and the vodka shop in all seasons. There are near to Taman some large oil-works, from which naphtha is said to be extracted in large quantities. It may be so, but I hear that their original owner is bankrupt, and he was a Russian ; so that as the present proprietors are Americans, and as such less likely to be able to protect themselves from local frauds, I should not feel inclined to invest my bottom dollar in the Taman Oil Company.

Such a wretched place did we find Taman, that we were glad to leave it and commence our journey inland at once. In describing a journey the traveller as a rule looks to the scenery to supply at least a very large portion of his description ; what then shall the luckless traveller do, who has literally no scenery to describe? The road is a beaten track by the telegraph posts, with, every sixteen or twenty versts, a white house with a straw yard and some sheds at the back, and a black and white post with a bell roofed in on the top of it in the front. This is the post station. The country surrounding it is apparently waste, and, except for a few flocks of sheep, an old hooded crow or two, and maybe a bustard, quite untenanted by living things. Always the snow beneath and the jingling bells in front, and this with no incident to rouse one, naturally ends in sleep.

Towards evening we came in sight of a larger group of buildings than any we had hitherto seen, and this we found was Tumerŭk, our resting-place for the night. As far as we could see it was a larger town than Taman, with the inevitable green-domed church, a good spacious bazaar, barracks I think, and a neat little club-house. We were told that Tumerŭk derived its wealth from the sturgeon fishery carried on to a very great extent in its neighbourhood. We were also told there were two good hotels in the place, and set off in high spirits to search for them, a comfortable bed to follow a good supper of sturgeon and caviare being things as welcome as they were unexpected. We searched diligently and found the first hotel, a moujik's drinking den or ' cabak.' There was a table with a man under it, and many more nearly ready to follow his peaceful example, but no beds and no supper. At last we found the grand hotel, a gaunt white house near the bazaar. With doubting hearts (for the place looked deserted) we beat at the little door, but got no response. After nearly ten minutes spent in mutilating our knuckles and damaging the door, a fellow in shirt and slippers turned up, looking as astonished as his besotted face would allow him to. The 'cazain' (master) was away, he said, and spite of his boasting anent the capabilities of his house, we soon found there was no food in it but black bread—no servant but himself. But he managed to find us a room in fair repair, with a couple of the usual wooden bedsteads in it, and this we took. To our horror we found the stoves had not been lighted for a month, and were out of order, so that the cold indoors was greater than that without. Still it was too late to seek a lodging elsewhere, so we had some of our own stores cooked, a dram of Tumerūk vodka from the cabak, a small charcoal stove put in the middle of the room, and then rolling ourselves in every fragment of clothing we could find, and almost regretting that we had ever left our comfortable quarters in Kertch, we proceeded to reap the reward of our long drive in a deep and dreamless sleep.

Towards morning I half awoke with an idea that the house was attacked, so violent was the noise that aroused me, and at once jumped up to see what was happening. But the moment I was out of bed a strange giddiness seized me, and turning round I fell, and remember no more until I found a friendly telegraphist endeavouring to rouse me with libations of cold water freely applied. Gradually I came round, but with such an intense headache and utter inability to use my own limbs, that I had rather have remained insensible. I was utterly unable to help in rousing my poor friend K., and as my senses came back to me I became seriously alarmed lest our morning callers should have been too late to save him.

The truth was, something was wrong with the charcoal stove. Every aperture through which ventilation could be effected had, Russian fashion, been hermetically sealed for the winter, and my friend and I had had the narrowest escape from asphyxiation possible. After immense efforts we brought him round, but in spite of the bracing cold and the rapid driving, we both suffered from racking headaches and extreme lassitude for the rest of the day.

The travelling during this second day was of a more interesting nature; the country being covered in many places for miles with jungles of a tall reed called 'kamish,' in which pheasants are said to abound, and boars and roe to occur not infrequently. After getting out of the reedy land we came to a tract of another nature, bare and rock-strewn ; and here, within half a mile of the station at which we slept, I was surprised to see numbers of foxes hunting about in the snow for food. I should think that at one time a score must have been in sight simultaneously. As soon as we had taken in our rugs and ordered the samovar, I took my rifle, as it was not yet dusk, and tried to stalk one of these little red rovers, without the least compunction, as foxhounds are probably a blessing of civilisation with which these barren lands will never be acquainted. But though I stalked a good deal and shot once or twice, I did no good until I got to a frozen lake, some three-quarters of a mile from the station. Here I wounded a fox and followed him for some distance over the ice, and in doing so came across the remains of some large animal lately torn to pieces by brutes of prey.

Having given up my fox, I was meditating what manner of beasts these might be, when my answer came in a long, weird howl. No need to tell any one what that sound is. Instinct teaches every man to recognise the wolf's howl, and once heard it is not easily forgotten. The first howl was followed by another and another, and though I have no wish to pose as a coward, I frankly admit I wished I was anywhere but three-quarters of a mile from a house, and all the distance two feet deep in snow, which would not bear my weight on the surface. The wind, luckily, was from them to me, so that, though I walked back at my best pace, plunging frantically into deep drifts every few yards, from which I was spurred on by ever-recurring wolf music, I saw nothing, though I heard a good deal of my grim serenaders. It was a retreat, I admit, undignified, if you will ; but if the wind had been in another quarter it might have been worse. Over our tea that night the station-master spun many a long yarn of the doings of the wolves, highly coloured perhaps, but true in part, I believe. Next morning their tracks were numerous by the post-road, and they must evidently have been about in some force.

After another day's journey, passing through a few Cossack villages, with their green-domed churches and walled enclosures, we at last came in sight of our journey's end, Ekaterinodar. This is the first town of any size on this side the Caucasus, and at first sight even this is more forest than town. The trees have just been sufficiently removed to make room for the houses, but wherever no house actually stands the forest has not been interfered with. The effect was extremely pretty, now that the snow had loaded every tree with its white plumes and given the streets a hard white covering ; but in summer, when the acacias (which predominate here) are in blossom, Ekaterinodar must be as lovely as it is malarious. In

summer and early autumn fever rages here, and
even now every man and woman that we pass in
the streets has a yellow wizen face that tells of
the ravages of this Asiatic curse. Here at last
everything is genuinely Asiatic except the buildings. The grotesque combinations of top hat and
long boots are not seen here. The denizens of the
streets are tall Cossacks with high sheepskin hats,
with a crown all scarlet cloth and gold braid;
short broad-shouldered Tartars, in loose blue garments, belted at the waist with bright-coloured
shawls; women in short petticoats and high boots
with bashliks over their heads. The shops are
most of them open magazines, with no glass front,
but instead an awning in front of them, and inside
a broad counter, on which the proprietor sits
cross-legged with cigarette or long pipe in mouth.
The wares for sale consist chiefly of pelts brought
in by the Tscherkesses from the neighbourhood; and
here, in the examination of them, my friend and I
spent no small time, as a great deal of the natural
history of the country may be gleaned from these
middlemen, and many a good guide and hunter
be secured from among their clients.

I shall pass over the two days we spent here
as shortly as possible. My friend had his work
to do, and my own time was filled up by chatting
with the officers who frequented the hotel at
which we were staying. It was whilst thus

engaged that we first heard of the existence of a large royal forest of some twenty-nine square versts in extent, which lay only some fifteen versts out of our course on the return journey. To make up our minds to visit it, having secured letters of introduction to the royal forester (Col. R.), was the work of five minutes, and next morning saw us with a friend in our sledge, who knew the colonel, dashing with buoyant spirits over the glittering snow. When the long line of darkly-wooded country first caught our eyes clean cut against the frosty blue sky, the stars were already in the heavens, and an occasional bark told us the foxes were all abroad, busy in their nocturnal forays.

After a drive of half-an-hour through dim forest rides, a fire glimmered ruddily through the trees, and the deep baying of hounds told us we had almost arrived. The forester's house was a small four-roomed cottage, with a wattle enclosure round it, while outside the enclosure a few huts and a huge bonfire betokened the presence of the score of Cossacks who formed his staff. Throwing open his door, our host rushed out to meet us, a little wiry man, with a ruddy complexion, bright merry eye, huge grizzled moustache, and the most cordial manners possible. Once inside the cottage, the samovar was soon steaming comfortably, and a supper of caviare and roebuck broth, with the meat to

follow, was discussed with an appetite which even the
schnapps could not increase. Then bed was proposed, and my friend being a German, and of a
certain age, readily fell in with the proposition. Not
so the writer. To sit still or go to bed, now
when all the longings of one's life were almost
granted, hearing the veteran sportsman before me
discoursing calmly of the boars that had broken
into his enclosure the night before, or the stag
which he had shot a few nights before that, was too
much for my boyish impatience; and my kind
old host, seeing it, was as pleased at my keenness
as amused at my impatience. Going out, he found
one of the Cossacks was just preparing for a night
hunt, and returning asked me if I would care to
accompany him. Of course I jumped at the offer,
and was starting forthwith. But my host called
me back, and making me leave my own useless
garments behind me, dressed me in a huge pair
of felt boots of his own and his fur-lined, much-
braided forester's coat. Thus attired, I must have
been too much of an attraction for my lazy friend,
who shook himself together, and being similarly
clad resolved to follow me.

The Cossack who was to be our chaperone was
a sturdy, ill-favoured fellow, in the wildest combination of sheepskins conceivable, but he seemed
to know his work, and was none the worse for
being silent. As we passed down the long forest

aisles, our footsteps, thanks to the felt shoes and the snow, were soundless even in that still night. Half an hour's tramp through a perfect fairy land of frozen oaks, with a carpet of snow at their feet, on which our guide silently pointed out many a fresh track, and then we paused. One of us was to stay here; I stayed, my friend took a position a quarter of a mile further on, the Cossack being at the same distance beyond him. My own post was at the foot of an enormous oak, and here I crouched, my long felt boots deep sunk in the snow, my back against the tree, and my rifle across my knees.

Now it was that I learnt how necessary it is to wear the clothing of the country. Sitting thus with my feet in the snow in tight leather boots, I must have either kept up the circulation by moving my feet occasionally, which would have been fatal to my chance of sport, or I must have had my feet frost-bitten. As it was, in my loose boots of felt, my feet were almost too hot; and of course the rest of my body kept about the same temperature as my feet.

Once my companions had taken up their posts the whole forest was still as death for some minutes. The stillness indeed was so great as to be oppressive, and the occasional sounds—an owl's weird hoot, the howl of a wolf, or the stealthy spring of an old grey hare—only heightened the effect by contrast. On every side I could look down long vistas of frozen hazels with tall oaks rising above them, through whose quaintly twisting limbs the intense metallic light of the winter moon gleamed down on the sparkling snow, or catching the icicles that hung in huge clusters from them drew from them all manner of pale prismatic colours. Every now and again a dark shadow glided over the snow, and a sound like a devil's low chuckling laugh told one that the substance of that shadow was the great eagle owl, whose strong silent pinions were creeping, a very shadow of death, over some doomed hare. At one time a company of wolves seemed to have gathered round, for as soon as a long vibrating howl had moaned itself into silence on one side, another took up the strain and startled the forest on the other. All round us this music was kept up, but not a single wolf showed himself either to my companions or myself. Suddenly there was a loud report as if an enormous piece of artillery had been fired, and as the echoes thundered through the forest, the whole seemed to wake at once to a fiendish riot of strange sound. Every prowling beast and weird night-bird screamed in concert, and then all was silence again. This was caused by the cracking of the ice on the Kuban some miles off.

After an hour of intense enjoyment of this kind, I was roused by a distant crashing, as though a regiment was noisily breaking its way through

the undergrowth. On and on it came, growing
ever louder as it drew near, until the noise in that
silent place seemed worthy of a herd of elephants.
It came straight towards where I lay, and my
heart beat so loudly with excitement that I really
believed for the moment that the approaching
beasts must hear it as I did; and in my anxiety I
even pressed my breast with my hands in an unreasoning hope of silencing it. The noise was now
so close that it seemed impossible but that I must
see the cause of it, when suddenly another sound
caught my ear. A slow scraping sound, painfully
distinct for a minute, while the other sound ceased;
then a rasping sound and a crash as of some heavy
body falling, followed by a thundering rush, a
glimpse of four splendid deer, magnified by the
moonlight, bounding across one of the hazel vistas
some four hundred yards off, a sharp, clear whistle,
and then as the sound of the flying deer died away,
the tramp of approaching footsteps, and all was
over. The Cossack arrived first, and behind him
my German jäger, woefully crestfallen, as well he
might have been could he have known what black
wrath filled his companion's heart. The deer had
been coming straight to me when my friend,
alarmed by the tremendous noise they made
amongst the frozen branches, had attempted to
swarm the oak under which he had been placed.
For a time he got on very well, and then losing

his hold on the slippery trunk, he came down on his back with a crash that unluckily frightened our game more than it hurt him.

So ended our first night's sport; but though we bagged nothing, no real sportsman I think would allow that a night spent amid such glorious surroundings, listening to the voices of Nature in one of her wildest moods, was a night wasted. At any rate when we got home my rest was the sweeter for my toil.

The day following this eventful night was spent in preparations for the grand drive fixed for the morrow; but though there was much to be done, our kind host arranged to give us some shooting in the afternoon of this day also. Lunch over, we took the hounds out—dark brown dogs with tan chests and points, looking as if they had a large cross of the bloodhound. The *modus operandi* of the day's sport was simple in the extreme. The whole forest was divided into sections, each containing one square verst. Round one of these the guns were placed, and then the forester and his dogs went into the thick of it, and in a few minutes the woods were full of deep-toned music. The dogs seemed to me to hunt everything they came across, from a stag to a running cock pheasant, and the business of the gunner was to kill and, if possible, to bag the game before the dogs did. There was a great deal of excitement, men shouting, dogs baying, guns firing, and hares scuttling to the right and left of you, while through all, with a beautiful pertinacity which hardly allowed him time to fire a shot, the veteran forester tootled away on his horn. This would have augured badly for our sport on the morrow but that the forest was immense, and we were only in an outlying bit of it, from which we probably drove some game towards our next day's ground. Although the snow was covered with tracks, we saw nothing but hares, of which we bagged about twenty.

The morning of Thursday broke as brilliantly as its predecessors, and the sun seemed if possible to glare with a harder light on the frozen snow. Outside our door the forester was apparently on the point of knocking down three or four Cossacks almost as excited as himself. His voice rose to a scream, his arms kept swinging about; even I knew enough Russian to hear that he was swearing awfully, and I had my fears lest something had happened to mar our day's sport. However, he finally calmed down, and presently I heard him calling a huge-bearded ruffian a little dove (golubchik), whom he had addressed as the son of the most immoral of the canine race not five minutes before. He was merely explaining some of the minor details in the business of the coming day, he told me afterwards.

About 7.30 a Cossack colonel, with a hundred

of his men, turned up. This was the local Nimrod,
and these the beaters he brought with him ; and
a wilder lot to look at, a more thirsty lot to re-
fresh, a noisier, more frolicsome lot altogether, you
could not find even at Donnybrook fair. With
the colonel came another Russian and a couple of
young Frenchmen, and this made up our party.

A huge sledge was in attendance for the sportsmen, and another for the game. The beaters were
sent on, and some of the more reliable entrusted
with a third sledge laden with eatables and a cask
of goodly dimensions. As the last Cossack disappeared down the forest drive, we turned back
into the cottage, lighted our cigarettes, and having
collected our ammunition, took our places on the
sledge waiting for us, and drove merrily to the
meet. On our way the overhanging branches
caught us now and again, sweeping one of our
number into the snow, amid peals of laughter from
all but the victim.

Arrived at the rendezvous, strict silence was
enjoined, the guns were posted, each a hundred
yards or so from the other, along one side of the
division, with orders on no account to leave those
posts until told to do so. Meanwhile the Cossack
colonel had taken his hundred men to the opposite
side of the section, and all being in readiness, we
heard his horn signal ' forward,' and then all was
silent as the grave. Every eye was strained on

D

the bushes and thick covert in front, every ear
intently listening for the patter of feet or the sound
of breaking brushwood. But as yet no sound:
even the Cossacks were too distant to be heard
as yet. Did some one move along the line? No,
every soul is still as we are. Again the crash;
the sound that set our hearts beating a few nights
ago, but now far less startling in the daylight than
it was then in the shadows and stillness of night.

Here they come trooping towards our line, four
does and a tall stag in front, half trotting, half
walking, tossing their dainty heads up and down
as they approach. They advance straight towards the oak at which I saw my German friend
posted, and I reluctantly hold my hand that he
may make the best of his chance. Nearer and
nearer they come, and yet no shot breaks the stillness, though they are almost past him. Suddenly
they throw up their heads, and with a rush are
lost in the forest beyond, without a shot having
been fired at them. My friend had of course
broken the rules, left his own tree, and gone off to
one which seemed to him to have greater attrac-
tions. Thus the deer had for the second time
passed him unfired at.

Soon the shots began to ring out, at first only
a dropping fire, though towards the end of the
drive the firing was so frequent as almost to
resemble file-firing. After the red deer a wild cat

came towards me, moving softly over the snow; and as my eye followed him I became aware of some dozen grey forms that had risen suddenly ghost-like all round me: one old hare sitting absolutely under my tree and gazing apparently rigidly into my face. There she sat, listening to the shots, without stirring for some five minutes, until in the open between two great oaks a fine red fox came trotting stealthily towards us, his broad heavy brush spread, and seeming to trail on the snow behind him, which threw his whole graceful, undulating form out in bold relief. It seemed against one's English nature to shoot him, but it had to be done, and a charge of heavy shot rolled him over on the snow. It seemed like shooting a friend.

By this time the cries of the beaters had drawn very near, some of their forms even showing from time to time in open places. Three quick springs and an abrupt pause in the bushes in front of me now arrested my attention, but thinking after a time that it was only another hare, I singled out one of these long-eared gentry, and rolled him over. As I did so two roebucks broke covert, and galloped rapidly past our Russian friend on the left, who, making a neat right and left, laid them both on the path.

This was the shot of the day. A bugle now sounded a warning to turn our backs to the beaters and only shoot as the game passed us, thus avoiding the chance of bagging a beater. The hares came thick and fast, and as they cantered steadily away, a large number of them were bagged. When we came out on to the path there were four roes, a red deer, of which I had caught a passing glimpse as she crashed along the line, my fox, and thirty-seven hares. My fox I say, but I was doomed to find myself mistaken. It seems after he had been to all intents and purposes killed, he had crawled along the line and lain down to die in front of the Cossack colonel. This worthy gave him the *coup de grâce*, and claimed him in consequence. The red deer too, whose throat a Cossack's bullet had cut as neatly as if it had been done with a knife, staggered on towards the colonel, and here, as its knees trembled preparatory to lurching forward in death, that gallant officer put a charge of small shot in its haunch, spoilt the venison, and secured another easy prey. The rule of the chase is here opposed to the English rule, and, I think, to common sense. With us the man who inflicts the first wound, with the Russians he who deals the last, obtains the quarry.

After two more beats, in which more game of the same kind was bagged, we repaired to the sledges at the cross rides for refreshment. I was much amused by the doling out of the vodka to the Cossacks. The cask was mounted on the sledge and there tapped, the forester, with three or four to help him, forming the Cossacks in line, and giving each man his nip in rotation, which he pitched straight down his throat in true Russian style, without ever giving the liquid time to wet the sides in passing. As the men went down after taking their nip, I noticed they coolly fell in again at the other end, and in time got another turn. One enormously tall fellow in a white sheepskin hat, which must have been double the height and circumference of an English 'topper,' with a crown of green cloth, got three drams in this way. But his hat and his height betrayed him, and put an end to the affair.

During the rest of the drives the sport varied very little; first came the wolves, slinking out almost before the beaters had entered the other side of the covert, then the deer, wild cats, and foxes in regular succession, and last of all the roes and hares. If there had been boars or bears I believe they would probably have followed the wolves and preceded the deer. But there were none seen all day.

When the game was counted out at evening the bag was one red deer, nine roe, two wild cats (splendid yellow tabbies, half as large again as a large domestic mouser), three foxes, two skunks, much prized for their pelts, and 175 hares, and this divided amongst some twenty guns, of whom two-thirds acted only as scarecrows to the game. The sport was good and wild enough in itself, but poor and without charm as compared to the still hunt of the night before.

Arrived at the forester's house, the hares were given as wages to the beaters, who exchanged their skins for vodka from some neighbouring drinking shop, and made a vast stew of the carcases. With an enormous bonfire blazing, they made themselves merry on this rough fare until late into the night, dancing wild, graceful flings and reels, and singing national songs, in which a tone of melancholy and depression seemed to run through the warlike character of a border ballad.

The whole scene was one which Turner's pencil might have gloried in, but no pen could do justice to the wild figures in their ragged sheepskins and mountainous hats of many-coloured wool, lit up by the long red flames, and backed by the hoary forest heavy with its months of snow.

In the morning before leaving Crasnoi Lais we saw a very curious instance of the sagacity of wolves. A herd of roebuck had settled down in fancied security in a hollow in the midst of one of the forest sections. A pack of wolves had discovered them there, and when we came in the morning the forester showed us plainly by their spoor their method of attack. At every few hundred yards round the entire circumference of the 'quartal' a wolf had entered it, and the whole pack gradually converging towards the centre had surrounded and killed three of the roes, which in rushing from one wolf must have dashed right into the jaws of another. My friend told me that he himself had been witness of another instance of the wolf's cunning whilst driving on the post-road in winter. A cow and her calf were feeding by the road side, and two wolves were endeavouring to carry off the calf. One of them kept frolicking about in front of the cow, rolling on the ground or snapping at her nose, to distract her attention, the calf meanwhile getting under her mother in rear. Here the second wolf attacked her, and seemed in a fair way to accomplish his object when my friend drove by.

The natives have many wonderful tales to tell of wolves, of which perhaps the most incredible is that if, when you are pursued by a pack, you have the presence of mind to squat down on your haunches, the wolves will come and surround you in a similar attitude, and after some time spent in contemplation will slowly retire, leaving you unmolested. I can only say that the man who had faith enough to put this to the proof would deserve to live to tell the tale. It is in spring, when the she-wolf is followed by a party of her grim suitors, that the Tscherkesses and Cossacks most dread this animal, and then they say they are extremely dangerous, and that if you are unlucky enough to wound the lady, nothing but their death will release you from the attacks of her enraged suite.

Having bid a hearty adieu to our host, and taking a couple of roebuck with us to testify of our prowess to envious friends at Kertch, we got under weigh next morning on our return journey. On our way I wounded an old wolf which I saw slinking round some kamish (reed) beds by the roadside ; but though I followed him far into the reeds I never bagged him, and could by no means get another fair shot at him with my rifle.

Three days' fast travelling saw us back at Kertch, the heroes of the hour ; for though Ekaterinodar with its forest is so near, the Russian sportsman is of so unenterprising a nature that none of our comrades knew it except by report. The comforts of our English consulate were none the less appreciated after the cold bare rooms of a Russian post station in the Caucasus, and we both agreed that though such sport was glorious, a comfortable home to return to was a blessing mightily to be desired.

CHAPTER III.

ODESSA AND MISKITCHEE.

Mountaineers and Shikarees—Outfit—Journey from London to Odessa
—Snipe-shooting on the Dnieper — A drunken yemstchik—A
collision — Prince Vorontzoff — Aloupka — Yalta—Livadia and
Orianda—Miskitchee lake—A Tartar butcher—Native hovels—A
shooting party on the lake—A dreary bivouac.

It was not until the August of 1878, three years
after the events recorded in my last chapter, that
a passage in a recently published book on the Caucasus drew my attention again to my old hunting
grounds. It was Mr. Freshfield in this work ('The
Frosty Caucasus') who wrote that in all his travels
in the Caucasian mountains he had seen little more
game than a couple of tame bears in a Tscherkess
village.

This struck me as strange, and as I was at that
time meditating a sporting tour in some as yet un-
chosen locality, I decided to go to the Caucasus for
myself, and test its capacities to the utmost of my
ability as hunting ground for large game. Since
my return from Asia I have seen Devouasseux, Mr.
Freshfield's guide, who tells me that the author
was too intent on his favourite pursuit of mountain-

climbing to have much time for looking for game. And indeed the book itself leads one to infer this. The climbing of almost impracticable mountains and the pursuit of great game could not be combined by any one. To achieve success in either pursuit is enough for most men.

After passing a week in preparing my outfit, which was by no means a formidable one, I was ready to start. An 'express rifle,' a double-barrel smoothbore (C. F. No. 12), fitted with metal cartridge-cases, which when inserted converted the gun into a muzzle-loader, a suit of moleskin, one of Rouch's photographic apparatuses, and a pair of Dean's field boots, were the chief items in my outfit. The first three articles are indispensable, the other two absolutely useless, as I was unable to work the one, and had but little occasion to test the other. Besides, I believe Mr. Dean's boots are not much good without the dubbin supplied with them, and this my servant promptly lost. No doubt properly used with this, they are as excellent as their many advocates believe them to be.

The most difficult thing to get was a really good map of the Caucasus, containing the names of the principal small streams and villages. This I afterwards secured in Russia under the name of ' Map of the Caucasian Isthmus,' by Professor Dr. Karl Koch (' Karte von dem Kaukasischen Isthmus.' Berlin. 1850). In this map most of the important villages are marked, and the names are sufficiently like those given them by their inhabitants to enable a stranger to recognise them.

The journey from St. Katherine's Docks to Odessa, *viâ* Vienna, has nothing in it worthy of record. Most men who travel nowadays have seen as much of it as they care to. For my own part, having made the journey several times, I think the things that have made most impression on my mind are the gradual improvement in the railway carriages, from the time you leave our English abominations until the time you find yourself surrounded with at least all the necessary conveniences of life on the last stage to Odessa; the gradual diminution in pace, until some little distance from your journey's end it amounts to little more than a crawl; the sudden clearing and brightening of the atmosphere once you have crossed the channel; the predominance of blue in all the dresses of the French peasant; the absence of fences to make a run interesting, if runs took place in this land of vulpecides; the disappearance of the rook, and the appearance of his grey-backed congener the hooded crow in his place; the multitude of magpies, and the loquaciousness of one's travelling companions. I am afraid my readers, if I have any, will at once put me down as unobservant, but it may only be that first impressions are lost if the same journey is often repeated.

Arrived at Odessa, my old chief and kind friend, Mr. George Stanley, Her Majesty's Consul-General there, received me with great kindness, and to him and Mr. Mitchell I am indebted for much valuable information and many acts of attention. During the few days I stayed at Odessa I had one very excellent day's snipe-shooting with Mr. Stanley on the Dnieper, during which we bagged fifty-six snipe in an hour between us. Of these, I am in honesty bound to admit, that Mr. Stanley, whose hand had not forgotten the cunning acquired in Egypt, bagged by far the larger share.

On our way home we had a specimen of the driving of Russian yemstchiks, which would have considerably lowered them probably in the esteem of their ardent admirer Sir Robert Peel. Our fellow seemed a little the worse for vodka, and as soon as we got away from the house at which we had been staying, we had proof that his looks did not belie him. The bracing air roused his spirits; his horses were 'little doves' and 'sons of dogs' in the same breath, his whip whirled about, and tossing their heads in the air, the team (in which there were two young ones) took the bit in their teeth, and went away straight across the steppe, over gullies, with a bump that would have smashed any springs had there been any, down slopes at a rate that took your breath away, and all the while the yemstchik laughing and swearing, and not minding one bit. Two of his crimson velvet cushions dropped off into darkness behind him, and this probably sobered him. At last we got on to the track, and though the pace was still violent, we were comparatively safe here. Once we collided with a droshky, the driver of which was unusually moderate in his oaths at the accident, and passed on quickly and disappeared. We discovered afterwards that a valuable piece of the harness of our own troika had been lost, carried away by the droshky in the collision probably, seeing which the droshky man had held his tongue, and made off with his prize.

But our troubles were not yet over. As we neared Odessa there was a sharp turn in the track. As we turned I saw our danger, but there was no time to avert it ; and in the twinkling of an eye we charged a telegraph post. The tall thin post passing between our off leader and the shaft horse, cut clean through every atom of harness, and set the young one free. For a moment he stood stunned and trembling, and then with a snort betook himself off into the darkness as fast as legs could carry him. This finally restored our driver to a state of most solemn sobriety, and for the rest of our journey we were conveyed at a safe and moderate pace by the remaining two horses. The fellow was lucky enough to recover his horse next day, but not without considerable trouble and expense. I believe he and two or three hired comrades spent the night on the steppe looking for the stray horse.

After this I bade adieu to my kind friends in Odessa, receiving as a last kindness from Mr. Stanley an introduction to Prince Vorontzoff, who, luckily for me, happened to be travelling by the boat in which I had embarked. This introduction stood me in good stead, as his Highness, who speaks English like an Englishman, gave me letters of introduction at Tiflis, by exhibiting the address and external signature of which I was able to allay the suspicions of the Cossacks on the Black Sea, and otherwise help myself. I owe Prince Vorontzoff many thanks for his ready kindness to a stranger, and repeat them with the same sincerity with which I tendered them when he left the boat for his lovely place at Aloupka.

Aloupka is to my mind the finest castle in Russia, in the most picturesque position. It is a strange mixture of the half fortress, half castle, of early feudal times, Moorish magnificence, Russian luxury, and English comfort. In the distance it looks massive and glorious, with magnificent timber, gardens, and vineyards stretching down to the sea at its feet, the grey summit of Aïé Petri towering over it from behind, and away to the right the Bear Mountain, couched with his head on his paws, looking ever seaward.

Yalta itself is the Eden of Russia perhaps, but it is an Eden in which most of the inhabitants are invalids, all the hotels infamously exorbitant in their charges; and life, unless one is addicted to the process of the grape cure, excessively monotonous. The palace of Livadia is beautiful, but would, I think, scarcely please ordinary English taste as much as the magnificent foliage (artificially arranged) at Orianda (the Grand Duke Constantine's seat), or the stately beauty of Aloupka. The mountains round Yalta and as far as Theodosia are extremely fine, and I know of few things more beautiful than some of the views to be obtained from their pine-clad sides. I believe a few roe and chamois are to be found on them, but these are at least partially preserved.

Arrived at Kertch I was at home again, and soon in my old room at the consulate. A right merry time we had of it, and, as was natural, devoted a couple of days to our old friend Miskitchee, the lake that 'best of all lakes the fowler loves,' on these Crimean steppes.

Miskitchee is the Tartar name for a village some sixty versts from Kertch: the lake, which adjoins the village, shares with the latter its name. The lake is a piece of shallow water some two miles long by half a mile broad, and nowhere deeper than up to a man's waist. It is for the most part covered with the high reed called here 'kamish,' and on the mud banks round its edges and in the little lagoons within the reeds myriads of wild-fowl play by day, and chatter and feed all night. Here have I had many a good day's wild-fowling, passed many a merry night. and had at least one adventure, which, as far as I remember, was somewhat in this wise: I had been staying at the house of the chief farmer in the village, a Greek or Armenian—I forget which—for some few days, on a shooting expedition. One morning, about six o'clock, I was tramping over some damp steppeland, where pools were frequent, and snipe should have been more so, but were not. After an hour spent in looking for something to shoot, I had almost resolved to be off again to my favourite lake, when I heard a voice calling to me in Russian. Looking up I saw a Tartar, rather a smart one too, in a fawn-coloured robe and the inevitable sheepskin hat, standing upright in a big flat cart, with a troika of capital horses before him. On coming closer I found he was inviting me to take a seat in his cart. assuring me that he, too, was a sports-man, and had to drive over a part of the steppe that morning where game abounded. Having no gun with him, he would show me where sport might be had if I liked. However, roubles in those days were rare with me, and I feared that if I accepted the lift I should have to pay a considerable fare, so I declined as graciously as possible. My friend persisted, and at last I told him frankly that if he gave me a passage to these happy hunting grounds of which he spoke it would have to be a free one, and include a return before nightfall. He consented at once, so without more ado I got into his cart, and drove off with him.

After a verst or two I began to find my friend was no 'blagueur,' for in a very short time we had bagged several hares and a few quail. His sight was the most marvellous I ever met with. Standing up in his cart, as he drove rapidly over the uplands, he would from time to time pull up suddenly, exclaiming, 'Vot zeits!'—Lo, a hare! at the same time pointing to some distant object on the ploughed land or prairie. It was no good my looking, for I could discern nothing, so that I had to dismount and simply trudge for one or two hundred yards in the direction he indicated, until sure enough, from under my very feet, the hare started, until then utterly undiscernible to me.

And now the object of his morning drive was revealed to me. On a hillside near us was a mighty flock of sheep, tended by a few ragged Tartar lads and one grey-headed shepherd, with the usual retinue of huge mongrel sheepdogs—brutes who go for you on every opportunity. Hailing the old shepherd, a bargain was soon struck, and we dismounted to choose our sheep. My friend plunged in among them, and after regarding many with the eye of a profound connoisseur, chose four. To choose them was easy, to secure them seemed less so. Kicking off his shoes and rolling up his long loose sleeves, the purchaser tried to approach his purchase. The more he advanced the more rapidly the sheep retired, trying in vain to lose himself amongst his comrades or substitute another in his place. But the Tartar was not to be done, and in a quarter of an hour three were secured, caught by the hind leg, jerked over on their back, all four legs tied together, and bundled into the cart. Ambitious of imitating my friend, I too took off my boots, and made frantic efforts to collar an innocent-looking beast. After an enormous waste of time I did get hold of a leg of mutton, though not, I believe, the right one. The jerk was neatly given, but alas! not by the right creature. In a moment I was sprawling, and in another the whole flock was romping over my breathless body. How I extricated myself I know not, but when I did I sat me down, feeling sheepish in more ways than one, and resumed my boots a wiser, though a sadder man.

Having got our whole cargo on board, we set off for the nearest Tartar village, killing on the way another hare. By the way, whenever I killed anything, my guide insisted on cutting its throat

and breaking its legs, a superstitious observance,
I have since heard, common to all Mahometans.
Arrived at the village, an old man (the moollah I
think he was) climbed to the top of a low hovel in
the middle of the straggling main street (if streets
there are in Tartar 'aouls'), and shouted himself
hoarse in the Tartar tongue. What he said I knew
not then, but from subsequent events I believe it
was to the effect that the good butcher, Lotso, had
brought with him five fat sheep, all or any of
which he was prepared then and there to convert
into mutton, if sufficient customers were forthcoming. Any one who wanted mutton, to raise
his hand. After a great deal of talking all by
himself, the moollah came down from his perch,
and a crowd forming round him, a tremendous
row ensued. It looked like being a free fight, but
it was soon over, and perhaps the Tartar house-
keepers may take to themselves the credit of settling
on the joint for the day sooner than their English
representatives at home.

The purchases being settled, a sheep was selected from the cart, and carried to a stone trench
hard-by, its throat cut, and the whole operation of
skinning and dismembering completed in a very
few minutes. Meanwhile a number of gaunt curs,
drawn by the smell of blood, had crowded round,
and so hardy were they that it was all a dozen
Tartars could do, whirling their knouts round the

butcher as the whips do when the huntsman is breaking up his fox, to keep the brutes at bay. Then the meat was parcelled out, the money paid, cash down, the entrails, tied up in the skin (butcher's perquisites), thrown back into the cart, and after a drink of sour cream at the dirty brown hands of a Tartar princess, we were on our way for the next village, to repeat the same process.

And now all our sheep having been slaughtered and sold, the gloaming came on, and with it a hunger on my part that made me anxious to get back to my quarters at the friendly Armenian's. Turning to the Tartar, I suggested our return, when he coolly informed me that I had better make up my mind to pass the night at his house at J——, naming a village of some half-dozen houses, at which an execrable murder had occurred some months previously. It may have been the memory of this, or it may have been his ghastly handiness with the butcher's knife, or perhaps the thought of my cosy quarters at Miskitchee, that made me resolve that go to that place I would not. Accordingly I reminded him of his promise. All the satisfaction I could get was that if I wanted to go back I must walk. Did I know in which direction Miskitchee lay? Yes, out yonder, over that low line of hills. A grim laugh, and the assurance that Miskitchee was in an exactly opposite direction, increased my suspicions of my quondam friend, as I knew by certain landmarks that he must be lying. A moment's consideration showed me that a walk at this hour, even supposing I did not lose my way, would end probably in a night on the steppe, at the mercy of this man or any other who chose to stalk me, and surprise me in the dark or in my sleep, to say nothing of the absolute necessity in case of my leaving the cart of abandoning my game. So I changed my tactics. He had no firearms, and sat on the edge of the cart. I had my gun, and sat behind in the body of it. Mustering what little Russian I knew, I let him understand that I held him to his promise; that I had heard of J—— and its evil reputation, and didn't mean to go there; that I knew the track now on our right was the home track; and that, if he refused to take it, I would blow him off his cart with a charge of No. 5. This was a rough argument, and he seemed nonplussed. He tried to argue me into going another way; he tried to laugh me out of my suspicions—he even began to bully. I simply watched him, repeated my proposals, and sat still. Meanwhile the horses were pulled up. Then my friend tried to slip off his seat, and so get out of his awkward position in front of my gun's muzzle. I cocked my gun with a click, and brought it in a line with his back. There was a moment's hesitation, and then with a curse he took the right road at a sulky pace.

All that drive I never took my eyes off him,

and never let go my gun. Gradually he seemed to become better tempered, and when we got within half a mile of Miskitchee he turned and spoke to me, to assure me that further than that nothing would induce him to drive me.

Satisfied now that I could get home in safety, I got down, taking a couple of hares and some birds with me, leaving the rest for the Tartar, and walked off to Miskitchee, thankful to have got off so well. On my way back I thought I had probably been over suspicious, and made a fool of myself. However, on my arrival, I found I had been searched for all day, and great anxiety had been felt for me. It seems my butcher was of more professions than one, being indeed the most notorious horse-stealer on these steppes. He had camped near the village the night before, and made several inquiries about me, having seen me returning from shooting that night. He had also expressed great admiration for my gun, a rather handsome breech-loader. This, together with the fact that the butcher, one of my host's best horses, and myself had all disappeared simultaneously next morning, accounted for the anxiety felt, as well as for the butcher's objection to return to the village that night.

Such was one of the memories Miskitchee called up in my mind. But on this my last visit I saw little to remind me of my adventure. The Armenian had, I believe, gone, and the whole village looked asleep in the sunshine as we passed it by: a straggling group of one-storied hovels, with the sunlight glinting on rows of yellow gourds on the thatch; a dark, good-looking Tartar girl in a scarlet cap and many ringlets, much bespangled with small gilt coins, standing in a doorway, round which there was some sort of an enclosure. At another cottage door, with his legs in the mud of the main street and his quarters on the somewhat drier mud of his dining-room floor, lounged, cigarette in mouth, a pink-shirted Russian moujik. Inside the hovel, if we had had time to look, we should probably have seen a heap of bedclothes between the roof and the top of the oven; this would be the baboushka's (grandmother's) bed. A wooden bedstead with more disarranged clothes on the floor; here the rest of the family, mother and father and brats, all sleep; a filthy, open fireplace, in one corner; a ragged woman, of ape-like propensities, combing a dirty child in another; and on the floor two more half-naked brats, fighting over the family loaf of black bread, from which they are in vain endeavouring to hammer a morsel with the back of an axe. From a blackened greasy beam overhead, adorned with a few strings of onions and withered apples, a dim light shines down upon the whole, proceeding from a tin of mutton fat, which makes the whole interior as unsavoury as it is ugly.

Gladly, then, we left the village behind us, and drawing up our droshkies under the lee of a high natural embankment beside the lake, prepared to pass the night there.   A hole was dug in the earth and a subterranean fire made to cook over.   Our bourkas stretched over the droshky made a kind of refuge between the wheels, into which we could crawl and sleep in case of rain.

These and other little preparations having been at least started, we began our shooting. Two guns went round the lake, one on either side ; one worthy sportsman might have been seen arraying himself in Mr. Cording's famous hose ; another, simpler and perhaps wiser, divesting himself of all the trammels which civilisation has thrown round the lower limbs of bipeds. The wading party, Cording's follower, and 'the unadorned,' made through the shallow lake for the reed beds in the centre ; here carefully concealed to reap the benefit of the stalking party on either shore.   The fifth gunner, a tall thin German from Riga, the very best of good fellows, with the longest of legs, had taken to himself a large biscuit-tin, the which he had deposited on a small sand-bank in the middle of the lake.   Seated on this, in his trim attire, which no campaigning could ever make less natty, with long limbs overspreading all the surrounding country, our friend B. awaited the dodgy duck. The men in the reeds had the best of it, though the shooting was hardest there, and as we had no retrievers we never got a quarter of the birds we killed. The isolated gentleman on the biscuit-tin got a few long shots, and as his birds all fell in open water, got most of what he killed. But, alas, when he attempted to rise to gather his birds, he was distinctly seen to stick. Vain were his efforts to rise erect. The misguided biscuit-tin had sunk into the treacherous mud bank, slowly but surely; the part next upon it had followed, and the pride of Kertch had apparently taken root in the wastes of Miskitchee. However, fate was kind, and by the united efforts of his friends he was rescued from his ignominious position.

The shore shooters came back tired but happy, though their bag of one cormorant, several red-legged gulls, and a large variety of waders, with a few duck, was rather ornamental than useful. The man of the biscuit-tin and 'the unadorned' contributed some mallards, teal, and a couple of pintail, with a few snipe; and after counting out the bag, all drew round the fire to imbibe the cheering 'tchai' (tea). But why this gap? Our friend in waders is still absent, and yell loud as we like we get no response from the little reedy island in which he was last seen. For half an hour we waited, and then we heard a gun fired right in the middle of the swamp. Again we shouted and fired, and this time got an answer, but it was not until the sky grew dark and the smoke from our fire could be plainly seen against it, that our friend found his way out of the maze of reeds in which he had been wandering round and round for nearly a couple of hours.

After our pipes had been lighted, the rain came down in torrents, forcing us all to creep under the droshky, and a very close fit we found it. However, by curling B.'s legs three or four times round his waist, we did manage it, and lay there smoking and listening to the old German jäger's ghost stories, culled from the forests of Germany and the plains of Asia, until far into the night. And never had a teller of weird legends fitter accompaniments than the million voices of the lake at our feet and the ceaseless pelting and buffeting of the storm without.

One more shot at the duck in the morning, and then we turned homewards. My time I felt was getting short, and it was high time that I sailed for the Black Sea coast, although I was nothing loth to have delayed these two weeks, feeling that now I was tolerably certain to escape the Circassian fever which is so prevalent in early autumn.

CHAPTER IV.

THE RED FOREST AND BLACK SEA COAST.

Journey to Taman—Downpour on the steppe—Tscherkess bourkas—
Long-tailed horses—Absence of cultivation—The Moujiks—Causes
of political discontent in Russia—Veneration for the Czar—Cheap-
ening supplies—A Russian writer on Englishwomen—Post stations
—A terrible tragedy—Hotels—Ekaterinodar—The fair—Russian
tea—Russian police—Bivouacking with Cossack foresters—Exciting
sport—Shooting a white boar—Sad disappointment—Pheasant-
shooting—A Cossack colonel—An execrable journey—Caucasian
women—Great consumption of supplies—In a Cossack saddle—
Mineral springs—A scorching bath—Lotus-eaters—Incidents of
the road—An insolent Tartar—Parting.

On Saturday, October 7, I left Kertch for Ekaterinodar, intending to have a week's sport at my
old quarters in the Crasnoi Lais (Red Forest),
having written to that effect to Colonel R., the
forester, about a week before.   My impedimenta
were a portmanteau, my gun and rifle, together
with a pointer (Calypso), which I had purchased
from an old shooting companion at Kertch.   My
intention was to have some shooting in the Suran
district, where bears are said to be plentiful, to
stay a few days at Vladikavkas, thence to pass on
to Tiflis, and from Tiflis across the little known
Mooghan Steppe to the Caspian.   But it is hardly

worth while to mention my plans, as they nearly all suffered change, and it would have been better for me if they all had.

At Taman, whilst the horses were being harnessed, I was kindly entertained by the chief of the Russian Telegraph station, from whom I gained a good deal of general information. I may say once for all, that wherever I went I met with the kindest attention from the employés of the Telegraph Companies, whether Russian or Indo-European, and I heartily commend to their kindness any one who may be inclined to follow on my steps. But the jingling bells, whose ceaseless monotony was to be my only music through many a day to come, warn me to drink up my coffee, light a pipe for the journey, and be off.

The country round Taman had improved somewhat since I saw it last. People used to declare nothing would grow there; but now that some Greeks have settled round the town, fine onions and other garden produce are daily sent in, grown within a mile of the bazaar.

Once well out on the steppe, in a flat open cart, with no shelter of any kind and retreat impossible, down came the pitiless rain. No fitful April shower, but a good conscientious downpour, large drops and plenty of them, for the rest of the afternoon. Here, then, was my first omission in fitting out for an expedition. An umbrella would have looked ridiculous, and been for various reasons useless; but the umbrella of the country, the Tscherkess bourka, should have been among the first of my purchases.

This bourka, without which no one thinks of travelling in this country, is a large piece of felt, of a good quality, extremely light for its size, and really waterproof. It fastens round the wearer's neck, and hangs like a bell-shaped tent from his shoulders to his knees. Bourkas vary in texture and quality, as well as price; some being white, others black; some as rough as a Skye terrier, others almost as smooth as a greyhound. The best are black and almost smooth, and cost as much as thirty or forty roubles (four or five pounds). After his kinjal and his horse, I almost think a bourka is the Cossack's most valuable possession; and rolled in these things, I have seen the hardy fellows sleeping placidly on a wet truss of hay in the midst of a perfect November deluge.

After going for a verst or so, my yemstchik came to his first halt. The horses here wear their tails, like the ladies' trains at home, preposterously long; and a dozen times in our drive of twenty versts, had we to pull up whilst the driver wrung out the mud from one of these sweeping appendages, and tied it up into a less comely but more convenient bob. Without this the horses could not have done the distance at all. As for myself, I was speedily sodden through, while my face was like that of a plaster cast with its eyes bunged up.

It is a pitiful thing to see all this useful land untilled, and all the peasantry and the country itself so poor. My friend the Russian telegraph clerk told me a few more reasons besides the perpetual ' prasnik ' for the want of agricultural energy and success in the Caucasus. The very abundance of land is an evil to the short-sighted Russian peasant. Here in the Caucasus I am told every ' soul ' (the Russian phrase for every male subject) is allowed sixteen dissatines (acres) free of charge, and he may choose his land pretty well where he likes. The result is, the moujik argues with himself pretty much after this fashion : ' In this particular spot where my cottage is, my corn won't grow well, elsewhere it would grow better, and in a third place another crop would find a fitter soil.' So on this principle of not trusting all his ventures to one bottom, he takes a few dissatines here and another few ten versts off, and still more beyond. In this way he wastes an infinite amount of time in making perhaps a threshing floor at each different farm, or in conveying the crop from one farm to another to be threshed. Add to this that water has often to be fetched from afar, that his tools are of the rudest, and that his men are, even if all were workers even in the English sense, far too small for the acreage, and you have some reasons for the want of that agricultural wealth which Russia ought to possess. It seems the greater pity, since the moujik is such a frugal, hard-living man, and barring vodka and 'prasniks' might do wonders. He can turn his hand to anything, is always cheerful, and almost his only glaring vice is drunkenness. A peasant family here, I am assured, will live in what is to them comfort, food and clothes and all included, for from eighteen to twenty roubles a head, *i.e.* from 2*l.* to 2*l.* 5*s.*, per annum. But then we must bear in mind that meat is a thing a Russian peasant rarely eats. In spring black bread and an onion ; in summer black bread and arboose (water-melon) ; in winter black bread and cabbage soup, with a dry fish now and again as a *bonne bouche*, suffice for his simple wants. Then, too, his liquor is infinitely cheaper than that of our beer-drinking peasantry. For three copecks (about a penny) he can get nearly half an English tumbler of the abominable neat rye spirit, in which he delights, and some of them will even drink spirits of wine and petroleum, which, I presume, is even cheaper than vodka.

The proprietor of the oil-wells at Tcheerilek, Mr. Peters—since, I regret to say, dead—has himself told me that some men working on his estate thought as little of tossing off a 'stakan' (small tumbler) of petroleum as I would of drinking the like quantity of Bass. In addition to these things, the moujik's clothes are as simple and inexpensive as his diet : in winter a toga of sheepskin, with the woolly side in, a scarf round his waist and sheep-skin hat on his head, a pair of long boots that cost him more than all the rest of his outfit, but are un-rivalled for their long wearing qualities ; in sum-mer a calico shirt ; and summer and winter you may see his wife and brats going about, in snow or sun-shine, with nothing but a single linen garment between them and the weather. His winter outfit is perhaps a trifle costly, as compared to the rest of his expenditure, but then it is wonderful how long one suit of clothes will last a moujik ; and like a wise man he always prefers old clothes to new, so long as they will hold together.

With such a thrifty peasantry, and so much valuable land, surely better results might be obtained.

I believe that the whole of the misery of Russia, her political discontent, her Nihilism, and the foul crimes of which it has been the cause, are due, not to the autocratic form of government under which she exists, and to which, in spite of the outcry of the few, the majority of Russians are firmly wedded, but to the utter want of religious training amongst all classes, and to that widespread corruption in the official world, from which all who come in contact with it suffer continually. Were there less com-pulsory military service, more religious training, greater encouragement given to agriculture, and more inducements held out to foreigners to settle in the waste places of Russia's vast empire, so that by their example they might teach her own people how to make the best of the natural advantages they enjoy, there might then be a chance of happiness and prosperity for Russia and her people.

There is in every Russian moujik an inherent love of the Czar, a personal loyalty to him, which deifies and renders its object infallible in the eyes of his subjects, and this takes much to eradicate. Could this feeling be fostered rather than destroyed by the injustices of petty provincial officials, who to the peasant are the only direct representatives of the supreme power, regicide and revolution would be things unknown.

The only complaint I ever heard from peasant lips in Russia of the Great White Czar was, he is too far off, he is deaf, our voices cannot reach him through the crowd of rascals who hedge him in.

To-day I myself was destined to dine on peasants' fare ; and though the bread was black and damp, it was wholesome, and hunger gave the meal the only sauce it needed. My night was passed on a wooden sofa at Tumerûk, with my pointer for a pillow, a style of repose that at least ensured early rising.

At 5 A.M. I was in the market chaffering with the peasant women for supplies for the journey.

Ikra (fresh caviare) was nearly two shillings a
pound, and fresh butter tenpence.   It is one of the
unpleasant characteristics of the Russian tradesman
that you must always bargain with him for the
merest trifle.   It is only fair to say for him that it
is the fault rather of his customers than himself;
for in Kertch, where we were known, the tradesmen. knowing that the English residents did not
care to haggle about a bargain. would ask the price
they meant to accept in the first instance, instead
of adding on an extra charge to be gradually taken
off to please the customer.

Whilst waiting in the post-station for my horses
to be put to, I chanced on the following passage in
a Russian book of travels, by one Ivan Goutcharoff,
which I have taken the liberty of translating for
the benefit of my readers.   Speaking of his sojourn
in England, he says : ' I did not make the acquain-
' tance of any families, so that I only saw the women
' in the churches, shops, opera-boxes, streets, &c., so
' that I can only say (and that to prevent your being
' offended at me for neglecting this subject) that they
' are very beautiful, well built, and of a wondrous
' complexion, though they eat much meat and sweets
' and drink strong wine.   Yet in other nations you
' will not find so much beauty as among the masses
' in England.   Don't judge of English beauty (as
' Russians too often do) by the red-haired gentlemen
' and dames who come out from England under the

'name of skippers, machinists, tutors, and gover-
'nesses, above all governesses. That would be a
'grand mistake. Beautiful women don't leave Eng-
'land for this. Beauty is capital. Women as a race
'are worth nothing in England if they have not
'some special talent. One foreign language or ac-
'complishment for children is no great thing, so it
'only remains to go to Russia. The greater part of
'Englishwomen are tall, well built, rather proud
'and calm; according to many even cold. The
'colour of their hair is of never-ending variety.'
Such appears to be the judgment of one who evidently believed himself a connoisseur, and had had,
moreover, an opportunity of studying the far-famed
Circassian belles in their own land.

These Russian post-stations grow worse and
worse; what may be the acme of evil at which I
shall arrive before I reach the Caspian, I dare not
fancy. They are bare of all save a wooden couch;
no carpets, no provisions, no anything, except
the thirstiest of what Mark Twain calls 'sea-side
chamois.' We passed to-day a Cossack village on
the border of a large lake surrounded by 'kamish'
jungles, said to be the scene of a strange tragedy in
the Russo-Tscherkess war. ' A band of Tscherkess
warriors here met a party of Cossacks, who utterly
routed them, and the wretched natives took refuge
in the depths of the 'kamish' jungles. Here they

stayed till nightfall, when the myriads of venomous mosquitoes, which make their home amongst these reeds, drove them out, preferring death at the hands of the Cossacks to slow torture from their insect foes.' This is only a tradition, my authority my yemstchik ; but from what I have seen of these pests myself, I have little doubt of its truth.

The cold is getting quite severe already ; all the quail have gone, and last night there was a full orchestra of wolves outside the post-station. At the end of three days we pulled up at the St. Petersburg Hotel, Ekaterinodar, and if anything can be worse than post-travelling in Russia, it would be the disappointment you suffer in the so-called hotel accommodation. One of a long corridor in the stable-yard, with only too ample ventilation, my room stands a whited sepulchre, with an iron bedstead, a wooden table, a mattress, sheet, and dirty cushion, no washing utensils of any kind, no bedclothes, a wicker chair, a broken bottle half full of doubtful water, and bare boards beneath. Such is the lodging. For attendance, one dirty little boy about twelve, and a pigmy for his age, waits apparently on every one in the house. The cooking, though not first-rate, is the hotel's greatest attraction. Some one talks about man's heartiest welcome being at an inn. If he had ever tried a Russian inn, he would have reconsidered that statement. Most of the guests at the *table-d'hôte* are officers, from which one would infer that regimental messes are not in vogue in Russia.

In the morning after my arrival at Ekaterinodar I was up betimes, and, with a friend whose acquaintance I had made on my first visit, proceeded to the fair outside the town to purchase the indispensable bourka. Thanks to his exertions, I was, in little more than an hour, the possessor of a good bourka, sheepskin shouba and cap, all purchased for about 4*l.* Attired in the costume of the country, and speaking the language fluently, if not well, I am less likely to attract the attention of the natives, who, I am told, being for the most part Mussulmen, are bitterly set against the English just now, ascribing, as they do, the misfortunes of the Turkish Empire to our cold friendship, for which they have, I fear, a harder name.

Ekaterinodar must be a prospering town, for I am told that seven years ago there were only five stone houses in the place, and now there are upwards of a thousand. The old houses were built of reeds washed over with a kind of cement. The fever, too, I am told, is on the wane, and, indeed, it had need to be, for some few years ago there was no worse fever den in the Caucasus. But now as the cart-tracks through the town begin to look a little like streets (though still of the roughest), with every here and there in the most fashionable quarters a hundred yards of uneven pavement, and, by the help of constant pruning and uprooting, the houses begin to peep less blindly through the trees, while a tolerably vigorous town government prevents the deposit of filth in the public thoroughfares, the back of the fever has been broken.

The wonderful richness of the soil is sufficiently shown by a statement made to me by a settler here to-day: ‘If I don't clear my garden three times a year from new growths, I should be unable to force a way through it at the end of a twelvemonth.’ It was in his garden that I saw this afternoon some of the largest gourds I ever set eyes on, some weighing over eighty pounds, while he assured me that they sometimes reached as much as 120 or 130 pounds. The people here make a substance called cassia of them, on which they live, and with which they feed their pigs.

Trade seemed to be very brisk in the town. The fair was crowded, the shops full, and the streets alive with conveyances of every description. The number of military stationed here appears considerable, and the barracks are fairly imposing edifices.

Ekaterinodar boasts of two cathedrals, of which the old one, now in disuse, is to my mind the finest. At night I visited the fair again, and a very lively scene I found it. Out in the open stood numerous little tables, at which nips of vodka and other liqueurs were dispensed, for the most part by German Jews, to little crowds of half-drunk Cossacks. Close by, through the open doorway of a tent, you caught the glare of a huge fire and your nostrils a savoury smell of roasting mutton. Feeling hungry, I entered at one of these open doors, and found myself in a Kalmuck refreshment booth, with two or three dead sheep hanging round the tent-pole and a big semi-subterranean fire at the farther end. Here several wild-looking Tartars were devilling little knobs of mutton on a skewer; and purchasing two or three of these skewers, with their savoury burden on them all hissing from the coals, we made the best meal I have yet partaken of in the Caucasus. To wash this down we ordered Kalmuck tea, evidently quite the thing to drink here. The tea is pressed in huge cake-like bricks, and is apparently of no very high quality. A square of this is hacked off, boiled down in a pot, and the tea served up in one soup-bowl between two, with a spoon apiece. It is correct to add to it milk, huge lumps of butter, and pepper and salt to taste, when it resembles soup a good deal more than tea.

It was not until 3 P.M. next day (Thursday) that I managed to get my 'podorojna' (travelling ticket) and other things in order. At that hour it was really too late to start on my long drive to the Red Forest, but I was so sick of delays that I determined to get as far as I could that night, and trust to luck for the rest. My yemstchik, who had only a misty notion of the whereabouts of our

journey's end, was a most melancholy fellow, and
regaled me for the first hour or more with stories
of horrible murders and atrocities which had lately
taken place in or near Ekaterinodar, and would
have made the fortune of 'Lloyd's Weekly.'   They
spoke little for the efficiency of the police in the
Caucasus; but then a more miserable lot than the
Russian police generally, I never saw.   They are
the smallest and worst men (physically) in the
army, and, as such, are drafted into the police
force.   They wear a sword which they use to protect themselves against dogs, attacking small curs
with this formidable weapon with the greatest
ferocity.   I speak here of what I have seen.   If
they have a chance they are, I am assured by Russians, more likely to assist thieves than to hinder
them, and the following true story, which came
under the knowledge of a British Consul, may serve
to illustrate their ordinary conduct when applied
to as protectors of person or property :—

   'A certain lady, resident in the Crimea, but not
a native, found her silver forks rapidly disappearing
in a manner difficult to explain.   These forks were
twelve in number, and marked with a crest or mo-
nogram.   One only remained at last, and in despair
she searched the box of a Russian servant in her
employ, whom she had reason to suspect of dis-
honesty.   Here she found the eleven missing forks,
and, without disturbing them, sent for the police,

made them search the servant's box, and thus the culprit was taken red-handed. The servant was removed to prison, so were the forks. Time passed, nothing was done. At last, tired of waiting, the lady applied to know what was to be done in the matter, and how soon; at least, she pleaded, the forks might now be returned to her. The answer was, that it was necessary that the police should have the other fork in order that they might identify the eleven as her property. In a weak moment she sent her twelfth fork to them. The set was complete. In a short time the servant was released, and in spite of all her expostulations this luckless lady never saw her forks again.' This occurred in the Crimea; the Caucasus is, I believe, under military law, yet before I had passed my six months in the country, I was destined to become so familiar with stories of murders and atrocities committed here from day to day, as to think little of them.

Meanwhile, thinking and chatting of these things, we had found our way by 10 P.M. to the forester's cottage. A huge fire was blazing outside, at which half a dozen grim-looking Cossacks were smoking and toasting their toes. Inside the cottage the cigarettes had gone out, and puffing a last long whiff of smoke through his nostrils, the head-forester had betaken himself to dreamland. The Cossacks told us he had guests to-night, and had not expected me. Remembering that a man roused from his first sleep is not always in his sweetest mood, I determined not to disturb mine host, but instead took my place amongst the Cossack guards by the fire, and in spite of their looks of wonder and ridicule, prepared to be comfortable in my own way. After some delay a kettle was produced, and taking some tea from my game sack, I soon brewed the odorous beverage, by sharing which with my rough companions I gained considerably in their good graces. The night was fearfully cold, and the stories the Cossacks told almost unintelligible to me, owing to the patois in which they told them, so that my pipe once out I was ready to turn in. One thing I ought to say for these men, uncouth as they appeared When I knelt for a few minutes before turning in, every one of them rose, left the vicinity of the fire, and remained respectfully standing until I was on my legs again ; and I may add, that wherever I have met Cossacks I have found the same outward respect at any rate for religious observances, and it is my firm belief, that though prone to many vices, they have more faith and a greater respect for the nobler qualities of humanity, than most of their more enlightened fellow-countrymen.

I slept that night in my bourka on the droshky, and when I woke, the bourka, which was black the night before, was silvery with rime, while my moustache was quite hard frozen. The forester's cheery greeting, and the hot breakfast that followed it, were welcome things indeed after my hard night's rest; and on inspection I found that I had as usual dropped on my legs at the Red Forest. The guest spoken of by the Cossacks was a certain Colonel H., a German, who had come a long way for a few days' sport with my old friend, and great were to be the drives in his honour.

Our first day was very unproductive, however; for though we got some red deer on foot in front of the sleuth-hounds, we never saw them. The second day was as bad, until the afternoon, when, on our way back, we heard in another quarter of the forest a furious crashing, accompanied by short fierce snortings. Old R.'s little wiry figure actually stiffened with excitement, and his eyes became more prominent even than their wont, as he gripped my arm till it ached. 'Kabân!' (boar) was all he seemed able to get out, and, indeed, I was little less excited myself. Motioning to the German to guard the corner of the quartal where the rides crossed, he stole stealthily along a ride towards the sounds, stopping every now and then to listen, but never letting go my unfortunate arm. The sound was close to us, and now even my untrained ears told me that the sound was much like that of pigs in deadly strife. All at once my vivacious little friend dropped my arm and pointed to something in the dense brush. The trees grew so thick here, and interlaced their limbs so closely, that the forest shade was as dark as a summer night, and I could see nothing. My friend gave me little time to look, for clapping his rifle to his shoulder he seemed to take a haphazard shot into the thick of it, and let fly. Then there followed a louder snorting, with the rending of more bushes in hurried flight, and at last I had a glimpse of three dark forms tearing through the covert. One seemed much larger than the others, and at him I fired. To my own astonishment, for the shot was a very hurried one, he lurched forward, evidently hard hit ; but he instantly recovered and went on. I had a faint idea that some one was calling me back, telling me that I ought not to follow a wounded boar in thick covert ; but as my hackles were now fairly up, I crept and ran as well as I could after my wounded game. The other two guns made for various rides to cut off any of the three boars that might come their way. Once or twice I viewed my beast for a moment, but never well enough to fire in my cramped position.

Meanwhile, the forester had been making what he called music on his everlasting horn, and some of his hounds hearing it were soon on the track of the game. Hot, breathless, and almost in the dark, among the nearly impenetrable thickets, I was on

the point of giving up the chase when I heard the
dogs baying something not far ahead of me. To
creep to within thirty yards or so of them did not
take long, and then crouching behind the bole of a
huge oak, I waited for my eyes to get used to the
darkness. Gradually I began to make out the
dogs' sterns waving eagerly to and fro, and then
under a leaning tree-stump, in the very heart of the
shadow, the indistinct outline of their enemy. The
music all this time was maddening. The dogs'
clamour never ceased. The boar kept half growling, half grunting. while through it all in the
distance came the tootle of our forester's horn.
Suddenly the mass moved, and a dog went flying
belly uppermost, and his yells were added to the
discord. But this movement of the boar's was
fatal to him, as it brought him into a more open
position ; and seizing the opportunity, I rolled him
over with my 'express.' Rising he tried to charge,
but though I fired again, I believe it was unnecessary, as he was too hard hit ever to have reached
me ; still I had seen a man killed by a wounded
boar, and I naturally preferred to keep this one at
a distance.

This was the first really large game I had
killed, and I rushed up to him and gloated over
him with all the abandon of a boy. I have said I
had seen a man killed by a boar, but I should
have added it was his dead body and not the event

which I saw. Moreover, I had never seen a wild
boar before this morning, and now as I contemplated my fallen foe a strange uneasiness beset me.
There was something so homely in the innocent
face of that dead pig, that my heart for a moment
misgave me. But I banished these foolish qualms,
the reaction after my triumph probably; and as I
heard the tootle of my friend's horn approach I
sat myself down on a broad side of bacon and
indulged in a victorious whoo-oop. And now the
bushes part asunder, and R., taking in the position
at a glance, bursts into a cheer and loads me with
praise. But, alas! what is this? As my friend
approaches, slowly the gay smile fades, the ap-
plauding voice is still; the horn drops from his
nerveless grasp, and the merry little visage
lengthens out in a telescopic fashion truly awful
to behold. 'Moe domaschne kabán!' Those were
the fatal words that first left his erst joyous
lips—' My own house pig!'

The blow was too awful, too sudden. In my
pride I fell. Gradually the fact was borne in on
my already half-awakened mind: 'wild boars are
black, but this beast was white.' I had come some
thousand miles to slay a beast which I might have
found in any sty at home; I had accepted my
friend's hospitality, and rewarded it by slaying his
one cherished porker. How I smoothed him down
I don't know, but I did it somehow. As for

myself, I never quite recovered until I had slain
a veritable wild boar long afterwards. The fact
was, this wretched animal had broken out of his
sty some months previously, and betaken himself
to the forest to take his fill of love, chestnuts, and
other pleasant things. He had apparently been
making too free with the lady friends of his black-
skinned brethren, and at the moment at which we
arrived was doing battle with two of them for his
offences. In the dark his own master had not
recognised him, so that there was ample excuse
for me, and there was even a good side to this
mishap, inasmuch as we were all getting very
tired of roe-deer's flesh, and this forest-fed bacon
was a grateful change. Dragging him home with
a sapling affixed to his snout, was the poorest part
of the joke.

During the next day I did not recover my
spirits sufficiently to try for big game, so the
German colonel and myself devoted it to pheasant-
shooting. The covert consists of thick reed-beds,
the birds are of the original stock from which our
English birds are derived, and in no way differ from
them in size or appearance. We killed very few, my
dog proving utterly useless in thick covert, in
consequence of which I gave her away on the first
opportunity. I had no right of course to expect
that she as a pointer would be useful in covert, so as
the quails had gone and I should have very little

open shooting for some time, I thought it better to part with her. I am told that throughout the Kuban district, the tremendous frost of 1876, together with the floods of the same year, destroyed most of the pheasants. They certainly seemed scarcer than they were during my previous visit.

At night, sitting up for big game, I saw a few woodcock flitting bat-like across the rides, but let them alone for fear of disturbing better game. The night was lovely; the fleecy white clouds, floating through the network of dark branches, produced a most charming effect. Of all the bird-mimics I ever met, commend me to the owls you meet with here. At one moment they bark like a fox; at another, yell like an evil-minded infant; at another, you hear them grunting like swine, and creep on noiseless feet towards the spot, rifle ready in hand; and then the wretches shriek out in eldritch laughter at your mistake, and flap clumsily off to repeat the trick further on.

My last day in the Red Forest was spent in an 'ablouva' (drive), which, being utterly mismanaged, resulted in nothing but a wild cat and a few hares. In the evening the German colonel and myself had a very hot discussion about the habits of the pheasants. He apparently had shot both the ordinary and the silver pheasant in different parts of Asia, and stoutly maintained that the pheasant never roosted on a tree or bush, but invariably on

the ground. My own assertion that with us the
pheasant roosts in trees as a rule, and seldom, if
ever, on the ground, was ridiculed by both the
German and the forester, which, as both appeared
to be fairly keen observers, would lead one to believe
that the perching of our pheasants is an acquired
habit, and not common to their wild congeners.

As we wended our way homeward, we heard
in front of us the bells of a troika, and on the
bridge we overtook it. The horses were stopped,
and a volley of Russian salutations, in a voice
that might have shaken the clouds, greeted us,
while slowly from the folds of a dozen or more
wraps, a grim, gaunt figure of an old Cossack
colonel, about 6 feet 3 inches in length, unrolled
itself. The old gentleman was vociferous to a
degree, and much given to kissing and bebrothering
his friends. Having hugged the forester several
times, almost shaken my arm out of its socket,
and given a multitude of directions to the driver,
whom he addressed alternately as 'son of a dog'
and 'little dove,' he unearthed a quart bottle of
vodka, and patting it fondly, conveyed it to the
forester's hut, there to give his host a drink, and
tell us all about himself. Although very red-faced
and very grey-haired, this veteran was about as
fine a Cossack as any I ever saw, with the bois-
terous manners of an English schoolboy, added
to the peculiarities natural to a Russian. In about

ten minutes he had put me through the usual
catechism, to which time and experience had
taught me to submit with the greatest placidity.
Who was my father? What was my trade?
Was I rich? Married? Why did I come here,
&c.? To all these questions I had regular stereo-
typed answers. But when to the last I answered
that my only object was to kill big game, the old
gentleman's interest considerably increased. He,
too, was a sportsman, and knew the Caucasus
better than any man living, having spent his
whole life in fighting in it. At this very moment
he was on his way to an estate of his, three days'
journey from the Red Forest, on the Black Sea
coast, where bears and boars (if one were to
believe him) were so numerous as to seriously
impede one's movements. Would I come with
him and see for myself? Naturally, as an Englishman I imagined little was meant by such an
off-hand invitation as this; but to my surprise
the forester backed up his suggestion, assuring me
that if I did not assent I should miss a chance I
might never get again. Only half credulous, and
never expecting it would come to anything, I
assented, and, before I well knew where I was, my
things were bundled into the tarantasse, myself
after them, the old Cossack on top of all, the
farewells said, and I was under way again for
Ekaterinodar.

The days of preparation passed in Ekaterinodar had in them nothing worth recording ; I gave up my portmanteau finally and for ever as too large to travel through the mountains on horseback, and bought myself instead some Tscherkess saddle-bags, in which I stowed three flannel shirts and a few other things. My gun, too, I was obliged to leave behind, and thus on the morning of our departure my entire kit had been reduced to a rifle and small saddle-bags, half full of cartridges and gunning implements. We were to have one other travelling companion, an excessively corpulent cavalry officer ; and if I had little luggage, this worthy made amends for my deficiencies. Pillows innumerable, bags and food enough to last through a campaign, while, as to bottles, I really began to think he must be starting as a peddling wine or vodka merchant. All this, as well as our three selves, had to be piled on one fourgon, or four-wheeled open cart, and when all the luggage had been stacked on it, and our hapless selves perched on top, we presented a picture of about as unlikely a group to travel far without falling out by the way as could be readily imagined. The old Cossack got wedged between two of the largest packages, and was thus pretty safe, but the 'plunger' and myself, sitting each on some shifting packages of loaves, sardine-tins, or what not, had an exceedingly merry time of it. Briskly our horses trotted along in the keen morning air ; the roads were hard with frost, and as the heavy cart lurched from rut to rut, and bounded from hole to hole, we two resembled nothing so much as a pair of erratic human shuttlecocks. As luck would have it, both of us returned from our aërial flights in time to go on with the cart, but at what an expense of finger-nails and other bruises none but ourselves can tell. As for the 'plunger,' the exercise acted on him like a rough sea passage, and before long he was grievously ill, and I frankly admit that in another hour I should have been as bad.

The road on leaving Ekaterinodar runs through marshes, and has been raised and constructed by Government engineers, who receive a regular subsidy to keep it in repair. With the money they apparently do what they like. The governor has not heard of the state of the road, or having heard does not interfere ; the result is that it is so infamous that passengers prefer a mere track at the side to the engineers' road, which is practically unused. And this seems to me to be the universal way of doing things out here. The Government seems liberal enough, and anxious to promote the people's welfare ; more than that, considerable sums of money are expended to this end, but owing to the vastness of the territory, difficulty of transit, and want of trustworthiness in its agents,

the good intentions of the Government are too
frequently frustrated.

Never was I more heartily thankful than when
we came to what was (for us) the end of this execrable road ; and when at the Tscherkess village of
Enem we saw our horses waiting for us, I felt
almost content with the instruments of torture which
Cossacks call saddles upon their backs. The 'aoul'
(village) was fenced about with wattled walls,
and seemed a busy, thriving little place, but as far
as I could see contained none of those lovely
women of whom one has heard so much in 'Lalla
Rookh' and elsewhere. And perhaps I may be
permitted to say here that neither at Tiflis nor in
Daghestan, nor elsewhere in the Caucasus, have I
seen, either among the peasants or the upper classes,
one single face sufficiently beautiful to attract a
second glance in London. I had heard so much of
Georgian beauty that, like the aurochs, it was one
of the things I had come to look for, and, like the
aurochs, I never found it. I have brought back
several photographs of typical Caucasian faces,
bought at various photographers, who seem to me
to have always chosen the best-looking people they
could find, yet even so they are by no means
strikingly beautiful. The men, if you will, are
many of them magnificent, and as handsome as
they are well built ; but for the women, even
those who have good features are so totally devoid

of expression, so extremely animal in their appearance, as to almost warrant the Turks' conclusion that they possess none but physical properties, and are as soulless as they are insipid. Moreover, they are most of them so wonderfully alike that cases of mistaken identity must be common, even with the most devoted husbands.

By the way, Tscherkess and Cossack are frequently used amongst the Russians as terms of reproach, equivalent to robber and swashbuckler respectively, and no Circassian ever calls himself Tscherkess.

Here at Enem I got the first insight into my companions' ideas of travelling. We had perhaps been on the road a couple of hours, and had breakfasted as heartily as men can do, yet here we were doomed to repeat the process. And to save further reference to it I may say that our vast supply of stores was by no means unnecessary. Every two hours throughout those three days we had a grand feed, while in the intervals the 'plunger' nibbled and nipped, the Cossack only nipping and smoking perpetually. If these fellows require as much food campaigning as they do travelling, they must be a difficult lot to provide for.

At Enem we hoisted ourselves into our Tartar or Cossack saddles, things in which you sit as it were in a narrow deep valley between two gables, your feet thrust into things like a couple of fire-shovels, with the corners of which you poke up the ribs of your Rosinante if he is tired or sluggish. Here, too, the English equestrian meets with a novelty in the pace of his horse, which has been taught to go at a kind of amble called 'enokod,' at which pace the beast travels about twelve miles an hour with very little fatigue to the rider. Very few of the horses trot properly, and if they do, and you attempt to rise to the trot as men do in England, you meet with so much banter that you are inclined to wish that they did not. The horses are for the most part small, and possessed of wonderful endurance, but there is one breed of horses in the Caucasus that looks all over like making into good hunters—I mean the Khabardine. They are larger, finer, and faster animals than any others that I have ever seen in Russia, and their price is proportionately higher. A good Khabardine costs from 200 to 500 roubles.

As we journeyed on from Enem the country became more hilly and more wooded, and at every turn we encountered the pretty little trout stream Pseekupz. How often we crossed that stream before we reached the sea I should be afraid to guess, but it seemed to me that we were almost as often in the water as out of it, and it is this small stream that when flooded stops this road to the Black Sea for nearly half the year. We stayed for the night at some mineral springs about forty versts from Enem, beautifully situated near the Pseekupz, with high, well-timbered hills all round. Most of the trees are young oaks, which were now lovely in their russet robes. But there are, besides, wild pear and apple, with everywhere a thick undergrowth of hazel. At the mineral springs is a Russian military hospital, and the doctor in charge was our host for the night. The hospital is built to hold some 300 people, and it was believed that this place would in time become a fashionable bathing-place for the Caucasus. Hitherto, however, the military have had it all to themselves. There are a few good houses in the place, and Government is erecting baths over the springs. The springs themselves are of hot water, strongly impregnated with sulphur, which comes down from the hills at a temperature of $42°$ Reaumur. I saw some of the water, which was colder, of a dull bluish grey, and stank horribly. These baths are supposed to cure rheumatic affections, and my friend the Cossack pretended to have obtained great relief from them. Nay. so enthusiastic was he that, after taking them both internally and externally, he insisted on my doing the same. Being in extreme need of a tub, I complied with his whim as far as an external application went, and was parboiled for my complacency, feeling a good deal worse when I came out than I did when I went in.

The springs run through a white stone which, though extremely hard on the surface, pulverises at the touch the moment the outside layer is removed. I am myself ignorant of geology, but I was assured that this was quartz of a very high quality, and excellently adapted for the manufacture of glass. If this be so, a glass factory here would, one would imagine, be an extremely remunerative speculation, with any quantity of timber and water-power immediately at hand, and no rival factory nearer than Moscow, especially as glass is in the Caucasus a very dear commodity, bad glass bottles costing from ten to fifteen copecks. In the evening and in the morning we saw the worst side of the village by the springs; for on both occasions a dense white fog rolled up from the valley high up the hills, completely hiding them from view, while the dew lay on the grass like rain after a very severe thunder shower.

We left the springs early, and shivered in our saddles as we waded through the rolling fog clouds, although in a few hours' time the heat was quite oppressive.

I noticed to-day by the wayside a large quantity of mistletoe, and have since remarked that its abundance is not restricted to this one part of the Caucasus. The insects by the wayside were 'hyale,' clouded yellow, red admirals, painted ladies, and

several varieties of white butterflies. I also
noticed some large pale yellow butterflies, which
may have been the common brimstone, but I
believe were not. I am pretty sure too that I
recognised one 'comma.' We passed through one
or two villages inhabited by 'plastoons' (Russian
settlers), who in spite of the richness of the soil appeared to be in the most abject poverty. On every
face the fever had set its yellow seal, and all the
women over forty were hideous enough to frighten
Macbeth's witches.

Truly, this Caucasus must be the land of the
lotus-eaters, yet what sorry beings these lotus-
eaters are. All round them such beauty as Ten-
nyson has dreamed of; mountains clothed in gold
and purple, with the sea murmuring round their
bases ; wealth to be had for the taking, from the
too luxuriant soil ; and yet here the peasant smokes
and moons away his life, content to cull in idleness
just enough to keep body and soul together, and
only doing just enough work to provide for himself a crop of that weed in the consumption of
which he wastes life and energy, as well as the
money and opportunities that might be his. Each
village where Russians lived seemed to me more
wretchedly poor than the last, and it became a
relief to see how few and far between the villages
were. The Tscherkesses, who made a garden of at
least some parts of their native home, might almost

feel revenged in contemplating the utter failure of the race which has supplanted them.

But for us the day was no day of idleness, but rather one of considerable toil and difficulty. The road grew exceeding steep and rugged, and the little baggage cart which we had endeavoured to send on by our men came to grief, and was broken beyond repair. The driver, who was on the top of the baggage, probably asleep, got a bad fall, and was rather seriously hurt. The tripod of my photographic apparatus was broken, and the stock of my rifle snapped short off at the pistol grip. The 'plunger's' store of eau-de-Cologne, without which this hero felt it impossible to travel, was also lost in the general disaster, and he, poor fellow, had very bad times throughout the day, having had too much to eat and too much shaking up after it. For a cavalry officer, too, it was somewhat undignified, when ascending one steep little ravine, to slide off over his horse's quarters ; and for a man of his weight it must have been as painful as it was ridiculous. Laughter went a long way towards leaving me as helpless as he was, for a more ludicrous sight than our gallant companion rolling off behind, it would be difficult to conceive.

The night was, if anything, worse than the day, for my old friend the Cossack, having a great deal of pain from an old injury near his spine, determined to cure it with hard drinking : the result

of which was that he became helplessly drunk, and
the 'plunger' only irritably so. In this condition
the nature of the man showed itself, and he amused
himself by baiting me, a stranger, and his friend's
guest, for the amusement of his servants. At last
his insolence became so intolerable that, risking all
possible consequences, I got him by the scruff of
the neck and gave him such a shaking as he had
not experienced even during the rough ride of the
last few days. It was, of course, extremely unpleasant for me, but my host was too drunk to
interfere, and there are some things which a man
cannot stand.

Next morning, after having spent the night
awake in a state of siege, uncertain what my quondam friend's servants might think fit to do to me, I
had a wretched ride in my own society to Duapsé,
the little seaport town which was to be the end of
our journey. The 'plunger' neither apologised nor
called me out, as I had thought he might, but the
good old Cossack behaved like a gentleman, and
although, of course, we were glad to say good-by to
one another at Duapsé, we parted good friends, and
I believe he exonerated me from all blame in the
matter.

CHAPTER V.

HEIMAN'S DATCH.

Duapsè—Tscherkess emigrants—By the sea-shore—Superb scenery—Drunken guides—A Cossack station—Bears—Take possession of a ruined villa—Hiding our provisions—Wild swine—Astray in the jungle—A rough breakfast—Boars in file—A missfire—Forest fruit—Lose our horses—A panther—Night-watch—Shooting in the dark—On the trail—*Barse*—A friendly Cossack—Deserted by my servants.

AT Duapsè there is an English (Indo-European) telegraph station, so, though unexpectedly thrown on my own resources again, I was much better off than I might otherwise have been. The Englishmen gave me a cordial welcome, and were very good to me. Duapsè, I am informed, is built on a graveyard, in which are buried numbers of the victims of the Russo-Tscherkess war. In 1864, after the final subjugation of the Caucasus, some 200,000 Circassians left the Caucasus for Trebizond, at the invitation of their conquerors. They were for the most part conveyed in small Turkish vessels, in which they were so crowded, starved, and exposed, that not more than half ever reached their destination, the others dying *en route*. Of these a very large pro-

portion died near Duapsé, and were there landed
and buried, or left to bleach, according to the means
of their friends. Their graves are still marked
by little mounds and inequalities in the ground
throughout the place. On their miserable journey
they sold everything they possessed, and I have
frequently heard in Kertch and in the Caucasus of
girls being sold for a few roubles, and valuable
daggers (the last thing almost that a Tscherkess
parts with) for about the same. Now Duapsé is
a vilely squalid hole, with two telegraph stations
and a governor's house. The steamers from Odessa
and Poti touch here, if it is fine, once a week, but
if there is any sea on they cannot come in, as I
was hereafter to learn to my cost. Why Duapsé
exists, and still more why it has a governor, I
never could conceive.

It was, then, with a feeling of intense relief
that on October 21 I left Duapsé behind me and
turned my horse's head southwards along the
Black Sea shore. I had managed to engage a
couple of Russian peasants, Ivan and Yepheem, to
guide me to some happy hunting-grounds of which
they knew, some fifty versts from Duapsé. Taking
three horses, we loaded each with as much provisions as he could carry, and then climbed on top
ourselves. It was difficult work to so adjust yourself and baggage, as to keep your seat over the
boulders. Grip was, of course, impossible, and

balance, with a shifting basis under you, almost as much so.

The road lay between the base of the cliffs and the sea, and as these two were in close juxtaposition, your horse had at one time to wade and at another to creep from boulder to boulder, in places where even a goat would have to move with caution. This lasted for fifteen versts, and these fifteen have in rough weather to be avoided, and a long circuitous route in the hills substituted for them. After leaving these stony places, the road winds up into the hills, and here the eye had a feast indeed. All the way from Ekaterinodar the scenery had been beautiful, but here it was superb. Range upon range of hills, as far as the eye could see, one behind another, and each range higher than the last, until far away one caught the sheen of snow-peaks against the sky. The autumn foliage was a never-ending glory. One shrub in particular caught my eye, of stunted growth, with a long oval leaf, which was now of the most brilliant shades of red. This shrub grew in immense clumps, and the effect at a short distance was that of vast beds of scarlet geranium.

But the road in the hills was almost as bad as the road by the sea, and after having done some twenty-eight versts in the whole day, our horses were done up, and so were we. Just after noon my men stayed behind for some time, and I, thinking nothing of it, rode slowly on. In about half an hour they rejoined, looking mightily pleased with themselves, and very drunk. They had discovered a large bottle holding about three pints of vodka, which I had brought with me for our use during the next fortnight. This they had quietly sat down to the moment my back was turned, and finished it. It was no good my making a row about it; I was in their hands, and determined to bear with them, at least until I found out where game was to be found, after which I could decide whether to keep them or try alone. Meanwhile they had finished their grog, and as I did not mean to give up mine, they would be punished by enforced abstinence for some time to come.

A Cossack station in the Caucasus is about as strange a place to pass the night in as can well be imagined. Ten or a dozen privates, with the manners of monkeys in the Zoo, all sleeping in the same room with yourself and their officer, a youngster generally little better educated than themselves, and thoroughly hail-fellow with them all. Such is your company. Your couch the top of the 'petchka' (oven), if you like heat and dirt, and are inclined to pay for the berth; if not, as much room as you can get on the floor or on a form, with a Cossack's boots next your head and a Cossack's head next to your boots. For supper we got some barbel, and a fish they called 'golovin,' which one of the soldiers had caught ; and though tired enough to turn in gladly even here, we were, I think, even more glad to turn out again at four next morning.

On our way we came across signs of bears ; in the first instance, in the face of a Greek settler we met, whose nose and mouth had apparently got discontented with their original positions, and had altered them according to their own fancy. On inquiry, we found that two years ago the Greek had been frightening bears from his orchard, when one of them had attacked him and, striking him on the head, peeled the face off his skull almost, and left him still living in this condition. He was found, and the face replaced as well as possible, but his whole appearance was hideously distorted.

A mile or two further on we came across fresh tracks of a regular family of bears, who had been down to the high-water line looking for waifs and strays whilst we were sleeping at the Cossack station.

Mid-day found us at our camping place—a ruined datch or villa belonging formerly to General Heiman, built on an estate given him, I believe, as a reward for his successes against the aborigines. But the house was never finished and the land never reclaimed. Where once the Tscherkess had magnificent orchards, nothing now remains save here and there a fruit-tree, still bearing fruit though sparingly, choked by the luxuriant growth of forest trees. Through the doorless doorways and windowless frames of the ruined villa, the big trees branch in, creepers and blackberry bushes grow merrily inside, while from the very hearth, disturbed by our intrusion, a scared woodcock bustles away. The spot had evidently been used as a camping place by drovers before our day, for all round the white skulls of cattle bleached on the shore and on the sward, while remains of campfires were numerous, although there were none of recent date. All this warned us to be careful, so that our first step, after turning out our horses, was to secrete all our provisions, &c. in a hole beneath the flooring, and to destroy, as far as possible, all traces of our presence.

Having done this, we turned to the greenwood, and indeed it was not far to go. Two dozen strides, and we had almost to cut our way through the dense undergrowth. After a time we forced our way to more open forest, and here we parted. Not twenty minutes afterwards there was a report that set the forest shrieking. Something came crashing down hill past me, and rumbled away into silence down a deep tree-covered gorge. In a few minutes I arrived on the scene of action, and found Ivan and his mongrel pointer gloating over a fine sow he had slain. Having gralloched her, we hoisted her on to the top of a blasted and broken oak, and, there impaled, she presented to us a ghastly, and to the jackals who soon arrived a no doubt very tantalising, appearance. However, we left them to their own devices and, feeling sure of pork chops for dinner, continued our hunt.

Twice I heard swine close to me, and both my men saw game again during the afternoon; but the covert was so dense that we none of us got another shot, and, what was worse, all lost our way. The sun, which had been our guide, went down all in a moment, and left us in the dark without a compass to steer by. For two hours and a half I struggled through jungle that tore me to pieces, and threw me down every few yards. I climbed out of a ravine up the white face of a cliff, gun in hand, which cliff I inspected by daylight on another occasion, and would not climb again for the best day's shooting that man ever had; and at last, fagged and bleeding, came upon Ivan resting, with his pig up aloft keeping watch for him.

After getting the pig down and finding Yepheem, we started on the back track; but, though the track had been comparatively easy by daylight, with no pig to drag along, we lost it in about five minutes now. In another ten minutes we were completely lost, and, realizing the fact, prepared to meet it. We had, fortunately, between us two boxes of matches, furnished with which Yepheem gave us an occasional glimmer of light, by which Ivan hewed away with his kinjal through the tangled creepers, while I plodded wearily on behind with the pig in tow. Two hours of this kind of thing, added to the previous day's work, was more than I could stand; so we sat down, made a wood fire, and, by its light, divided the sow longitudinally.

It was no good waiting for the moon to rise, as she was in her last quarter; so Yepheem shouldering one half, and myself the other, we floundered on again, to arrive at last at the ruin about midnight, dead beat and starving, to say nothing of being saturated with the blood of the pig, and lacerated all over by the thorns of that abominable creeper the 'wolf's tooth.' Then, after one long pull at the whiskey bottle, I lay down and slept where I was, too tired to wait for the chops which the men were frying by my side.

Nor were my men much less tired; for when I woke with a shiver at dawn, one of them was asleep with his skewer of grilled pork almost untouched by his side. Of this I speedily relieved him, and, raking together the embers of the fire, which my men had made under the flooring the night before, I re-cooked the kabobs, and breakfasted, not perhaps sumptuously, but with an appetite that made amends for any defects in the cooking.

Whilst the men still slept, I went down to the sea for a swim and a look at the country

round us. Looking from the sea you saw nothing
but endless hills, growing gradually into mountains, as they receded farther and farther from the
shore. Everywhere they seemed covered with
forest, the greater part of which was composed
of Spanish chestnut trees. Except a solitary
eagle, a few porpoises rolling about near in shore,
and one of my men coming down now to collect driftwood, there was no sign of life anywhere.
After helping to light the fire and brew the tea, I
sent Yepheem to look for the horses, which were
nowhere in sight, and meanwhile Ivan and I took
our rifles and tried another part of the forest.
We had gone but a very little way when the
dog gave tongue, and was evidently driving something through the bushes towards us. Ivan ran
in one direction, I in another, to cut off the
game. Standing behind a big tree at the foot
of a small hill, covered with rhododendron clumps,
I heard a rustling through the covert, such as
some small animal might make if quietly forcing
his way through. I never dreamed it was our
game, but was still intently listening for the crashing charge I was beginning to know so well.
Looking in the direction of the rustling, I was
thunderstruck to see three magnificent grey old
boars following one another in single file down
hill, straight to my tree. The almost cat-like
noiselessness with which large and clumsy animals

can move about in thick covert, is almost more wonderful than the tremendous noise even small ones make when so minded. I picked out the leading boar, fired, and with a thundering rush they were gone. How I could have missed him I don't know, but I apparently did clean, and for the rest of that day I found it harder than ever not to speak somewhat unadvisedly with my lips when a long loop of ' wolf's tooth ' caught me up under the nose, or a hazel wand flew back and cut me over the ear.

Later on in the afternoon we were all three walking abreast, with perhaps a hundred yards between each gun, when I caught a glimpse of Ivan stealthily scrambling up an old stump, from which elevated position he aimed carefully, for what seemed about five minutes, at something almost under his feet. Then followed the click that denotes a missfire, and a great crashing amidst the rhododendron bushes, as a big brown bear scuttled away in undignified flight. Some minutes afterwards, whilst Ivan with many curses was descending from the stump, his valuable piece went off, luckily damaging no one.

Except some wild boars seen by Yepheem, this was the last game we saw during the day, although we came across regular roads made by bears and swine, and one patch of several acres, which from the broken fruit-trees and trampled state of the ground appeared to be a regular bear den. The quantity of fruit one meets with in these Circassian forests compensates in some measure for perse- cutions of the 'wolf's tooth' and other thorny creepers. Large apples, walnuts, grapes, 'fourmar' (an edible berry for which I do not know any other name), medlars, blackberries, dewberries, and a kind of scarlet plum, occur frequently, and where- ever they occur the trees are smashed into ruins by the bears. You begin to get some notion of the power of a bear when you have seen the enor- mous boughs he has broken in his greed for fruit. To-night the jackals were calling all round us, but the wily little beasts never gave me a shot.

In the morning Yepheem woke us with the pleasant intelligence that our horses had been stolen. A drover had passed along the coast whilst we were shooting the day before, and suspicion immediately settled on his party. Of course after this news there was no hunting for us to-day, for while Ivan and Yepheem scoured the country for our missing steeds, I had to sit at home and watch. At nightfall the best news they could give me was that the Cossacks on the station at which we had slept on our way hither had lost six of their horses at the same time.

I had time during the day to examine the insect life about our camp, and amongst the butterflies I noticed all three meadow browns, quantities of very large brimstones, a fritillary, and a wood argus, whilst amongst the moths I recognized quantities of the gamma and the humming-bird hawk moth.

When we went down to the shore to bathe, huge shoals of what looked like bass were playing close in shore, but alas we had no means of securing any, though they would have been a noble addition to our ill-found larder.

Last night, whilst writing up my journal, with my legs dangling from a rafter, and a great wood fire burning by my side, by which the men lay curled in their bourkas, the wind that came moaning through the open places in the wall brought with it a sound between a child's wail and a wolf's howl, which was so distinct from the jackals' cries that it arrested my attention at once. The men sprang to their feet simultaneously, and with excited faces whispered 'barse' (panther). At our backs was the ruined doorway through which the forest trees stretched their arms ; in our front was the huge empty window place with thickets of briar and thorn half blinding it, and right under it the sound seemed. For a moment I believe the same feeling was on all of us, that the next event would be the entrance of our serenader by either door or window. However, this wore off at once, and snatching up my rifle I crept to the window place to try to make out the beast in the moonlight. But outside all was a maze of shadowy limbs and dark places, with every here and there a brilliant patchwork of moonshine; and though I went outside and carefully beat all round our camp I could not catch sight of the barse.

To-night, having had a lazy day in camp, I was by no means in a hurry to roll myself up in the least draughty corner, so taking my rifle, having constructed a night sight for it, I betook myself to the beach to await our last night's visitor should he repeat his visit.

The hills near Heiman's Datch come down almost to the high-water line, so that sitting hidden under some drift-wood I had the forest close at my back, and a little above me; so close indeed as to suggest the possibility of a sudden spring from the bushes to my hiding place if any beast had the courage to try it. Before me lay some forty yards at most of strand, and beyond a perfectly calm and silent sea. Far up in one of the valleys at my back two wolves were answering each other, and away towards Dnapsé I could hear some jackals fighting over some carrion they had found.

But for a long time nothing happened, except every now and then a rustle in the forest at my back, that made me start and bring my gun to bear on its dark fastnesses. I had almost made up my mind to give up my watch and return to the ruin, when a figure like the grey ghost of some large hound was just visible against the sky line. It was too dark to see even the barrels of my rifle, but aiming as best I could, I fired. The figure bounded forward and trotted briskly along the coast from me; so pitching my rifle low, and well in front, I fired again. Then the beast vanished. For a minute or two I waited, expecting to see it again, or at least hear it making off, and then, loading my rifle, I went up to the spot at which I had last seen it. But whatever the beast was, it had vanished, and feeling that I had wasted a couple of hours and a couple of cartridges in missing a jackal, I went back to my roost in the ruin.

However, on the morning after my night-watch, when we went down to bathe and collect driftwood for our fires, my man Ivan suddenly called to me to look at something he had found on the stones. On inspection it proved to be large blood drops, on the very spot, as near as I could tell, on which my shadowy visitor of the night before had stood. Following the blood track along the shore, we momentarily expected to find a dead jackal, as, from the quantity of blood, the beast must have been very hard hit. Some two hundred yards along the shore the trail crossed the mouth of a little mountain stream, with a bed of soft clay on one side of it, and through this the trail went. Our astonishment may be imagined when along with the blood marks we found the fresh tracks of a large panther (or more properly leopard), which had evidently been the beast wounded by me in the dark the night before. Of course the search was now prosecuted with far greater ardour, at least on my part. As for the men, they have so many yarns about the much dreaded barse, that they were not as keen as they might have been; and when the trail turned from the shore and entered some extremely dense and dark thickets, they came to a stand, and nothing would induce them to enter the forest with me. Unfortunately the dog was of their mind, so that after wandering blindly about for some time, tearing myself to pieces, and losing my temper terribly, I had to give up my search, with the conviction strong upon me that a noble and (in this part of the world) rare quarry was lying dead within a stone's throw of me.

'Barse' is the name given by the peasants on the Black Sea coast, and in fact generally throughout the Caucasus, to any feline animal larger than a wild cat; and this indiscriminate use of the word occasioned me a good deal of trouble. Too often when they tell you of barse, the animal they refer to is only the lynx, of which there are at least two varieties in the Caucasus, and which is extremely numerous on some parts of the Black Sea coast. The natives trap it for its skin, which is one of the commonest in the furriers' shops of Tiflis and Ekaterinodar. But that the leopard or ocelot (the snow leopard of India) does occur not uncommonly in the Caucasus, even on its western coast, I was assured by Professor Radde, the courteous director of the Tiflis Museum, who showed me great kindness in going over his collections with me during my stay in that town. And even had I had no further confirmation than the tracks I have above alluded to, I should feel convinced that the beast I wounded was an unmistakable leopard.

Returning from our tracking operations, we were startled by seeing a strange figure moving about inside our camp, evidently looking for anything light enough to carry away. Remembering our horses, we never for a moment doubted but that this was one of the gentry who had stolen them, returned possibly for the saddles. Had he been, he would have had fleet feet to have escaped, for we went for him like terriers for a rat. But our anger was turned to rejoicing when we recognised the face of a friendly Cossack from the next station, who had brought our horses back with him, and was looking for nothing more valuable than a still smouldering ember to light his cigarette by. Our horses had joined his 'taboon' (herd), which had been pasturing in a valley somewhere between our camp and his station, and he had there found them the night before.

On hearing this good news Ivan and his chum announced to my disgust their intention of going straight back to Duapsè, before any further accidents happened, alleging as their reasons that their wives could not do without them any longer. As a matter of fact, I presume their own appetite for sport was satiated, and their appetite for vodka becoming daily more unendurably keen. As no words or promises of mine could turn them from their resolve I gave in to them, merely stipulating that they should leave me one of their horses to take me twelve versts further up the coast, to the hut of a Tscherkess telegraph watcher, who lived by that irrepressible mountain torrent the Golovinsk. To this they agreed, and I moreover managed to persuade the Cossack to accompany me to Golovinsky, as another Cossack station at which he could rest was not far from the watcher's hut. So we parted company, my men and I, and I don't think I suffered any great loss from their defection. My reasons for wishing to go to Golovinsky were, that a report had come down the coast that in the extensive chestnut forest round the watcher's hut bears were more than usually numerous, the man himself having recently killed two by shooting from a platform in a tree during the night.

CHAPTER VI.

GOLOVINSKY.

THE Cossack and myself, having seen the two Russians round the first little promontory, unearthed a small quantity of whiskey which I had managed to save from their insatiable thirst, and with this and a pork kabob made a very fair lunch, and laid the foundation of a good understanding between us. Then we piled up a pyramid of odds and ends on the back of each little horse, and made the whole fast with cords. The equestrians' enviable position was astride the summit of the pyramid of luggage—a position difficult to retain when gained, and almost impossible to attain unaided. However, after many failures the Cossack hoisted me on to my place, and providing we never went out of a walk I felt fairly safe. How the Cossack got up was a miracle, but he did it somehow; and we proceeded at a walk through the shingle, that forms the only possible pathway along this part of the shore.

We had not gone far when it seemed to me that I was gradually leaning over more and more towards the sea. I tried to regain an erect position, and then I became aware of my situation. My girths had got slack, and my saddle, with its huge pile of luggage, of which I was the highest point, was gradually turning round under my horse's belly. Seated as I was, I was utterly helpless; I could not readjust my saddle, and a voluntary descent, except head first, was impossible. So I waited the course of events, and in a few moments lay sprawling on the ground, half buried in pots and pans, bourkas, and other impedimenta.

This was our only misadventure, however, and about four o'clock we came in sight of the watcher's hut—a two-roomed wooden shanty, knocked up in the roughest way possible, standing on the edge of the shingle, with a big brown bear-skin stretched over the roof to dry. A more utterly miserable-looking hut cannot well be conceived; but the skin on the thatch consoled me, proclaiming as it did the vicinity of the game I was in search of.

After much shouting and hammering at the board that constituted the hut's one door, a wild Robinson Crusoe-like fellow came shuffling out. Tall and well built, but taciturn and clumsy to a

degree, Stepan was not a favourable specimen of
the benefits of woodland isolation to mankind.
Instead of giving me a kindly welcome as, to do
them justice, all Russian peasants had hitherto
done, he eyed me in the doubtful manner in which
some big dog might eye a too familiar stranger
before snapping at the would-be caressing hand.
His face was shrivelled and yellow with fever, and
a frequent deep cough formed no pleasant accom-
paniment to our cottage life. Gradually his
sullenness gave way to surprise at the presence of
an English gentleman in those evil places, for such
he evidently deemed Golovinsky; and when I explained to him that I wished to hire his services
and the use of his hut, as well as to put all game
killed at his disposal, his delight knew no bounds.
His terms were a rouble a week, that is about
half a crown; but that seemed so unfair to me that
I trebled it, and added to it a promise of ten
roubles additional for the skinning of the first
bear I should kill; and considering that he gave
me house-room, black bread, and his whole time,
I think 7s. 6d. per week was not an exorbitant
charge.

However, he was delighted, and though rather
startled to find that his whole larder consisted of
some black bread, onions, and pork fat ('salo'),
I consoled myself with the reflection that with the
addition of tea and sugar, which I had brought

with me, we should be able to hold out for a week at least, in which time I should probably have obtained my coveted bear-skin.

Outside the hut all was beauty. The hut itself was as nearly as possible the centre of a bay of fairly high hills, enclosing a couple of hundred acres or so of plain covered with low shrubs. Beyond the first chain of hills, which was wooded to the top, rose another and a higher chain, and so one after another, in successive semicircles, they rose range above range, until far away in the sapphire sky shone the white glory of the snow-peaks. Out at sea a long line of pelicans lay tossing on the little waves, like a small fleet riding at anchor. Within the hut all was squalor and filth. The place consisted of two rooms, in one of which was a telegraphic apparatus of the simplest kind, with a handle like that of a barrel organ, and a face like the face of a clock with letters in place of numerals. This was the deity of the place and Stepan's pride and fear. Near it was a camp bedstead, and here the list of the furniture ends. The other room was merely a shed, in which such cooking as we had to do was done; and though the appliances were of the simplest, we never taxed them overmuch. The floors throughout were of mud, and several inches deep in refuse, dating from the time of Stepan's arrival in his den.

Borrowing a spade and cutting down a large bough for a broom, I soon had a clear floor, and by dint of hard work had in an hour's time got a fairly clean place to move about in. Stepan retired to the shed, and, in spite of my protestations, took up his abode there. Had it not been for his cough I should have fallen in with this arrangement readily enough; but as it was, I felt he required the best accommodation the shanty afforded. However, in the shed he remained, and for the rest of my stay I had his best room to myself.

There were, besides Stepan and myself, three other residents at the 'telegraph station,' as he loved to call it—to wit, Zizda, Lufra, and Orla, three large cross-bred dogs, devoured by mange, with which Stepan hunts the boars that abound in the thicket at the back of his house, killing on an average, so he tells me, half a dozen in the year. In spite of the numbers which inhabit the adjoining forests, this small bag is not very much to be wondered at, when the impenetrable nature of the covert and the almost utter uselessness of Stepan's gun are taken into consideration.

Russian peasants have amongst them the most wonderful fire-arms in the world, which, as a rule, they buy in the bazaars at from three to five roubles (i.e. 7s. 6d. to 12s. 6d.) each. I have frequently seen the grebe-shooters along the shore

at Kertch using old rifle-barrels worn thin, tied on
to a rough stock, with flint lock, &c., the whole
thing being compounded of the remains of some
venerable weapon in use in the Russian army
immediately after the invention of gunpowder.
Stepan's was no exception to this rule, and yet
I distinctly remember seeing him put in charges
which I would not have ventured to put into my
high-class breech-loader.

After putting the house in order, Stepan loaded
his valuable weapon with a good charge of powder
and two bullets, the first in its naturally smooth
state, the other chewed into a rough-edged mass.
Thus prepared we sallied forth and reconnoitred
the little plain within the hills. Everywhere the
tracks of bears, boars, wolves, and occasionally roe-
deer presented themselves to our eyes, but of the
animals themselves we saw nothing. Pheasants
rose several times from the bushes at our feet, and
Stepan tells me Golovinsky is a favourite abiding
place of theirs, in consequence of the quantity of 'phaisantchik' growing here, upon the
yellow berry of which they feed. The pheasants
have no bad taste in berries, for when ripe I
know no berry much pleasanter in flavour than
that of the 'phaisantchik,' in spite of its acidity.
The flavour strongly resembles that of the pine-
apple.

Of course, as pheasants abound here, Stepan

has no fowling-piece, and I have left mine behind
at Ekaterinodar. You would imagine that living
as the Cossacks, Stepan and many others, do, in a
state of semi-starvation in the matter of meat from
week to week, with an abundance of game birds
round them, they would become good shots and
keen sportsmen, or at the very least turn trappers,
and so supply themselves with food. And yet it
is not so. Not one Cossack amongst the many I
have met was a sportsman, and this perhaps their
want of sporting rifles and ammunition may account
for ; though, if they were allowed to use them, no
better rifle than the Berdianka, with which they are
supplied, could be desired. But that neither they,
nor the settlers and peasants, should have any idea
of trapping, is most strange. In all the Crimea and
Caucasus I never saw or heard of snare, or pitfall, or
any of the hundred and one devices for killing game
without fire-arms, which other nations use. The
only thing of the kind I ever heard of, was told me
by a German settler, who assured me that in some
places they caught pheasants by inserting small
cones of paper, limed inside, into the earth ; in the
bottom of each cone a pea is placed and others
strewn around. The pheasant, after finishing the
peas scattered on the surface of the ground, finds
the pea at the bottom of the cone, and, in trying to
peck it out, hoodwinks himself with the limed paper
cone, and being blinded becomes frightened, and re-

mains cowering on the ground, an easy prey to the trapper. But I could never hear of any one amongst the Tscherkesses, Cossacks, or 'plastoons' (settlers), who had either done this or heard of its being done; and I believe I am right in saying that the Russians, at least in the Crimea and Caucasus, know very little of trapping, and indeed of woodcraft generally.

I had passed the first part of this my first night at Golovinsky, sleeping as well as I could in my only too well ventilated quarters; and rising while it was still dark, Stepan and I had wiled away the time in chatting of the snares and traps with which different nations used to kill their game. As we chatted he busied himself on a pair of rough sandals or mocassins he was making for me from the skin of a wild boar he had killed in the spring. As soon as they were finished, he steeped them in water to soften them, and then, first wrapping my leg round with canvas, he fastened on the sandals, winding the long laces round and round the canvas until they fastened just below the knee. Thus I was booted and gaitered *à la mode Circassienne* in a very short time; and as the dawn slowly broke over the mountains, and the stars grew pale and died in the grey of morning, we left our hut and walked hard to warm ourselves in the soft rain that began with dawn.

On our way to the forest, which began at the

foot of the first range of hills, we had to ford that turbulent trout stream, the Golovinsk, and as its waters come straight down from the higher peaks, and are fed almost entirely by melted snow, right bitterly cold we found it. Chilled and wet to the waist, we forced our way through a weary half hour's work in thorn brake and strangling creeper, while the gathered rain-drops ran in streams down our necks and up our sleeves from every bough we touched.

At last we gained the more open chestnut forest, and here we found how great a boon the rain really was to us. The leaves, which the day before had sounded like small minute-guns under our feet, firing a warning to every beast in the forest, were now soft and silent. Arrived among the chestnuts, Stepan and I separated, he taking a line along the base of the hill, I choosing a parallel line much higher up. To-day the dogs had been tied up, and our *modus operandi* was simply to walk as silently as possible through the forest, stopping every twelve yards or so to listen, and trusting at least as much to our ears as to our eyes to find the game.

For over an hour I stalked noiselessly on, hearing nothing but the rattle of the falling chestnuts, the patter of the ceaseless rain, and the screaming of the everlasting jays. It is easy to understand why the Indian, whose whole life is spent more or less in the chase, becomes such a silent, self-contained being. The whole chase is a school for silence and self-restraint. Should you tread carelessly, a twig breaks and your chance is lost; should a thorn run right up under your nail from end to end, you must not complain; and should the bitter blows dealt you in the face by the rebounding twigs, or the tearing and strangling of the thorny creepers, at last extract an exclamation, your chance is over for the day.

For over an hour I bore all the malice of the forest fiend silently and uncomplainingly. But at last, in an evil moment, a long trailing loop of thorny vine hooked me under the nose, and pulling up that tender member to an unusual angle, held it firmly hooked in its painful position. Then I fear the wrath within me boiled over; and as I released my mutilated proboscis, I spoke unadvisedly with my tongue. Hardly was the imprecation out of my lips when there was a short sharp snort, and a black object flashed past me downhill at a hundred miles an hour. A quick snap-shot failed to stop him, and so I passed on, reflecting that my little explosion had cost me probably the only game I was doomed to see that day.

But this lesson taught me caution, and a short half-hour afterwards, whilst I was creeping noiselessly along a kind of natural cutting, I was suddenly aware of a big black thing moving in the hazels high above me. The creature looked as if it was browsing, and might have been anything from a cow to a rhinoceros, for any distinguishing feature that I could discern. However, in such a position, I argued, it must be game of some sort, so, raising my rifle, I aimed as nearly as possible into the middle of it, and fired. The yells that followed my shot were proof positive that I had hit something, and before I had time to turn, an old bear was coming straight down to me through the brushwood, 'puffing' furiously as he came, like an excited locomotive engine. I had time to notice that his mode of progression was curious and lop-sided, lurching as he did on to his hams at every step, and when he was almost on top of me, rolling over the cutting in which I stood : only avoiding me by a few yards, he went crashing downhill, taking another bullet with him as he went, and lodging under a fallen tree far down the hillside.

Here for a time I left him, making the woods hideous with his snarling and moaning ; and after some ten minutes' shouting I managed to get my guide, Stepan, to come to me, white and shaking with fright. He explained to me that he thought I had been certainly killed, and in consequence of this, I suppose, believed I should want his services no more. Standing in the cutting, I pointed out to him the place where Bruin lay, far down through an almost impenetrable thicket of blackberry-bush

and wild vine. Stepan did all he knew to induce
me to leave the bear to die by inches, and come for
him next day ; but this seemed to me not only
unsportsmanlike, but uncertain : so leaving him to
watch Bruin, I crawled into the thicket, and began
forcing my way by a game-track under the bushes
to the place where he lay.

It was a difficult path, and the creepers hampered me sadly, so that it was not without a considerable quickening of the pulse that I heard
Stepan screaming, 'Look out, Barin (master),
for heaven's sake, here he comes!.' The bushes
parted about ten yards below, and slowly pushing
his way uphill came the bear, swinging his head
from side to side, throwing the blood and foam
from his jaws, and moaning and sobbing hideously.
As soon as he caught sight of me he gave his
jaws a kind of vicious snap, and even managed to
increase his pace to a trot. It was difficult to fire
in my cramped position, but I managed to do it,
and, thanks to his extreme proximity to my rifle's
muzzle, the ball went right through his head,
passing through a large oak sapling beyond, leaving a hole in it as clean drilled as if it had been
done with a hot iron.

The bear, when we came to examine him, was
a very old fellow, quite black, and with a skin in
anything but a good condition. However, being
my first bear, we skinned him with great care and

much exultation, and brought home his head, tired but rejoicing.

It was still early when we got back to our hut, not more than mid-day, in fact ; but the weather was of the roughest, and our uprising had been an early one, so that we were not sorry to pass the rest of the day in cleaning our bear's skin and preparing his flesh for our evening meal. And fresh-killed bear's meat takes a considerable time in preparation, and when the animal happens to be as old and wiry as the beast killed to-day, not forty cooks with forty rolling-pins could ever beat his flesh into a reasonable degree of tenderness.

The Cossacks on the station won't eat bear's flesh, though they only get meat once a week here ; and partly for that reason, and partly because with their single-barrelled rifles they consider the risk too great, they never molest the bears. So little in fact do they know of their comparative harm-lessness, that they gave me quite an ovation when I came back loaded with spoils to-day, and for the moment I figured as quite a Nimrod to an ad-miring audience of eleven semi-savages.

I had heard a great deal in time past about the excellence of bear's hams, and the delicacy of bear's paws stewed, but I felt that another of the pleasant illusions of my youth had been destroyed when I encountered to-night the mass of boiled black whipcord, which, in spite of its unpleasant flavour, was undoubtedly real bear's ham. As for the paws, Stepan and myself baked them *à la mode* in a little subterranean oven ; but on unearthing them we could find nothing but skin and leather, with bones and bony sinews, and certainly nothing to eat. Even our dogs did not seem to make much of them.

In spite of the poor quality of our food, we made, however, the heartiest of suppers, having been strangers to meat for nearly a week ; and with a storm raging outside which seemed to threaten a repetition of the disastrous flood that swept our cottage away last year, we slept the sleep of the weary but successful.

The next day, Saturday, was a red-letter day for me. Rising rather later than usual, we tried the other side of our bay of mountains, and, in spite of the noisy wind, with great success. Hardly had we forced our way through the growth of briars at the bottom of the hill into the chestnuts above when Stepan, turning round, beckoned me to stop, knelt down, and aiming deliberately, fired at something which the bushes concealed from me. On going up to him I found that he had fired at a boar standing end on to him some thirty yards off, and, as might be expected, with his extraordinary weapon, had only succeeded in frightening the beast.

Angry at the luck which had given Stepan

such a chance to throw away, I pushed noisily through the thickets, never dreaming of finding any more game, at any rate for another half mile. Yet hardly had we gone three dozen paces from the spot whence the last shot was fired, when our ears caught the sound of a bear's even step close to us, and approaching still closer. Slipping silently behind a couple of trees, we waited with our hearts in our mouths. Softly and deliberately the steps drew near, with a sound closely resembling the step of a man slowly picking his way through the forest. Every now and then the bear paused to give a loud snuff of inquiry, which, luckily for us, the constant shifting of the wind in these narrow valleys completely baffled. At last I got a glimpse of her passing slowly through the bushes, and stopping every now and then to pick up the fallen chestnuts in a leisurely way as she paced along. I waited for a minute or two until I could see her grey shoulder plainly through the rhododendrons. Then I pulled, and wheeling round with a short sharp cry, she disappeared in the higher covert, followed in her retreat by a snap-shot from my second barrel, which evidently did not take effect.

Uncertain whether the bear was killed outright or only wounded, Stepan and myself were somewhat shy of following her into her stronghold. At first we both tried climbing trees, hoping to get a view of her thus; but finding that of no avail

I persuaded Stepan to follow me at a distance in a careful survey of the place in which we had last seen her. Poor beast, she had not gone far : the moment she was out of our sight her strength failed her, and when we found her she was lying stone dead, not sixty yards from the spot where the bullet had reached her.

' Express ' rifles are terribly destructive little weapons. This second bear was totally unlike the one killed the day before, at least in colour : for while he was black, her coat, a very fine one, was of a soft light brown, so light as to be almost grey.

On examination we found that she was a year-ling, and was returning from her morn'ng's work, the ruin of half a fine chestnut-tree, when we met her. Some of the boughs she had managed to break were almost as thick as a man's waist. On looking at her fore-arm after Stepan had skinned her, I could not but reflect that the stories one meets with from time to time, of hand-to-hand con-flicts with bears, require a large grain of salt for the swallowing.

Leaving Stepan to finish the skinning, I wan-dered on somewhat higher up the hillside. I had not left him a quarter of an hour when I again heard the peculiarly soft regular tread of a bear above me, and after waiting patiently for about five minutes, I caught a glimpse for a moment of the head of an exact counterpart of the bear then under Stepan's hands. Unluckily for me, she sighted me at the same moment, and with a loud sniff plunged straight downhill at a pace that, even had the covert not concealed her, would have rendered my chance of hitting her extremely problematical. I saw from the direction she had taken that she would pass almost over Stepan, and I hurried on to be able to lend him a hand in case he only wounded her. But I waited in vain for the report of my man's mighty blunderbuss. Sitting engaged in the sanguinary task of disrobing our dead bear he had suddenly become aware of what appeared to him either the shade or the enraged sister of the deceased charging furiously down upon him; and oppressed with a consciousness of his guilt, Stepan fled red-handed from the avenger, leaving his gun to take care of itself.

Poor Stepan, who was originally I believe no coward, but in days past, according to his own version, a mighty hunter, was an instance of a man who had suddenly lost all his nerve, and this occurred as follows. One day, when suffering severely from fever, he was walking along the dried bed of a mountain torrent, when, on turning a sharp corner, he almost ran into a large bear. For a moment they stood facing one another. Stepan, having no weapons, thought his last hour had come. There was an awful noise, something struck him on the face, and for the time the hapless Tscherkess passed away from this bear-haunted world to a land of oblivion. On returning to his senses, he was surprised to find no bear, and no bloody wound upon his scalp. Further examination showed him, however, that a bear had stood facing him, and it was probably the gravel thrown up by its hind feet as it slewed round in headlong flight, that had struck Stepan, not stunning him as he supposed, but merely in his weak state frightening him out of his senses. Since then until now my man had only shot at bears from a platform in a tree at night—a style of sport extremely free from danger, as, although Bruin can climb, he very rarely if ever attempts to do so in pursuit of a foe.

Living, as Stepan had lived all his life, in bear-frequented forest lands, he had many a story to tell of 'Michael Michaelovitch,' as the peasants call him. On one occasion he and a friend had observed an apple-tree well laden with fruit, some seven or eight versts from their village in the forest, standing unclaimed of any man, almost sole relic of some once prosperous Tscherkess village. Stepan and his friend, who lived at some little distance, arranged to meet at the tree one morning early, and gather the fruit, to be shared amongst them. Arrived at the tree, Stepan saw some one already engaged throwing the apples down. Thinking his friend was trying to steal a march on him, the irate Stepan heaped all manner of abuse on him, accused him of spoiling the apples by throwing them down; and, at last, getting no answer, fairly yelled with rage, and began to throw things into the tree. Then the shower of apples ceased, and, with a gruff snort, a huge old bear came tumbling out of the tree, almost on top of the terrified villager. As usual in these cases, Bruin was just as much frightened as the man, and shambled off as quickly as possible, leaving the apples to the friends.

All the Russians and Tscherkesses with whom I have talked about bears, say there are two kinds in the Caucasus—the ordinary big brown bear, and a smaller one, that lives in the higher ranges, has a kind of white shirt-front to his coat, and is much fiercer and more carnivorous than his brown brother. Dr. Radde, however, of the Tiflis Museum, tells me there is only one kind; and though I have myself seen great variety in the sizes and coats of different individuals killed on the Black Sea coast, I can well believe he is right. Still, I fancy the higher ranges of Transcaucasia are very little known; and it may well be that a variety of the common bear, differing considerably from the specimens found on the coast, is to be met with nearer the snow-line. The peasants tell wonderfully circumstantial stories of their favourite's craft (for, in a way, the bear is a great favourite with the moujik, and hero of many a droll story): how that he lies in ambush for the unsuspecting roe or wild goat, and pounces on him, or knocks him down with a log used club-fashion, as he passes. Or, again, that lying hid on a ledge overlooking some favourite pass of the túr's, he rolls huge stones on his prey as it browses beneath him, and then, having killed it in this way, climbs down and dines at his leisure.

Of course all these are mere peasants' stories, but as they have been told me repeatedly by peasants who have lived amongst the beasts of which the stories are told all their lives, I give them for what they are worth. There may be some grains of truth in them.

After putting my bear's skin out of harm's way, and leaving the hams to take their chance till we returned, Stepan and I continued our hunt. In a deep glade, where no sunlight came to disturb the drowsy stillness, something bounded to its feet with a great noise, and hurried off unseen, making the whole forest re-echo with its short sharp barks. The cry was new to me, and I imagined all manner of grim beasts from whom the sound might have proceeded, and regretted intensely my evil luck in not obtaining a shot. Stepan, however, consoled me by telling me it was only 'cazeole,' the roebuck of this part of the world, which answers—so an old Indian sportsman tells me who has shot many of these 'cazeoles,'—to the Indian 'karkee.' Indeed, all the game found in the Caucasus is the same as, or very nearly allied to, species found throughout the mountains of India.

Later on in the day, whilst exploring a rhododendron thicket at the very summit of a high hill, shut in and encircled by still higher eminences, I heard something bolt from me through the rattling covert, and then pause, and with a loud sniff try to get my wind. Apparently getting it, the beast changed his course and proceeded at right angles to the line of his first rush, and then halting, again tried for my wind. Luckily for me, shut in as we were by the higher peaks, the wind kept veering round; and, thoroughly puzzled and beaten, the unlucky beast kept changing his course until at last I, standing behind a tree, saw a long grey snout and a pair of gleaming white tusks peering out of a thicket some thirty yards in front of me. The quick eyes sighted me at once in spite of my tree, and I had hardly time to fire before the owner of the eyes had retreated out of sight. Quick as the shot had to be, however, it was wonderfully effective, and the boar went crashing head over heels from top to bottom of the hill, there to rest still as sudden death could make it until I could get down to him. The bullet had gone in at the front of the shoulder, and traversing the whole length of the spine, had perfectly pulverised it, remaining buried just under the hide near the root of the tail; whence I extracted it and still preserve it, smashed and flattened as it is, a memento of the wonderful force of the 'express' (450) rifle.

Laden with spoils, the bear's skin and head, as well as the tidbits taken from the boar, we hurried home, to send up the Cossacks for the rest of the boar, which would be a welcome addition to their perpetual cabbage soup.

CHAPTER VII.

DENSE COVERTS.

To recount day by day our adventures whilst hunting at Golovinsky would certainly be wearisome to the general reader; and even the keenest sportsman has enough blank days of his own without reading the record of other people's. In spite of the fair beginning I had made, in the first two days of my stay, sport was not always as good or game so plentiful. Day after day, from dawn to dusk, often dragging our weary limbs home through icy torrents, by the feeble rays of a young moon, without whose light we had already been some time wandering in the forest darkness, we toiled unceasingly without getting another bear, although their tracks abounded everywhere.

Boars were at first fairly plentiful, and with them we did pretty well, though with them as with the few bears we did see, Stepan almost invariably got the shot and invariably missed it. Once he did hit an old she-bear, and a rare mess he very nearly made of it. I had got sick of seeing nothing, and was standing on an old log under which a bear had at one time made his lair, gazing idly down a long vista of forest below me. As I gazed I saw a small animal, which at the distance I could not recognise, being rolled over and over in the dead leaves by what was unmistakably a bear. I was on the point of descending to stalk her, when a report rang out below, and the old bear rolled over beside her cub. In another moment she was on her feet again, and using her fore-paw to urge him along, she was rapidly driving her cub towards me and away from the spot whence the report had come. As I watched, too much engrossed to think of firing, I saw her leave the cub and go at a really good gallop for something between her and myself. For a moment I thought I was the object of her attack; but a view of Stepan, his wretched old fire-arm as usual abandoned, bolting like a rabbit, revealed at once the true state of the case, and I made all haste to his rescue. Seeing me coming and Stepan stopping as I approached, the old she-bear turned, much to my surprise and infinitely to my disgust. Blown with my sharp rush and unduly excited, I missed the old lady entirely, or only hit her behind as she dived downhill through the high covert. Though we heard her once or twice, tramping about in the bushes and growling over her wounds, and though I am convinced she and the cub were within a few hundred yards of us whilst we munched the black bread and onions that made our lunch, we never saw either of them again.

Black bread and an onion sounds but a poor kind of refreshment after a hard morning's work, yet what real enjoyment that half-hour at lunch used to be to us, only those who really love forest life and nature at home can tell. All the mysterious rustlings of the forest, every breaking twig, suggested a whole volume of possible adventure to us. Coming but six weeks before from the stifling atmosphere of London, every breath of fresh air seemed full of fresh life, every forest sound replete with music. The chirping of the green frogs—those mysterious little *saurians* whose bird-like note is so pitched as rather to lead you from than to their hiding-place; the harsh shrill note of the handsome black woodpecker, whose crimson crest is the more distinctly beautiful as it is his only adornment; the continual chattering of the traitor jays, who seem always bent on proclaiming the hunter's presence; even the sharp rattle of the chestnuts, falling over-ripe from the trees; the droning of the bees, and the tiny but insatiable mosquito, combine, though in themselves not all harmonious, with the murmur of the sea and the whisper of the breeze.

to make a woodland concert, which to some ears no other music, either of the present or of Herr Wagner's future, could ever hope to rival.

Those mosquitoes were the only bitter drop in our mid-day draught of lazy pleasure. That they were *bonâ fide* mosquitoes I do not pretend, though we called them so, and hated them as much as if they had been, because, though mere microscopic midges, the lumps they raised upon us were worthy of the efforts of a Goliath among mosquitoes. From every rotten tree-stump rose a perfect steam of these evil little beasts, and being so small they could and did get through everything, and elude all vigilance.

There was another insect pest which used to cause us considerable annoyance : a kind of tick which dropped upon us unawares as we brushed against a bough, and creeping in under one's clothing buried its head unfelt in the skin, and there took up its abode. If not found and dislodged at night, the body of the creature would grow to such an extent that in the morning it had the appearance of a large wart growing upon you, and if left longer would swell to almost any size, taking root by its head and requiring infinite care in removing : for of such a bull-dog nature is the insect that it will allow its body to be torn from its head rather than let go its hold. If this happens the result is a bad wound, hard to heal and apt to fester. There are other insects in these woods, though of a less obnoxious nature; and from one class to-day we received a most welcome addition to our larder.

My man spent a good deal of his time in hunting for honey, and was wonderfully sharp-sighted when bees were concerned, noticing them at once across a valley, observing the line of their flight, and eventually tracking them to their secret hoard with a certainty that seemed almost like the result of instinct. These Tscherkesses have a way of making a rough sort of hive for the wild bees in trees to which the bees are partial, and I believe respect each other's hives when they come across them. Bruin, however, has less conscience than the Tscherkess, and if there is one thing which will tempt him into an indiscretion sooner than another it is honey. This man told me that once in a tree, with his nose smeared with honey, and stung all over by the indignant bees, the bear will go on feeding greedily, though the whole time he keeps crying and bemoaning himself for the pain given him by his tiny foes. At such times, so intent is he on his feast, that the hunter may approach him as closely as he pleases, and shoot him at his leisure.

The peacock butterfly was another insect of which I noticed large numbers from time to time round the outskirts of the forest; and indeed, in the whole of autumn in the Caucasus, I never noticed any butterflies, or only very few, which were not

familiar to me as British insects, while I saw specimens of almost every butterfly which occurs with
us at home. The most numerous, I think, was the
clouded yellow, and its paler variety 'hyale.'

The day we got our honey was a red-letter day
for us, for on that occasion our larder reached its
maximum of plenty; the boat, with stores from
Duapsè, turning up on the afternoon of the same
day. A bear's ham, some pork, black bread, honey,
onions, and a bottle of abomination, labelled ' Vieux
Rhum, Marseilles,' which I doubt not had never
been much nearer France than the Crimea, made
my servant's face beam with delight at the sight of
such unwonted plenty; but alas! from this day
our evil times were to commence; and so bare did
our larder at last become that the very flies that
then swarmed gave us up as inhospitable paupers
before the end of a fortnight.

On trying the part of the forest in which I had
killed my first bear on Monday, we could find no
fresh traces of game, although the place was quite
a warren of old boar runs, and full of beaten roads
made by the bears. The cause of the game's
absence was evidently the presence of the carcass of
my first bear, which, mangled by jackals, was
already tainting the air far and wide. Some large
game I did almost bag, but that was nearly being
a very serious matter for one of us.

As usual, we took parallel lines along the hillside, and though from time to time a broken twig betrayed the presence of the one to the other, Stepan and I were otherwise lost to each other. For over half-an-hour we had been stalking in this way, without any event occurring to wake the stillness of the wood, when from a point above me, and coming down wind towards me, I heard a sound like that of approaching game. Slowly it came on, and as the leaves were crushed softly under its heavy even tread, which stopped from time to time that the beast might listen or pick up a chestnut, I recognised the step as that of Bruin strolling slowly home after his early breakfast. Stooping to get a better view through the hazel stems, I saw them swing and shake some eighty yards above me, and caught a glimpse at the same moment of something lighter in colour than the covert passing through it. Instinctively my rifle covered it, and from that moment, for quite three minutes I should think, I followed the bear's every movement with my rifle's muzzle. Twice I half pressed the trigger as a larger piece of the creature's grey side was visible to me, picking his way slowly past me; but just as I was on the point of firing he turned and came downhill towards me. Thanking my stars that I had not fired a random shot into the brown of my game, I waited for him to come closer. There was twenty yards from me a little open space, and here, if he entered it, as he seemed likely to, I meant to kill him. Jealously my rifle followed his every movement, dreading a change of direction, and in another moment the shot would have been fired. The grey thing suddenly rose on end, or seemed to ; and parting the thorn vine with its fore-arms walked into the open my man Stepan !

For a moment I felt absolutely sick, and I don't think I was ever more unhinged in my life than I was for the rest of the day ; and when, later on in the heat of noonday, I was resting in a ravine by a small pool, half dozing after lunch, hearing the same pace just above me, and seeing a great patch of grey move through the bushes, I lost a veritable bear by not firing. So Stepan's folly nearly cost him his life, and cost me a bear. He had, it seemed, gone on too fast to the end of his beat, and getting tired of waiting for me, thought he might as well come back to meet me. Heard on the dead leaves, a bear's step as he moves slowly along, stopping from time to time to feed or listen, is wonderfully like that of a mocassined hunter stalking slowly over the same ground.

And now, day after day, the sport grew worse. Stepan was evidently but a very poor guide. Living, as he had done, for a couple of lonely years in his hut at Golovinsky, his spirit of enterprise had never led him to explore more than the two beats in which we had already been successful,

Beyond these two tracts of forest he knew nothing, and in this dense covert it is almost useless to attempt to shoot until you have first explored a little. If you do attempt it, you find yourself, sooner or later, lost in a dense mass of thorns, in which you cannot move without noise—in which, in fact, you can scarcely move at all. From above hang thick curtains of the abominable creeper which the people call aptly enough 'wolf's tooth,' which is so keen and strong that even my stout jacket of moleskin was torn by it ; while Stepan's clothes, though made of the toughest canvas, ceased to exist, in spite of all his ingenious patchings, by the end of the fortnight. A few boars and two more bears were all we could get ; and at last I consented to a trial of Stepan's vaunted pack. But not until we had tried every other method did I consent to having the forests disturbed in this way.

One day, after twelve hours' spent in the usual stalking, Stepan and I perched ourselves like ungainly birds each in a tree above a hole full of mud and water, in which herds of swine wallowed nightly. But our limbs grew cramped, and the moon rose higher in the heavens, making quaint patterns on the dark hole below, without our ever being disturbed in our night-watch. As the moon grew more dim, we climbed down again with aching limbs ; and as Stepan relieved his feelings by a hoarse cough long pent up, a sudden charge through the thickets close by, with indignant snortings, told us that the herd was just approaching as we left.

On our way back, as we crossed a small tributary of the Golovinsk, a big silvery thing slid off a stone into the water, and swam along the bottom of the shallow stream close by me. In the grey morning light it looked to my drowsy eyes like a large fish, and it was not until I heard Stepan's wretched old gun miss fire that I recognised in it a very fine otter; then, of course, it dived into deeper water, and was lost to us. Many of these, as well as a few sea-otters, are found between Novorossisk and Sukhoum, and my man showed me the skins of several which he had killed; but though I frequently saw their spoor, this was the only live specimen it was ever my luck to see.

Another long night we sat down under a juniper bush on the shingle that has, at some time or other, formed the bed of a broader Golovinsk, or has been brought down by the stream during its winter floods. On the opposite bank rose the hill forest, coming down in thorny thickets to the water's edge. Half a mile behind us, on our side the stream, the other forest began, and a quarter of a mile below us the sea kept moaning. On all the little patches of sand the tracks of game were numerous and recent, and we had good hopes of sport: indeed we needed them to keep us up through that cold night. On the far side of the river there was a large tract of sand and clay, which was one close-written record of the goings and comings of thirsty beasts. Yet all that weary night we saw hardly anything. At six we marched down to those icy waters of tribulation as men prepared to do or die—that is, to be miserable as comfortably as possible. Pitching ourselves and a flask of Marseilles 'rhum' into the bush, we arranged that Stepan should watch until midnight, and the morning watch should be mine. With a stone for a pillow, and my knees tucked up to my chin, I soon slept to the tune of the stream at my feet, to wake in about an hour's time shivering and wet through with the mist. The sound of a well-known snore explained to me how rigid had been Stepan's vigil ; and as two or three dusky forms bolted back into the thicket on the far side as I rose unwarily to kick him, I bitterly regretted that I had not kept watch all night through.

Resolving not to disturb my trusty henchman, I settled myself in the warmest corner I could find, and prepared to keep watch till morning. And I did so through all that livelong night, until the Pleiads had worked right round into the west : a little querulous wind arose, the stars grew greyer and greyer, there came a sudden bitter chill into the air, to which all the cold of the night had been as nothing, and then we knew it was morning.

A violent shake roused Stepan, and without troubling ourselves about more breakfast than a crust of black bread and the flask afforded, we went into the forest. Here we had a blank day; though had Stepan chosen to fire, he had a splendid chance at two bears; but as I was at some distance, he held his hand, apparently from prudential motives.

When we came back late that evening, empty-handed, to conclude our twenty-four hours of toil with a march of a mile over the bed of the Golo-vinsk—feeling its boulders through our worn moccasins as plainly as if we were barefooted; the small stones burning into our sore feet like hot irons, while from the big ones we slipped, risking sprains and breakages every other step, and getting clear of the stones only to plunge into the icy stream—when we were enduring all this, I might, I think, be forgiven if I said 'Amen' to the Russian proverb which my wretched guide kept repeating, to the effect that 'the chase is worse than slavery.' It does not say much for the sporting spirit of the Russians that such should be a favourite proverb among them; but in Stepan's case, where he had all his share of the toil and none of the enthu-siasm which novelty lent me to keep him up, it was a pardonable sentiment. Poor fellow, it was

quite tragic to see him, having crossed his enemy
the Golovinsk for the last time that night, sit
down beside its waters, and, casting the remnants
of a pair of mocassins into the stream, walk home
barefoot.

CHAPTER VIII.

HUNTING WITH DOGS.

AFTER our twenty-four hours of unsuccessful labour recorded in my last chapter, we were too tired and too tattered to take the field again next day. So we spent it in drying our clothes, mending and washing them, constructing fresh moccasins from the hide of one of our boars, and generally preparing for a campaign of another kind against our enemies the bears and boars.

In this campaign we were to be assisted by a canine force, consisting of three mangy curs belonging to Stepan, and one utterly useless beast, the property of the neighbouring Cossack station. Stepan's trio were, in their way, the three ugliest half-starved mongrels that ever were possessed with the pluck of a gamecock and the unreasoning devotion that never shows itself in anything

L

but a dog. Why they should have been Stepan's faithful slaves no human reasoning could explain. They could have picked up more by themselves than he could give them. Poor fellow, he never had any great abundance for himself. They had to sleep outside the shanty, were kicked if they put their noses inside, and were devoured by the mange, which their master never seemed to think of curing. As for breed they had none, or perhaps I should say they had a touch of every breed in them. Zizda was said to be in some way connected with a race which they called ' harlequin ; ' and if oddity of shape, oddness of eyes, and a general unevenness of colour and outline. entitle a dog to the name, old Zizda was a veritable harlequin. He was a large dog with huge paws, a very square head, wall eyes, a capital nose, and indomitable pluck, which had from time to time earned him the innumerable scars with which he was marked from tail to muzzle. The other two were utter mongrels. but staunch supporters of old Zizda in any emergency. They were an old bitch called Lufra, and a young dog. Orla, or ' The Eagle.' I cannot refrain from giving the dogs' names, because they were such real heroes in the chase. and good servants to me.

The first duty of our day of rest, then, was to feed our pack—a duty often forgotten. and appreciated by the dogs now as an unprecedented attention from us. This done, we busied ourselves in getting the skins of the game we had killed ready to send away, as a boat had been seen passing a day or two before, and having been signalled to, had promised, if possible, to call on its way back from Sotcha. It called to-day, took our skins on to Kertch, and left us a good supply of tobacco, the want of which we had hitherto keenly felt.

Another visitor turned up to-day to our utter surprise (for visitors are rare at Golovinsky)—the head gardener from the Grand Duke Michael's forest of Ardenne, who had been out hunting for two days and taken nothing. With him was a Greek from a colony somewhere near, who complained bitterly that though he and his fellow colonists had spent most of their nights about harvest-time on platforms or trees, to shoot at and scare the bears and boars, these gentry had completely destroyed the crop of ' koukourooz ' (maize), on which the Greek villagers greatly depend. When I found that in spite of the number of guns in the trees, not one bear or boar had been killed, I was not so much surprised at Bruin coming to look upon the noise as merely a military salute intended in his honour, which in no way interfered with his appetite.

From time to time during the day I managed to extract a little information from the taciturn

Stepan, but his lonely life has made him so reserved as to be almost inaccessible to the wiles of the inquirer. He is a Tscherkess who has abjured Mahometanism without apparently adopting any other faith; so of his religion he had little to tell. About his village and the life in it he said little more, and of the Tscherkess wars he absolutely refused to speak—though on that topic he evidently had more to say—from what seemed to me a fear lest any words of his being repeated might get him into trouble. So we fell back upon natural history, and on this topic he was fairly fluent.

Amongst other things he told me of some quaint habits of the hedgehog—for I presume it was the hedgehog and not the porcupine he meant; for the word he used for the beast was one which I did not know, being Tscherkess patois of some kind. But from his description the animal was either one or the other; and as the porcupine is only supposed, I think, to inhabit the Persian border of the Caucasus, the animal of Stepan's story was probably a hedgehog. He described a hedgehog perfectly, and then added that there were two kinds in the Caucasus, one with head and feet like a pig, the other with head and feet like a hound. It was one of the latter which he noticed one day under an apple-tree in the forest, collecting and carrying off the fallen fruit by rolling over it (so he described it) until she had impaled an apple on one of her spines. She then impaled another on the other side of her body, and thus laden, retired for some time, to return without her load, for two more apples. This sounds very unlikely to me, but as the fellow had no object in inventing the story, and invariably told me the truth as far as I could discover, I give it, as well as other yarns from the same source, for what it is worth. Of the same beast the Cossacks and Stepan assert that he kills snakes by seizing their tails in his jaws and then rolling on them, turning a somersault over them, in fact, so as to drive the spines into them.

I heard too, to-day, a quaint superstition about the common bracken, which abounds here, and on the roots of which the swine feed when there are no chestnuts or berries to be had. The Circassians say there is one moment in one night of the year (alas, my authority had forgotten which night), at the very stroke of midnight, when this plant blooms. The flower lasts but a few moments, in the which if any one has the good fortune to gather and preserve it, he obtains omniscience thenceforth. Talking of such things as the foregoing, and making fresh moccasins for the morrow, the day soon passed, and we rolled ourselves up in our rugs and were happy, though we went to bed almost dinnerless.

The sea rose to-night, and raged as the Black Sea sometimes does, in so wild a way that one almost forgets its habitual calm in these short bursts of Berserker fury. So close did the white waves come to our fragile hut, that we began to tremble lest the sea should wash through the ground floor (our only floor), as it had done once last winter; and in the middle of the night old Zizda, pressing close to the wall outside for comfort from the keen wind and driven spray, pushed his way right through the lath and plaster, and appeared wet and unceremonious by my bedside. Whether he found it much warmer inside than out I very much doubt. It must have been very bitter outside if he did. But by morning, though the waves were still white below, a bright sun was shining, and the rain-drops had been dried off the grass.

We gave the sun another hour or two to complete his good work, and then, at about nine, started for the forest with our pack.

The method of procedure was simplicity itself. Once in the forest each dog went whithersoever he pleased, and the whole team, cruising about at random, at last hit on the track of something and gave tongue. Then, with our ears only to lead us, we made to what seemed the likeliest spot to intercept the dogs and their quarry, and right good fun it was, though rough work in the extreme. Bad as are the briars and tangled masses of vine, I think the frequent ravines and hillsides, covered with their fine short grass, are infinitely worse.

Rushing pell-mell to the scene of action, you expect
to have face and hands lacerated as you go and
take it with equanimity, content if only you can
force a way at all. But having forced a way, it is
annoying to have your feet slip upon those dry
hillsides, and, perfectly helpless, feel yourself and
rifle rapidly gliding downhill away from the point
towards which, at so much personal inconvenience,
you have been struggling. It was better fun to
see Stepan, as he strove to descend a ravine, slide
helplessly down, sixty miles an hour, to a pool at
the bottom, into which he unceremoniously plopped,
pursued at once by Zizda, who followed his master
on his haunches, looking the picture of imbecile
misery. But for bipeds and even ordinary quad-
rupeds there is some excuse, seeing that Bruin
himself often comes to grief in these places. Witness the numerous slides on these banks, looking
as if Bruin had been diverting himself and his
family by the innocent amusement of trebogging.

Throughout the forest where we were hunting
to-day, we found every here and there the traces
of Tscherkess villages, whose occupants have fled,
some long ago in the old war time, and some only
last spring, to join the Turks in their war against
Russia. Even in the case of these latter no sign
of a house remained, only a piece of ground more
level than that which surrounded it, overgrown with
a dense jungle of briar; here and there a piece of

hand-wrought wood, a relic of some Circassian house furniture, and fruit-trees that were merged into the forest when their owners joined the Turks. These old ' aouls ' are very strongholds of Bruin, and his work is visible on all sides. Little pathways, beaten smooth through the briary places, torn-down branches of the walnut and apple, and bees' nests dug out where none but he could have got at them, all attest his presence.

It was from one of these old ' aouls ' that our dogs first got anything to make a really good stand. The ' aoul ' had been on the very summit of one of the chain of hills on which we were shooting. The site of it was covered with acres of dense briars, from the midst of which towered what had probably been the village pride, a patriarchal chestnut of enormous size. Here Zizda gave out his deep bass warning that game was afoot, and the other three curs made a chorus of it. I was down below in a belt of chestnuts outside the region of briars; and thinking that whatever the game was, it would probably break downhill from the thicket in which the dogs were baying it by a little track that passed me, i jumped on to a tree-stump and waited. Stepan was on the other side of the briars, quite close to the scene of action, and I naturally imagined would close in still more and get his shot. After waiting a good ten minutes, during which time neither game, dogs, nor Stepan appeared to move an inch, I whistled to let the latter know that I was coming to the assistance of the brave dogs which he was leaving to their fate. To force my way uphill through those briars was a labour worthy of Hercules ; and if the game should have broken through the dogs, there would have been small chance for the hunter fast meshed in that briary net. When at last I did get a view of the field of battle, so dense were the briars that I could not have swung my arms round where I stood ; and though I stood on tiptoe, all I could discern were the waving sterns of Orla and Lufra, the brave old veteran Zizda being too close to his quarry to be visible ; but from where I stood I could hear his sharp charges and the low snorts of rage which they elicited from the object of his attack.

Unable to see to shoot, I picked up a clod, and guessing the beast's whereabouts by the low muttered thunder that came from the roots of the chestnut, I heaved it over the dogs in the direction of the sound. Then for a moment the briars swayed as if an earthquake had moved them ; one of the dogs yelled as he was rolled over, with another scar added to his already numerous decorations ; and then, not ten paces from me, passing at a gallop went the biggest wild boar I ever hope to see. And I missed him. It is true that I had but a momentary glimpse at him as he shot across a yard of open, and I snapped at him as one would at a bolting rabbit; but I shall never forgive myself for missing his enormous broadside for all that. Far through the crashing forest I heard him, with the dogs at his heels, for almost ten minutes after I had missed him; but I never saw him again.

I had heard frequently previous to this of the immense size of these Caucasian boars when old and lonely, and have myself since seen the specimen in the Tiflis Museum killed by the Grand Duke or one of his friends at the Royal forest of Kariâs, which is said to weigh twenty-one puds; and as sixty-two puds go to the ton, this would make him about 780 pounds. But in my own mind I feel convinced that the boar that charged past me from his dark fastness at the root of that old chestnut was half as large again. Every angler knows that the fish you miss is the heaviest that ever rose at your fly; of course I may have misjudged the dimensions of my boar, and therefore ask no one to believe in his immense size, though firmly believing in it myself.

That boars should grow to an enormous size here, where they are never disturbed, and where every variety of food to which they are peculiarly partial is so abundant, is hardly to be wondered at. The forests are full of all sorts of fruit, of which bears and boars alone have the gathering;

patches of bracken, on the roots of which the boar feeds, are on every hillside ; at certain seasons of the year he finds quantities of fish washed upon the shore, and on these he riots. As for the chestnuts, some idea of their abundance may be formed from the fact that, kneeling in one place not purposely selected, to-day, I filled all my pockets with fallen chestnuts without once changing my position ; and yet their only use is to fatten the wild boar, who munches them husks and all, or more dainty Bruin, who eats the nuts, but leaves the husk in his path.

Once during the day I saw an old bear as I struggled through a veil of thorn vine up a slippery hillside, and firing brought him down with what was almost a bellow of rage or pain, in a succession of somersaults that took him past me down the hill at a pace that he would never have attained to by his ordinary method of progression. But, alas, on searching for him at the bottom of the hill where he should have lain, we found no trace of him ; and though the dogs followed for a while, a large stream which he had crossed foiled them, and sent us back empty-handed.

Twice during that day did I get into close proximity to big game without seeing anything. Once in the thicket, whence the old boar had charged. I had forced my way beyond all hope of a speedy return, when the sound of Stepan's gun

down below, and the sharp treble of the younger
dog's bark, told me something was afoot in that
direction. Straight towards me up the hill came the
dogs, and right eagerly did I look for a tree as
a coign of vantage from which to get a view of the
approaching game before he absolutely ran over
me. But there was not even a stump in reach.
Round me was perhaps a yard of almost open
space, but beyond this the briars formed a wall
impenetrable everywhere, except at the point at
which I had entered the little opening by an old
boar's run. To quit the opening by the only
apparent outlet, on my hands and knees, with my
tail to an approaching foe, did not seem prudent: so I remained where I was, hoping I should
see whatever the game might be before it saw
me. Suddenly, though the dogs were still only
half-way up the hill, struggling slowly through
the brake, as impenetrable almost to them as to
us, right at my elbow I heard a heavy breath
drawn, half sigh and half sniff, and then a soft
shuffling of feet in the hidden places of the thicket.
Almost directly this was followed by another and
another sniff, and I knew that a bear was deliberately walking round me, trying to get out probably by the road by which I had entered. I
would rather not have been there I admit, as Bruin
fairly cornered is an ugly foe to face; and I fully
expected that when the dogs arrived on the scene

he would go for his own private pathway, taking me as a mere obstruction *en route*, as I never for a moment doubted but that he was the beast the dogs had roused. As I stood expectant, a lovely wild cat, with a fine tawny skin, marked almost as clearly as a tiger's, stole snakelike across the opening, utterly unheeding me, and disappeared in the brake beyond. Expecting the bear in another minute I let the cat go, and regretted it directly after, for with a regular burst of hounds' music our pack dashed into the open, mad after their cat, and went raging on, taking no notice of the larger game close by. We searched afterwards, and found that a bear had really been there, and had stolen off by another of the hidden ' trapinkas '(game tracks) with which the whole brake was warrened. The dogs treed the cat, and we spent our luncheon hour in smoking her out.

The other occasion on which I got too close to big game that day was in a rhododendron brake, when our dogs, having bayed something on the other side of the hill. I was hurriedly forcing my way to them, when I became aware of sniffings and tramplings to the right of me and to the left of me, and plunging wildly on, nearly ran into something else advancing. Had the rhododendron clump not been exceptionally high (higher far than my head), I could have seen my game and had capital sport ; as it was, I was kept fumbling about in the thicket for nearly ten minutes, expecting every moment to run up against a bear, who was at the same time just as anxious not to come into collision probably as I was.

Tired and happy after a good day's sport, during which the fun of racing after the dogs had been a pleasant change from the ordinary silent stalking, we wended our way home, the dogs at last keeping fairly close to our heels. When we were down in the flat by our old enemy, the snow-fed Golovinsk, the moon came up hazy and dim, and the owls began their weird hootings ; then with a sudden rush the dogs left our heels, and were once more wakening the echoes with a nocturnal chorus worthy of the Demon Hunter's infernal pack. In the patch-work of moonlight we caught a glimpse of something scudding away before the dogs, and joined heartily in the chase, forgetting our fatigue in the excitement. After ten minutes' slow hunting in the briars they bayed him in a dense clump, where some larger trees shut out the silver moonshine and made midnight of the place. This wood being a favourite resort of bears at night, on account of the roseberries with which the place abounded, and of which they are fond, we went somewhat cautiously to work, and as we pushed out of the moonlight into the darkness we went shoulder to shoulder, literally feeling our way with our rifles. The dogs were right at our feet.

and, as I expected, were sitting heads in air under a tall tree, on one of the limbs of which I could just make out in the moonlight an excrescence which experience taught me must be a wild cat. Rifle-shooting by moonlight is not as easy as by daylight; and though the cat came down, I don't think she was hit hard; probably not hit at all, but merely dislodged by the bough beneath her being broken. However, be that as it may, when she did come down, she scattered the dogs right and left, and got clear away into the thicket again. Long after, when we were smoking the last pipe rolled in our rugs, we could hear them making music either over her or some luckless jackal which they had come across.

But this, our great day with the dogs, was the last on which fortune smiled on us at Golovinsky. From that day we got from bad to worse. No more boars fell to our guns, and on wild cats and fresh bear's meat even a hungry Tscherkess will hardly feed. But when our supply of bear's meat failed too, and nothing but a cheese rind remained, we grew desperate, and having heard of a place with a name fathoms long about ten miles from Golovinsky, where boar abounded, and had not been lately disturbed, we hired two horses from the Cossacks, and with one of them for a guide started to try our luck there. As usual, the guide knew as little of the way as we did, so that we spent nearly all the day in getting to our ground, and, on arriving, found not only no vestige of the hut which we had been told existed there, but no chestnut forests either.   Add to this that, though the scenery was even finer than at Golovinsky, the herbage grew more rankly luxuriant every hundred yards as we rode up the glen—the mist, which rose in a white wall round us, drenching us to the skin before we had been in it a quarter of an hour—and it will not appear so strange that, having toiled all day to get there, I gave the order at once for a counter-march, considering that to pass one night in this den of fever would be certainly dangerous, and possibly fatal to some of us.

I was not far wrong, as events proved, for next day, although I had beaten such a hasty retreat, Stepan and the Cossack were both down with the fever, and I had an attack of intense lassitude and headache, which, if yielded to, would probably have resulted in the same. Stepan told me the weather was becoming dangerously feverish, an east wind having set in, which is always the harbinger of ill to the Tscherkess on the Black Sea coast. Fever never comes, they say, when the wind is from off the sea ; but when it comes from behind the hills, then it is that the fever seizes its wretched victims.

As we climbed over the hills or up the watercourses to-day, the cold wind that was blowing would lull for a minute, and a soft hot blast come over us, just as if fresh from the mouth of some furnace. Then the fresh breeze rising would blow it off again. These puffs of hot wind recurred at long intervals throughout the day, and were, Stepan assured me, sure precursors of fever. Whether they really were so, or whether his croaking frightened us into it, I don't know, but next day we were certainly extremely ill. Stepan had genuine fever, and as all Russians and Tscherkesses do, lay down at once and gave the fever full play.

I had read somewhere of a doctor on the African coast who used to get his fever patients into a room with doors and windows shut, and there make them have the gloves on with him for a quarter of an hour, after which the fever left them. I owe that athletic doctor my best thanks for his example, and hereby tender them; for though I had no gloves, and no one to use them upon if I had, I acted on what seemed to me the principle of his cure, and, selecting the stiffest bit of country I knew, started on a solitary hunt with the dogs. At first I reeled, and my knees gave under me at every stride. I was sick and blind and dizzy, and felt altogether worse than I ever did, even after the first half-mile of a Rossall paper chase as a boy; but gradually things improved, as they always do if you stick to it, and I had the satisfaction of shaking off the fever, never to be troubled with it any more, though I have spent days in Poti, of which town Baron von Thiel-mann says, in his excellent book on the Caucasus, that 'no European has passed a night there and been spared the fever.'

It is my firm belief that abstinence from water whilst in the chase or on the journey will be found almost a safeguard against fever, and if, in spite of this, the mists and chills of the undrained swamps are too much for the traveller's constitution, a good bout of violent exercise, taken as soon as the fever seizes him, will free him from his illness in its infancy.

That the natives suffer from fever is not to be wondered at. They live so poorly that an Eng-lishman would die of want of nourishment alone, did he live as they do. They sleep out in mists that soak through and through a man as no rain ever could, and, worse than all, in the chase or on the journey, when heated and over-wrought, they lie down at every rill, and drink like thirsty cattle. I attribute my own freedom from fever to the fact that I never touched the water of the Caucasus for drinking purposes, except in the shape of one cup of tea in the morning and one at night, never drinking at all throughout the day; and though my tongue sometimes grew dry and seemed almost to rattle in my mouth, habit soon enabled me to do without water, and that without any great discomfort.

But, although I avoided fever myself, and believe that with these precautions a foreigner might well pass some time in the Caucasus and escape, more especially if he went in late autumn and returned by the end of March, I have no wish to describe the Caucasus, more especially the Black Sea coast and the neighbourhood of Ekaterinodar and the Kuban, as anything but a nest of fever. Where the vegetation is as rank, and marshes so frequent and of such extent as those round Poti and Lenkoran on the Caspian, the summer time is a dangerous time for even the most prudent.

For two or three more days, after our visit to the valley of mist and fever, I continued to hunt near Golovinsky, though my man was too ill to help me much. But day after day proved more decisively that unless I could get deeper into the forest than I had ever penetrated yet, my labour would continue to be but labour in vain. So I determined to return to Heiman's Datch, the old ruin where I got my first boar on this coast, and after spending a few days there in search of the panther which I had wounded, or another if he was dead, return to Duapsé and thence to Kertch. To this I felt impelled by a number of reasons, of which the bareness of our larder was by no means the least. For over a week chestnuts had formed the greater part of my fare, bread even running short, and as for meat we had none. Often at night I had had to tighten my belt as the best way of reducing the vacuum I had no means of filling. But this is a method of which Nature soon wearies, and I was longing greedily for even the good things of Duapsè.

CHAPTER IX.

RETURN TO KERTCH.

Of my second visit to Heiman's Datch I shall say
but little, as, though interesting to me, it would
only entail a great deal of repetition for the reader.
I killed two bears, I believe, of which I bagged
one, the largest specimen of a brown bear I have
ever seen ; his head, set up by Burton, of Wardour
Street, is in my library now, and in no way belies
my description of him.   With the boars we did not
do much good, but we at least did enough to get
a fresh supply of meat, though of the coarsest kind.
On one night I sent Stepan back along the coast
at his own request to fetch his dogs from Golovinsky.
It was a ten-verst tramp, and he chose the night to
do it in.   I regretted when he came back next
morning that I had not accompanied him, for on

his way he met a couple of bears at different points, both of which appear to have been much bolder by night than they ever are by day. He fired at one of them and missed him. The brute turned round and appeared to search for the origin of the noise; and if Stepan is to be believed he passed a very 'mauvais quart d'heure,' motionless behind a big piece of drift-wood, while Bruin sat up and watched for him. However, the wind was not right for the bear, so he moved off at last, leaving Stepan to pursue his course unmolested, but resolved never to fire at another bear by night, alone and on foot— a resolution to which he stuck religiously when, some half hour afterwards, he met another coming from the direction of his own cottage.

Arrived at home, he found the dogs had gone off to the Cossack station, and in their absence the bears had been down from the hills to visit him, overturning his hives, and even breaking the door of his hut. I felt doubts in my own mind as to whether the Cossacks had not been before the bears in these matters, but as it was a damage which could not be remedied, it mattered little who bore the blame.

Returning in the grey morning, Stepan had a chance at a sea otter, which he wounded but lost. I feel that it is only fair to say for Stepan that with a proper rifle he was not such an extraordinarily bad shot as his constant misses would imply; but a sight of the tool he used would convince any sportsman that with such a weapon the chief danger was to be apprehended from it by the person behind it. Stepan's way of loading, too, was curious : two bullets, one in its ordinary condition, the other chewed into a ragged lump of lead, over a heavy charge of powder : such was his ordinary charge : but when, as on one occasion, to this was added a second charge of powder and small slugs for pheasants, to save the trouble of extracting the first charge, with an extra bullet put in next day to meet all emergencies, the only wonder is that the weapon was not more fatal to Stepan than to the old she-bear into which he put this extraordinary broadside.

But now I must bid good-by to Stepan, whose last duty was to procure me a horse from the next Cossack station to convey myself and my bears' skulls to Duapsé. I bid good-by to my servant with hearty goodwill, for though a poor guide and worse sportsman, he was a faithful, obliging fellow, and honest in the extreme.

From Heiman's Datch to Duapsé is, they say, only thirty-eight versts ; but the road over the shingle at the foot of the cliffs was so bad that it took me from 8 A.M. to 6 P.M. to accomplish the journey. I did not stay even for food by the way, but plodded steadily on at a foot's pace among rocks and boulders, with the Tartar saddle galling my limbs, and a fierce sun pouring down on the grey cliffs, until everything appeared at a white heat, and all life seemed stilled, except for the myriads of lizards that revelled in the fierce sunlight at the cliff's foot. But all things must have an end, and at 6 P.M. I was at rest in the telegraph station, with a substantial dinner before me and a bottle of beer, which, if not Bass's, bore at any rate some faint resemblance to the beverage beloved of Britons.

On the Sunday morning, November 9, I received a polite message from the Governor of Duapsé to warn me that, as the Caucasus was still under military law, and not as yet entirely settled, I must oblige him by not going to stay in any Tscherkess 'aoul,' and if I neglected this warning, he added that my words and deeds would be watched. Moreover, he requested that I would bring my shooting trip in his district to an end. This sounded a formidable message ; but on interviewing the Governor I found him not by any means inclined to be unpleasant, and indeed his only desire appeared to be to prevent my getting into scrapes by meddling with politics, though, at the same time, he was evidently exercised in his own mind as to the real object of my visit to the Black Sea coast : as he, in common with all the other Russians I met, seemed to find it impossible to believe that any man would visit a distant land merely for sport. Several times I had warnings from various English residents in the Caucasus that I was suspected of being a British agent, and, as such, was fully described to the police, and carefully watched. Unluckily for me, the boat to Kertch only calls every Wednesday, so that I had three weary days to pass in Duapsè.

One of these I spent in a visit to a mountain farm belonging to a German baron, and worked by two young Germans, his bailiffs. Here I saw a collection of insects made on the farm, and amongst them recognised, in addition to the species I have mentioned as seen by me before, both the British varieties of the swallow-tailed butterfly, the small wood white, the marbled white, the privet, and the elephant hawk moth, as well as the death's head, which abounds here. There were also oak-eggers and stag-beetles, as well as another hawk moth of a delicate fawn colour, which was strange to me.

Returning from the hill farm I had an adventure which might have terminated worse. The road from Duapsè to the farm, which is situated at a great height above the sea, winds about the hill in zigzag lines. Over the road, which is steep and rough, hang the edges of the forest, and from time to time it crosses a rough wooden bridge, spanning a chasm of considerable pretensions. By daylight these chasms and their wooden bridges mattered but little, for though

the bridge trembled as the droggie passed over
it, there was not much chance of an accident so
long as you and your horse could see where you
were going.   After my day's shooting I stayed
late at the young Germans', waiting to share with
them their evening meal, so that it was already
dark when I prepared for my ride home.   I had
calculated on a moon, but, the night being stormy,
I was disappointed, and when I did make a start
it was on a young horse, in almost utter darkness,
and knowing very little of my way.   However,
the Germans consoled me by telling me that the
road to Duapsé was the only road from their farm
to anywhere, and it had no roads branching from it
—moreover, the horse knew his way.

At supper they had told me that one of them,
riding into Duapsé some weeks prior to my visit,
had been sprung at by some animal from the trees
overhanging the path; and though there was
not sufficient light to distinguish the beast by,
it was supposed by them to have been a lynx
or a leopard.   Not much distressed about this
danger, but anxious about the bridges, I started
on my lonely ride.   All went well until I was half
way to the river which separates Duapsé from the
base of the hill.   Then, as we got to the darkest
part of the road, where the trees overhung it most,
my horse suddenly turned back, and tried to bolt
for home.   In spite of all my exertions I could

not get him beyond a particular point on the road
home for some time ; and when at last I did drive
him past with heels and whip, he dashed away
with a sudden plunge, and, catching the bit in his
teeth, bolted as hard as he could gallop from that
point to Duapsè—or, rather, the river that gives
that town its name. It was no good my trying
to stop the hard-mouthed little beast with the
feeble tackle at my service, and, dashing through
the darkness over the roughest of roads, I could
only sit still, and hope that the sagacity and keen
sight of the horse might save both his neck and
my own. I had no time to feel nervous as we
crossed the first bridge, which seemed to rock as
we dashed over it—a couple of bounds, and we
were on the other side—but from that to the next
bridge my mind was tortured with visions of the
horse's feet slipping from under him on one of the
poles, and the inevitable fall that must follow.
But horses have wonderful eyes, and, if left to
themselves, see as well in a dark night, I think, as
their riders do by day ; and, in spite of the rough
road and the bridges, we were soon breast deep in
the stream, and half swimming, half fording it,
came in safety to the other shore.

Amongst other things which served to pass my
time whilst waiting for the boat at Duapsè was a
peasant's wedding supper. At the ceremony itself
I was not present, but I presume it was like all

other weddings in the Greek Church, with its
crowns held over the heads of the principal parties,
and its symbolical knotting of the handkerchief.
But the supper and its ceremonies were strange to
me.   During it the happy pair came in, not par-
taking of it with the rest, but merely presenting
themselves to perform certain ceremonies.   Of
these the first was to take a blessing from the old
people.   This they did, turning in succession to
each of the four quarters of the earth.   Refresh-
ments having been brought in, and all sitting
except the bride and groom, these latter handed to
each guest in turn a glass of wine or spirits, a cake
and a coloured handkerchief.   The cake you eat,
the handkerchief you were expected to pocket as a
wedding gift from the ' nouveaux-mariés,' and the
wine you drank ; but if in drinking it you were
maliciously inclined, it was open to you, without
appearing guilty of rudeness, to declare it was sour.
At the word ' gorko ' (sour) the wretched bride
and groom were obliged to exchange embraces in
public, and this as often as you chose to repeat the
sorry joke.   In return for the cake, wine, and
kerchief, each guest was expected to place some
wedding gift on the tray for the young couple, and
in this instance the gifts were made in every case in
money.

After these ceremonies had been concluded, the
chief actors retired, and left the guests to make

merry at their leisure. There seemed in this particular instance to be a chorus of old women engaged to sing, dance, and otherwise become objects of ridicule. These hideous old crones gained the goodwill of the guests, as well as innumerable drink-offerings of neat vodka, by singing lugubrious chants, to my uneducated ear more fit for a funeral than a wedding. This they supplemented by indecent antics on their hind legs, and a great deal of coarse buffoonery. The only musical instrument was one in great favour amongst the monjik class—I mean the concertina. As for the other guests (for I presume the old women were invited and not paid jesters), they sat down steadily to gorge and to drink, and so well did they stick to their self-imposed task of making beasts of themselves, that the wedding supper lasted until the morning of the third day, when its drunken harmony was finally marred by one drunkard beating a girl, and another breaking a bottle over the head of the first, at which crisis the law stepped in and took the supper party under its own protecting wing.

On Wednesday, November 13, I gladly shook the dust of Duapsé off my feet, and embarking in one of the Russian Company's steamers, passed pleasantly thence to Novorossisk. I was obliged to return to Ekaterinodar to recover my luggage and to obtain any letters which might have arrived for me during my absence at Golovinsky; and anxious to see as much of the Caucasus as possible, I arranged to steam to Novorossisk and proceed thence overland to Ekaterinodar. I hardly think I was repaid for my trouble, as the country through which I passed was not of a very interesting nature, and more like the neighbourhood of Tumeruk than of Duapse. At Novorossisk I hired a cart (fourgon) with two horses and a driver to take me to Ekaterinodar, calling at the Red Forest *en route*. The distance was 114 versts, and including stoppages, with the heavy cart behind them, the game little horses did the journey in thirty-three hours. It is wonderful what Russian horses will do and on what a little food they do it. Neither of the horses in this instance stood fourteen hands, and they got no corn whatever on the journey.

On our way to Ekaterinodar we stayed at a large village called Krimsky—a Cossack settlement I think it was originally; and here we encountered another of those fairs at which the Russian moujik buys and sells all he wants or wants to part with during the year. I wandered into the fair whilst the horses were being watered, and found it a medley of every race in the Caucasus, distinguished from one another not more by their varied and picturesque costumes than by the endless variety of their conveyances and beasts of burden. Fashionable droshkies, droggies of rough logs tied together with rope, lumbering fourgons, heavy 'pavosh-kas,' light carts, like huge ozier baskets on wheels, nearly six feet high, and the house on wheels, which the Mingrelian calls his 'arba,' were all ranged in rows to form the streets of the fair. Round about them stood the beasts who drew them, varying from a goat to a camel, from a pony to a team of six grey oxen. The shops are simply a sheet of canvas spread on the ground, perhaps under a partially-inverted cart—some few under a more pretentious awning; and here are laid out the trader's wares, whilst he for the most part sits cross-legged in the midst. The grandest shops, or booths rather, are generally those in which are sold the 'ikons,' or holy pictures, for which there is an immense sale amongst the pious Russian peasantry. They are gaudy pictures of the Virgin, or one of the saints, encased in a deep frame of brass, with much tinsel and tawdry ornament about them; but they are to be found in every moujik's cottage, and before them he pays his simple devotions to his God, night and morning, standing bare-headed with bent head, for barely a minute perhaps, but apparently in earnest during that minute. A little taper is kept always burning before the 'ikon.'

Next to the 'ikon'-seller, you detect by your nose, if not by your eyes, the 'shouba'-seller, for these sheepskin garments are excessively strong-smelling, even in their earliest stages. Close by, in the midst of a crowd of the ugliest old women on earth (and herein I do not malign the Russian 'babonshka'), is a pedlar selling knitting-needles and other housewife's gear. They must be hard to please from the noise they make, for the sound of their bargaining would silence the morning babel of Billingsgate.

At the back of the fair is a long row of fires on the plain, whereat the Tartar is cooking the savoury 'shushlik' (kabob). This is the refreshment-stall department of the fair, or at least a part of it; the other part is to be found at the little square tables at every corner, on which are a dirty bottle and two dirtier glasses, behind which stands a red-shirted moujik, and around him drunken Ivans and Stepans embrace and fight, or argue and abuse, for a Russian never fights as our English rough does. Never, perhaps, is too strong a word; but in my three or four years in Russia, though I have known men dirked in broad daylight in the bazaar, and have never entered a bazaar without seeing one or two rows going on, I have not seen two real stand-up fights. The Russian rough barks loudly, and possesses a fathomless *répertoire* of abuse, which he supplements with ready invention, but he rarely goes beyond words. At these tables too, 'Macha,' the demure peasant girl, as well as the 'staruka' (crone), are frequently to be found;

and when they take their glass they take it neat as the men do, and toss it off at one gulp as cleverly. Russian peasant women are hard-working, frugal, and the earliest risers in the world, being generally up before dawn ; but they are, alas! too often to be found on their backs dead drunk in the street in the morning. This is at least true of the Crimea and Caucasus. I can only speak of what I have seen.

At the Krimsky fair I discovered a show-booth, and as show-booths are not every day occurrences in such places, I proceeded to investigate it. A rough tent, with strange pictures of beasts roughly painted upon it, formed the abiding place of the show. Round this a red-bearded Persian continually prowled, with a long stick to thump the heads of penniless brats who, unable to pay for admission, kept trying to satisfy their curiosity by furtively lifting a corner of the canvas veil that concealed the mysteries within. Avoiding this functionary's stick, I paid twenty copecks (about 6*d*.), and entered. There was one other spectator besides myself, and, satisfied that this was the largest audience he was likely to obtain, the gentleman of the stick kindly followed me in and prepared to perform, leaving the little boys to see as much as they could meanwhile. In the tent, in spite of all its grand advertisements, the whole show consisted only of three small monkeys tied to a box, trying to get at the skins of two maneless (Persian) lions, stretched on upright sticks. These had been the glory of the show, but had recently departed this life, leaving nothing but the foolish-looking hides I now saw, to their bereaved proprietor. After exhibiting some fire-swallowing tricks, and a little serpent-charming, the Persian announced the performance over ; and after disgusting him by showing him that I knew all about the manner in which his deadly serpents had been rendered harmless, I left hurriedly, lest a worse thing should befall me.

My inspection of the fair was here cut short by the arrival of my driver, announcing the horses ready to proceed. I remarked that he seemed anxious and mysterious in his manner, so followed him quietly, and asked for explanations when we got outside the town. Then he confessed that lately two or three highway murders had been committed near Krimsky ; that the presence of such a collection of roughs of every race as the fair contained was not calculated to increase the safety of the road, and that his reason for hurrying me out of the fair was that he wished to leave unnoticed before dark. From the time I left Krimsky to the time that I reached Ekaterinodar I heard of nothing but robberies and murders, several of which I believe were substantially true, though that many of them were exaggerated is only natural. But it is hardly to be wondered at that there should be a good deal of this kind of crime in such an uncivilised, semi-settled district as the Caucasus, while in the Crimea, which is far more civilised and under the hand of the law, highway murders and burglaries are not unknown even in the precincts of the towns. The worst part of these highway robberies on the Russian post-roads is that you can never feel sure that your yemstchik is not in league with the highwaymen; in fact, I have heard Russians say that that was almost invariably the case.

However, we reached our journey's end unmolested; grateful as far as I was concerned for the only accident that occurred, as helping us more rapidly on our way. This was merely a chase given us by some infuriated moujiks, whose cart we ran into and considerably damaged, when, as usual in such cases, my yemstchik returned their curses and sought safety in flight. Such a jolting I never had before; but I forgave the cart even that, as it got me into Ekaterinodar half an hour earlier than I should have otherwise arrived.

To give some notion of the inexpensive nature of travelling here, I may say that the sum I paid the peasant for driving me the 114 versts from Novorossisk was fourteen roubles, and this at the then rate of exchange (ten roubles to the pound sterling) would be 1*l*. 8*s*. in English money. A meal which I had on the way at the ‘ duchan ’ of a small village we passed through, consisting of soup, chicken, black bread and tea *ad libitum*, for my man and myself, together with hay for the horses. cost fifty-five copecks, *i.e.* about 1s. 1d. Had I travelled by post from Novorossisk, I should have paid one-third less for my horses and travelled faster, owing to the fact that I should have had relays of horses and not the same pair the whole way ; but then I could not have gone out of the direct course, or stopped where I liked.

Arrived at Ekaterinodar, I found myself in a hot-bed of political discussion at the *table-d’hôte*, where, amongst others, I met a certain Loris Melikoff, a planter in the Caucasus, and brother, I believe, to the dictator. Remembering Prince Vorontzoff’s kindly advice, I carefully avoided being drawn into the conversation as long as politics were the subject, although some of the things these half-educated officers were pleased to say of England and her Premier (Lord Beaconsfield) were hard to leave unanswered. They could not, however, have paid him a greater compliment than they involuntarily did by the hatred which they expressed ; and consoling myself with this thought, I ate my dinner with an appetite unmarred by the contempt which they were pleased to express for a nation ruled by ‘ a Jew.’ This was everywhere the phrase which they hurled at my head, considering it in our case a bitter disgrace that our Prime Minister should be an alien, and totally forgetting that not one officer of state only, but two-thirds of their highest officials—in fact, almost the entire brain of their country—are alien, and principally of the race they most affect to hate, viz. the Germans.

It may be readily imagined that I soon tired of the society at the Petersburg Hotel, Ekaterinodar, and indeed, early on the morning after my arrival, I was at the treasury (' kasnochest ') applying for a travelling ticket. Of course I had to wait over half an hour, while half a sheet of paper was being filled in with a few signatures and my own name, and during that time I had an opportunity of observing some of the noticeable features in this public office. Most of the clerks were smoking cigarettes (those who were not had probably no tobacco) ; none of them used blotting-paper, but instead either blotted their manuscript on the white-washed walls or sprinkled it with sand from one of the many old sardine-boxes, supplied apparently by a frugal government to contain that valuable commodity. All expectorated with the freedom and frequency, if not with the accuracy, of the proverbial Yankee. Almost every clerk had some decoration, and all were in uniform.

But the ' podorojna ' was ready at last, and armed with it I started once more for Kertch. On the

road the relays of horses were scarcer than usual,
and in one place I was warned that at the next
station there was only one relay, and congratulated
by the postmaster (an old acquaintance) on being
in time to get it. As he spoke, a Russian officer
with a similar pass to mine and having heard the
same story from the yemstchiks, made vigorous
efforts to get off first and secure it. In this he
failed, and I started with a lead of half a verst or
more. But in a short time he came in sight, and
to my horror I found he had, by paying extra,
obtained another horse, thus driving four to my
three, a serious advantage over these fearfully heavy
roads.

The course was a long one, nearly twenty
versts, and by promising my driver a large 'pour-
boire' if we were in first, I so roused him that
before ten versts were done our rival was again out
of sight. As darkness had set in, I made myself
as cozy as I could on my bundle of straw, and
thanks to long practice slept none the worse for
the jolting.

I woke with a start. Those confounded bells
that the horses wear seemed to surround me ; for
whilst my own horses were shaking them furiously
in front in a last desperate struggle to keep the
lead, my rival's four-in-hand was jingling them
triumphantly just behind, as he momentarily
gained on us. It was no good, our horses were

dead beat, and every effort they made almost pulled
the wheels off in the heavy clay. The four passed
us in the darkness with a jeer from their yemstchik. But they too had had enough of it, and as
the lights of the post-station were now in sight,
they were content to keep just in front of us, going
like ourselves almost at a foot pace.

A bright idea struck me. The first 'podorojna'
presented gets the team, if both 'podorojnas' are of
equal urgency, and there is only one team to have.
We were now not many hundred yards from the
station. Touching my driver on the back, I told
him to take no notice of me : so ridding myself of
my wraps, with the travelling ticket in my hand, I
slipped off the tarantasse into the mud, and making
a considerable detour to escape observation—which,
owing to the darkness and the triumphant security
of the others, was not difficult—I ran my best, and
arriving considerably before the Russian officer,
handed in my 'podorojna,' and had the yemstchik
out after the fresh team before my rival entered the
office. When he met me coming out his face was
good to behold ; but when I had explained how
I had done him, he took his beating like a man,
and invited me to share his basket of provisions
and a bottle of wine before parting company. I
hope he had not long to wait for horses.

On the steamer which took me from Taman to
Kertch was a cargo of fish for the Kertch bazaar,

caught in the lake between Taman and Tumerūk.
They were for the most part carp, huge fellows
weighing from 25 to 30 lbs., and one of the fisher-
men told me they were frequently caught up to
40 lbs. in weight.   There were sturgeon too, from
the mouth of the Kuban, caught, so they said, in
snares, something after the fashion of our ordinary
rabbit snares, as they routed with their noses pig-
like along the bottom of the stream.   There were
too 'sudak' (Sandre), an excellent fish for the table,
and the hideous ' som ' (Silurus)—largest, I believe,
of Caucasian fresh-water fishes.   This whiskered
water-fiend plays the part of the pike in the Caucasian lakes and rivers, feeding on all other fish,
and anything else in fact that he can find.   From
what I have seen I should say the pike was rare in
the Caucasus, having only once seen one, and that a
very small specimen, near the Caspian.   The ugliness
of the ' som ' has led the inventive mind of the Russian moujik to create all sorts of legends regarding
him, such as his laying hold of the limbs of horses
and cattle as they crossed fords near which he was
lying; and even of his seizing, and thereby drowning, a man under similar circumstances.   They tell
too of his growing to vast proportions; one Russian colonel, whose home is in the Red Forest,
claiming, and being commonly reported, to have shot
one with his rifle while basking in the Kuban,
where it passes through the Crasnoi Lais, which

weighed over 200 lbs. I fear this sounds very much like fisherman's weight. What other wonderful stories of the monsters of lake and river I might not have heard, I cannot tell, for here the steamer was made fast to the Kertch jetty, and amongst the hearty congratulations of half a dozen friends, my second tour in the Caucasus came to a happy end.

CHAPTER X.

TIFLIS.

I ARRIVED at Kertch in an opportune moment, for on the day of my arrival the little town welcomed back one of its heroes in the Turkish war, and as he was an old friend of mine, I came in for my share of the merry-making. My friend and I were invited to a large supper-party, composed of all the young blood of Kertch, and were together fêted, he as warrior, I as sportsman, both fresh from a common field of glory (and discomfort) in Asia.

Of the Turkish war our friend had little to say, except that the discomfort had seemed to him greater than the danger, as the Turks were execrable marksmen with the rifle, and though capital artillerymen, none of their shells would explode,

This I have heard frequently both before and since.

The arrival of the old steamship 'Kotzebul' on Sunday put an end to all these gaieties as far as I was concerned; and leaving behind me a whole mass of invitations unaccepted from my hospitable friends at Kertch, I once more sailed for the Caucasus.

From Kertch to Poti we had a fair and pleasant voyage, over a sea calm and still as an inland lake, past a coast where mountains in the background sink into hills in the foreground, and the hills themselves run right down into the sea; while almost from the point where they touch the waves with their feet the forest starts upwards and clothes them to the very summit. On November 26, at Sukhoum, the skies were blue and cloudless, many of the trees still in their green foliage, some double-petalled wild roses in full bloom, and the temperature that of an English summer.

Sukhoum itself though, in spite of the lovely weather, is but a sorry sight. The houses are most of them ruins; the town is full of soldiers camping amongst the ruins and making confusion worse confounded; the gardens are already half absorbed in the wild growth that surrounds them; the splendid avenues of 'bignonia catalba' which once graced the town have been ruthlessly cut down, though useless I should think even for fire-wood; there is no church left, and I saw very few women. The streets are overgrown everywhere with belladonna, one of the commonest weeds here. But whilst meditating over the desolation of Sukhoum, and gathering its wild roses, the whistle of the steamer broke unpleasantly on my ear, and my friend and myself had the nearest escape of being left behind for a week, by the end of which time we should have had enough of Sukhoum I think.

On board the steamer I met a certain Col. G., a very well-known and successful sportsman, not only in the Caucasus but throughout Russia. He had spent three years between Elbruz and Sukhoum, and had devoted a great deal of his time to sport, but admitted that he knew very little of the country yet. It was his opinion that this district is richer in game than any other part of the country; and if by game you mean only large game, I entirely agree with him. In this comparatively small area he himself had either shot or seen shot aurochs (bos urus), 'ollen' (Russian red deer), roebuck, ibex, chamois, wild goat, mountain sheep (tûr), leopards, lynxes, otters, bears (of which he too said there were at least two kinds), jackals, and here, and here only, the black wolf. This is a beast of which I have heard frequent mention on the Black Sea coast, but have never seen it. It is probably only a slight variety of the ordinary animal, but I think, from frequent mention made of it, that it must be a variety which is more or less prevalent in this country. The best place for aurochs now is between the Pscebai and upper Zelenduk rivers, according to my friend. Col. G. told me of another animal, which he declares exists in the Caucasus on the Kuban river, to wit the beaver; but as I never heard of this creature's existence there from any of the natives of the Kuban districts, or from any naturalist, Russian or other, whom I have since met, I think this last statement of the gallant colonel's must be taken 'cum grano salis.'

Arrived at Poti, I found a very fair hotel for such a town, managed by an obliging old Frenchman; and though Poti is built on an undrained swamp, I escaped without the fever. I was met at Poti by an Englishman, who was at that time acting vice-consul for Great Britain, and was himself employed as agent to a large timber firm in England. To this gentleman, Mr. Carroll, I owe many thanks for his useful hints for my journey. The timber of which he exports most from the Black Sea coast, is, he tells me, box, of which large quantities are found in the adjacent forests; and the burr of the walnut-tree, an excrescence in appearance rather like a huge fungus, but hard and of most beautifully grained wood, out of which the thin layers are cut, which are used in England for veneering, etc. The cost of finding and transporting these woods from the forests in the interior of the Caucasus, between which and Poti com-munication is difficult, renders them extremely expensive.

From Poti to Tiflis I had two English-speaking fellow-travellers—a German landowner and an English mining engineer going to the former's property near Kutais to prospect for coal, of which there is supposed to be a large supply there. The coal, they say, is of good quality and in seams of considerable thickness. This engineer, who had seen a great deal of the Caucasus, assured me, in common with many others, that though not in sufficiently large quantities to be of any serious importance, there was undoubtedly gold in most of the small river beds between Batoum and Duapsè. From Poti to Rion the scenery is not very attractive, the first part being merely a cutting through a marsh forest, where all the growth is too rank, and so dense as to spoil the individual development of the trees which compose it : it has consequently a mean, stunted appearance—besides looking horribly suggestive of fever. At Rion, however, we were cheered by the sight of glorious snow-capped peaks in the distance ; and here, having met with a Government forester, to whom I told my story of wanderings in search of game, I was by him persuaded to stay and shoot for a few days in the neighbourhood of Kutais.

After unearthing the local forester, whose senior

my friend was, we prepared ourselves for any emergency, by a liberal consumption of the inevitable tea and 'papiros' (cigarette), and then drove to an estate of Prince Mirsky's, where we passed the night. In the morning we had a game drive, and killed a few roe deer, of which, Tartar fashion, these fellows eat the kidneys, still warm and raw, as soon as the beast was killed. I had the good fortune to kill a very large wolf as my own share of the bag, and a very handsome fellow he appeared when I first saw him, with his fore feet planted on an old stump and his hackles all up, looking savagely over his shoulder in the direction of the yelping curs which had disturbed him. He seemed a good deal more inclined to fight than to run, I thought. His coat was of that strange colour that I have so often noticed in the hares of the Crimea about the same time of year—a silver grey, turning at different points to what you might almost call rose pink.

Thanking my friends for the sport, and reflecting that an utter stranger in England would be very unlikely to meet with such random hospitality, I resumed my journey to Tiflis next day. The second half of the journey is far more interesting than the first, and in places the scenery reminds the traveller of Switzerland. The old town of Suram is one of the most picturesque glimpses on the way,—a huge ruin of a rough kind of castle standing on a little eminence, with the cottages of its dependent town brooding, chicken-like, under the shadow of its wing. The station, which is the end of the railway journey from Poti to Tiflis, is by no means Tiflis, as I found to my cost, but is put as far from the outskirts of the German colony, which forms a continuation of Tiflis beyond the Kûr, as it well could be. Tiflis, even by starlight, after a long, dull journey, and seen from a droshky, is a sight not to be forgotten. You feel in a moment that the town you are now in is as distinct from any you have ever seen before as anything well can be. In spite of the Grand Duke's presence and the sober little German colony, European civilisation is still only a resident stranger in the streets of Tiflis. The Tartar, Georgian, and Persian are all natural, and in keeping with the place, but the occasional high hat of Bond Street persuasion or Russian uniform is entirely out of harmony with the surroundings.

As we crossed the Kura bridge we were met by a long string of camels, and I was much impressed by my first meeting with these weird, soft-footed monsters, pacing through the silent starlit street, with their heads almost on a level with the roofs of the one-storied houses on either side, every now and then giving a low roar, but save for this moving on between bales like little towers, mute and noiseless as ghosts.

On this, my first night at Tiflis, I had little time to spend in admiring or wondering at the picturesque medley of men and things all round me. All my time was more than filled with hotel hunting. Not a single hotel in the town had a room unoccupied, though I tried more hotels in that one night in Tiflis than I ever imagined the whole Caucasus possessed collectively. The cause of this was simply that the Lord Lieutenant was about to leave Tiflis next morning, and all the gay world of the Caucasus was in town to bid him farewell.

At last I found a resting-place in the worst inn's worst room, high up next to the rafters that supported the roof, without any furniture, even the bed being represented only by the post-house couch, two feet too short for my legs. However, if my room had its disadvantages by night, it had its advantages by day, for in the morning the view from my fourth story (the only fourth story, I should think, in Tiflis) was superb.

The town lies clustered round the banks of the river Kûr, a broad stream, with steep banks where it passes through the town. Over its dark waters rise tiers of flat-topped houses with external balconies, where the ladies take the air and smoke their cigarettes in the summer evenings, if their husbands cannot afford to take them to the fashionable summer resort of Tiflis in the hills. Here and there fine modern buildings of European character mar the uniformly Asiatic nature of the scene, while in the streets splendid carriages run into rough log-carts on huge wooden wheels dragged slowly along by half-tamed buffaloes. Camels look pityingly down at you with mild, sad eyes, as they stalk past; Cossacks and gentlemen in the latest Parisian costume jostle each other on the pavement; at the street corners sit ferocious figures with moustaches several inches long, in sheepskin headgear, literally one-fourth the size of themselves, engaged in the peaceful occupation of embroidering slippers or cushions, which are afterwards exposed for sale in Abkhasian serais standing side by side with shops wherein the wares are fresh from the boulevards of Paris; and everywhere throughout this strange scene glide the Georgian women in their white mufflers, which resemble nothing so much as a sheet wound round their persons, showing only their faces and a few inches of many-coloured skullcap at the top. Here and there you see a Tiflis water-carrier with his skins of precious fluid carried on his horse's back; a Persian selling hawks, or a band of Swanetian minstrels in skullcaps of white felt. However, when I first looked out from my lofty post of vantage on the morning after my arrival, Tiflis was but barely awake, and the sights I have described above were only partly visible; the rest gradually appeared as the day got older.

As I sat on my balcony at six o'clock in the morning, with my glass of tea and that leathery ring of bread they call a 'bublik,' which forms the regular breakfast of a Russian, the only things stirring in the streets below were the 'dworniks' (watchmen), and a few lumbering peasants' carts coming into the bazaar. I was thankful, when the day grew older and the streets more lively, to leave my room and go in search of something more like an English breakfast, before beginning the business of the day; and though I had some difficulty in getting the waiter to supply me with anything more solid than aërated bread at such an early hour, I did eventually succeed in a capital hotel (the name of which I am sorry to have forgotten), which I thenceforth made my home.

My first business was, of course, to find out our English consul—a duty which, if travelling Englishmen always observed, would conduce materially to their comfort. It is besides a piece of courtesy which ought not to be neglected. To a Londoner, who does not know the way to any place, the first thing that suggests itself is to hail a cabman, whom he looks upon as an unfailing pilot. Acting on this belief in the unerring topographical knowledge of the race of Jehus, I hailed a droshky, and having carefully explained to the driver where I wanted to go, sank back in the cab, giving myself up in perfect trust to the guidance of my pilot, and rapidly forgetting everything but the scene in the streets we were passing through. A more perfect *mélange* than Tiflis is impossible. There are no two houses alike; there are no two groups of gossipers by the way speaking the same dialect; in every street there are a score of costumes belonging to different nationalities; and, as I afterwards found out, you can, by leaving these main thoroughfares, dive into yet another world and a worse Babel, by turning down towards the river and entering the bazaar.

Shops there seemed to be many and good; one of the best in the place being kept by a Scotchman. The most attractive to the European are those in which they sell Persian work, cushions, carpets, and arms. In making purchases in these, it is as well, however, to take a friend with you, who knows something of the wares offered for sale, as well as their approximate value, and the tricks of their vendors. By doing this I certainly in purchasing things to fit up a smoking-room at home spent barely 100*l.* in place of about 250*l.*, the sum to which the original demands of the tradesmen for each separate item would have amounted. Nothing annoys a foreigner more, I think, than this enforced haggling over the price of every purchase.

But to hark back to my cabman. After driving me all over Tiflis, through the main street, up back slums that finally ended in waste hillside, and into squares which had no exit, and contained nothing but shops on a kind of second story—after hailing and haranguing some dozens of passers-by —he pulled up, and told me with much complacency there was no English consul, but that he would find me two or three other consuls, French, German, &c., if they would do as well. For a moment I was puzzled what to do, as my hotel-keeper had been unable to give me the address I wanted, and I hardly knew where else to ask for it now my Jehu had failed me. But a telegraph-post gave me an inspiration. Where those tall slim posts are, there must be an Englishman or a German not far off; and telling my cabby to drive to the telegraph station, I soon found all I wanted, as well as a kind friend in the person of the chief of the telegraphists, Herr Günzel.

Our consul, I found, was just the man to help me—an old Indian officer and shikaree, to whom all my wants were perfectly comprehensible. To Captain Lyall I owe much for his ever-ready help and hospitality. With him and Herr Günzel I passed the next few days, calling upon the dignitaries of Tiflis, presenting my letters of introduction, and obtaining all the information I could collect relative to Lenkoran and the game to be found there.

With one solitary exception (Prince Gagarin, once governor of the Lenkoran district) I was told by every one that large game abounded, and tigers were things of everyday occurrence. Alas! I listened to the many, and, in spite of my own conscience, closed my ears to the one. One Russian gentleman upon whom I called showed me a letter just received from an Englishman engaged in writing a monograph on crocuses, asking for his assistance to obtain certain bulbs of this flower supposed to exist at Lenkoran. I did my best, as I promised my friend I would do, to obtain some bulbs during my stay by the Caspian; but as there were no leaves above ground, and as the natives don't take any notice of flowers, or know one from another, I was completely foiled in my attempt.

The number of musical instruments in the streets of Tiflis would lead one to believe that the population is a most musical one. My old enemy, the barrel-organ, turned up here in great force, especially about the German colony. The Armenians seem most fond of it, and during my short stay in Tiflis I twice saw a droshky containing a couple of Armenians evidently on the spree, with organ and organ-grinder crowded in on the top of them, playing away his hardest, while, with beaming faces which plainly testified that they were doing the correct thing according to their lights in the best style, they rattled through the streets. Those who know these people will tell you that it is their favourite folly, when they have had a little too much to drink, to engage an organ-grinder by the day, drive him about playing over them, until they have called at so many ' cabaks ' on the way as to render their seats in the droshky insecure, and then, alighting at their favourite drinking-den, enthrone their grinder on the table round which they sit, and to the tunes of their beloved instrument succumb gloriously to the united charms of Bacchus and Apollo.

Next morning they go home from the gutter with a consciousness of having spent a happy day, as a happy day ought to be spent, and regard its memory as a thing to be proud of. It seems a strange thing, but in Russia and amongst these people the peasants envy a drunkard instead of pitying him. Drunkenness is to them a highly desirable condition, and shame for it they cannot understand. The most popular Englishman who ever lived and travelled amongst the Caucasian tribes owed his popularity entirely to the enormous quantity of strong drink he could absorb without doing himself any harm. The Circassians themselves have an almost incredible facility for drinking large quantities of wine without any apparent harm.

A propos of wine, the wine of the country, or rather one of the wines of the country, the Kachketinsky wine, both red and white, is admirable, and far superior to any of the imported wines to be met with at Tiflis. There is another wine which

is a good deal drunk by the ladies, called ' Donskoi.'
It is something like Moselle, red in colour and
unbearably sweet to the palate. The people drink
vodka and rough native wine in their ' cabaks ' and
' duchans,' as well as a rough kind of beer, very sweet,
and more like what mead must have been than like
any beer of to-day. Tiflis itself is full of beer-
halls, but these are rather for the military and the
Germans than for the natives. These Germans
are, I fancy, an unpopular race in the Caucasus as
well as in Russia, not from any inherent vice in
their natures, but from the fact that, being more
civilised than their neighbours, they utterly refuse
to mix with them, living apart in their colonies,
with their own society, school, and church, prospering beyond any other settlers, and by their staid
sobriety and orderly, thrifty life, forming a contrast
to the life around them too favourable to themselves to be pleasing to their neighbours. ' Nemets '
and ' colbasnik '—dummy and sausage-eater—are
the sobriquets in which they rejoice.

On the fourth day after my arrival at Tiflis the
town, in spite of its novelty and ever-varying
scenes, began to pall upon me, and with some
difficulty I arranged a shooting expedition to the
neighbouring steppe of Kariàs. Here the Grand
Duke holds his shooting parties, and enormous are
the bags made, though the festivities are of such a
nature as one would imagine to interfere con-

siderably with the shooting. But, alas! for us, there were to be no royal forests with innumerable beaters and any quantity of boars and tall red deer. Our hunting grounds were the wide steppe-lands outside the viceregal preserves, where antelopes (*subgutturosæ*) and all the ruffians who are wanted by the Government at Tiflis do mostly congregate.

Early, then, in the morning, while the stars were making up their minds to retire for the day, and a faint pink was just stealing into the sky, our party rattled out of Tiflis; the English consul and myself on horseback, the rest of our party on wheels. Our way lay through the Tartar bazaar, where the fiery-bearded Persians and astute Armenians were already astir, and then over the broad Kûr, and through lands which but for the artificial irrigation of which the Kûr is the source would be absolutely barren. On our road we met a quaint cavalcade, if that may be called a cavalcade which contained but one horse: a vast train of donkeys, some brown, some white, several hundreds in number, part bearing bales of merchandise, and part their owners. Here and there amongst the troop a black conical tent ambled along, nothing visible but the tent with four thin legs trotting along under it. This was a Tartar or Persian on his donkey, his 'bourka' round his neck, hanging in loose folds to his animal's knees, and completely concealing man and beast. The caravan was on its way to Persia, and was the only one of the kind I ever saw, though trains of camels and carts are of frequent occurrence between Batoum and Tiflis.

Kariâs, or the black summer, is a name which this steppeland has earned for itself by the excessive virulence of the fever which raged there after the introduction of artificial irrigation. It is some thirty-five or forty versts from Tiflis, and, besides being the preserve of the Grand Duke and the refuge of Tiflis outlaws, it is the home of several bands of Tartars and one German planter.

It was to the home of this latter that we turned our horses' heads, after being ferried over the broad dark waters of the Kûr. All the road between Tiflis and this ferry had been bare and uninteresting: low grey hills, looking parched and lifeless on our right, a grey dusty steppe at our feet, and on our left the bare unlovely banks of the Kûr, with here and there a huge vulture sitting gorged and sullen on its shore. By the ferry a belt of low woodland lent some interest to the scene; but this was left behind as soon as the river was crossed; and far away on every hand stretched the level steppeland, so bare of succulent herbage as to appear anything but pleasant pastures for the many flocks of sheep and herds of antelope that roam over its surface.

An hour's ride, straining our eyes in a vain
endeavour to catch a first glimpse of the antelopes,
whose home we were invading, brought us to a
canal with a bridge and toll-house or something
of that nature; and the bridge once crossed, the
clamour of a dozen curs and the appearance of
several Tartars advised us of our arrival at our
journey's end. The planter himself came to meet
us—a young fellow speaking many languages as
well as his own, a mere boy amongst the worst-
looking gang of labourers man ever put eyes upon,
yet managing them fairly well, and making his
venture pay. His home was a mere hut, utterly
destitute of any of the comforts or refinements of
that civilisation to which he had apparently been
brought up; and it would indeed need to be a
lucrative venture which should tempt a man to
lead the life our friend Adolphe led. He had been
made a magistrate by the Tiflis Government, with
exceptional powers and privileges; but, as he himself told us, he was a magistrate merely in name,
unable to carry out any measure he might deem
necessary, utterly powerless to punish or bring to
punishment, and so used to the evils by which he
was surrounded as to have grown perfectly callous
to them. Murder, horse-stealing, and every other
crime are of almost daily occurrence. However
openly committed, it is impossible to convict, as
none dare witness against the perpetrators of the

crime, knowing full well that, should they do so, they would live in hourly danger of their lives from that time forth. And even in the rare cases in which the crimes have been fully proved, and the criminals safely conveyed to Tiflis, they have been set free again on one plea or another, until the name even of justice has lost all meaning in the land. In the six or seven years during which my host has lived at Kariâs he has had his horse shot under him on one occasion, has had a bullet put through his bourka on another, and on a third, whilst riding into Tiflis, a bullet fired from the rifle of a concealed assassin broke the jaw of the servant who accompanied him. If he makes himself obnoxious to any of his neighbours in the execution of his magisterial duties, his best horses are mutilated, his cattle shot, or his house fired. Labour is so dear and labourers so scarce that he cannot afford to choose those he employs, and though a man comes to him red-handed, he must engage him and be content. Thus it happens that his own men are the veriest scum of Tiflis.

One fellow who acted as my guide was wanted by the Tiflis police for murder, and a speech made by my host himself illustrated, I thought, as well as anything could, the utter lawlessness of Kariâs. ' We generally have mutton,' he said, ' though, as I have no sheep and don't buy it, I don't know where it comes from; some of my fellows steal it, I suppose.' Raids upon sheep and cattle are of common occurrence, and free fights take place between the villages. The cattle stolen are generally driven across the river and sold at Elizabetpol. Every village is, I believe, theoretically responsible for the misdoings of each of its inhabitants; and thus a man's neighbours are to some extent converted into amateur policemen, who watch and report his deeds. But as a crime is rarely the result of one individual's enterprise, the culprit is rarely run to ground; and even if he is, the village pays an inadequate fine, and there is an end of it.

Tiflis itself is under military law, and at the moment when I left it for Kariâs three men were under sentence of death for a glaring outrage committed in broad day in the streets. Two were to be hanged, and one, in consideration of his rank as a nobleman, though filling a menial position, was to be shot.

But the stories of the lawlessness of the Caucasus might be continued *ad infinitum*, were it not that they would become monotonous, and, as our consul himself remarked, the state of the country is so bad that an honest account of it would not find credence in England. I am tempted to say more on this subject than I might otherwise have done, because travellers who have recently written on the Caucasus, having kept much to the post-roads, and, luckily, escaped molestation upon them, have, I think, given too peaceful a colouring to their picture of the country through which they drove. In another place I may be able to say more of the safety of the Russian post-roads.

That the fever from which Kariâs derived its evil name was of an exceedingly virulent nature may be imagined from the fact that in one summer, out of a village of three hundred inhabitants, only nine were left alive. The whole place seems plague-stricken in summer, even the river having its disease, in the shape of a small worm, which, burrowing into the skin of those who bathe in it, eats away whole joints, until the part affected has the appearance of being withered. One man amongst those we saw at Kariâs had a withered finger-joint, which he attributed to this cause.

About ten o'clock we rolled ourselves up in our bourkas, thanking our stars that we were not settlers in the Kariâs steppe, though as a hunting-ground it is in every way desirable. Before turning in we were warned that we ought to be up early, and, thanks to the too lively nature of our couches, we were up long even before we need have been. At one o'clock the misty air feels chill and comfortless ; we were glad to busy ourselves vigorously in preparing our horses for the day's sport ; and, though we felt like blind men following the blind, we blundered on at a quick step after our guide into the darkness that encircled us. After going some three versts, that seemed to us thirty, we took our guide's advice, and, hobbling our horses, rolled ourselves in our bourkas, to lie waiting in the dark until the dim light stealing over the plains should show us the antelopes browsing within rifle-shot. But all our dreams had to be of the waking sort, for the intense chill made it too cold to sleep, and, though the grey dawn showed us no confiding herds, it was none the less welcome on that account.

Gradually around us there grew out of the darkness a plain flatter than all fancy can fashion, with never a tree nor a bush to break the monotony, or to afford concealment to any living thing. Round this there rose slowly on the sight a chain of low hills, with the river and the low mountains running at right angles to them ; and on the other two sides steppe unbroken to the horizon. And now we rose and shook away the chill and the torpor it had brought into our blood, and with a pang of regret for that tub which circumstances so often denied, we buckled our bourkas on to our horses, slipped cartridges into our rifles, and spreading out into line, shaped our course across the still dim steppe for the low hills beyond.

As the dawn brightened we began to fancy ghost-like figures flitted away over the horizon into the unseen beyond, and at last we made out clearly a herd of some thirty antelopes. As they scudded,

with short stiff tails erect over the plains—their
horns for some reason unnoticeable in the distance—
they looked to me quaintly like large grey dogs,
with none of the deer-like attributes with which
fancy had endowed them. Once we had found
one band, the whole plains seemed to be alive with
them, racing about from point to point or standing
rigidly at gaze. To see them and to long for a
nearer view was one thing, to obtain that view
quite another. Fired at continually by the Tartars, hunted by the sheep-dogs, though little hurt
by either, they were as shy as any living thing
could be. Stalking them was out of the question,
and they made all attempts to surround them
futile by breaking through the line almost before
it began to close in on them. Nearer than five
hundred yards we seemed doomed never to get, and
after half a day's ceaseless fag and a few wild shots
at impossible ranges, my friend L. got disgusted,
gave it up, and went home.

Towards mid-day we reached the low hills
which bounded the plain on the side farthest from
the canal and our home, and in my eagerness to
secure an antelope I found I had lost sight of my
companions with the horses. This troubled me
very little, as I knew the way back; and if I did not
find my friends before nightfall I felt quite capable
of getting back on foot.

All over these plains near Tiflis, and in fact

near any town in the Caucasus, large flocks of
sheep are pastured ; at Kariâs their shepherds are
Tartars, whose pens and huts are in the low hills,
at whose foot I had now nearly arrived ; but that
I did not know till later. Whilst still half a mile
from the hills, I noticed a large herd of antelopes
galloping for a point, to gain which they had to
cross my line of march about a quarter of a verst
in front of me. The herd looked as if it had been
recently fired at, and some of its members were
far behind the leaders, who had already crossed
me. Hoping that these laggards would not perhaps swerve from the line of the rest, I ran as hard
as I could to intercept them, and was rewarded by
two long shots, which apparently did not tell.

Though the shots did not affect the antelopes
they led me into a most unpleasant adventure.
Browsing at some distance was an immense flock
of sheep, and at the sound of my rifle a dozen of
the huge grey dogs who guard these flocks came
racing towards me, loudly manifesting their dis-
pleasure at my presence as they came. Often
before had I been annoyed by these gaunt beasts
in the Crimea and elsewhere, and even known them
board a traveller's cart as it passed through one of
the Tartar villages they infested, but never before
had I seen them look so much in earnest as they
did to-day. They were all round me in a minute ;
and though still preserving a discreet distance,

deafened me with their hideous din, and resolutely
baffled all my attempts to break through their circle.
Picking up some stones, I tried to free myself in
that way from my tormentors, without any result,
until a larger stone than the rest caught one of their
number on the leg, and set him howling lustily.

Then the shepherds, who up till that moment
had been enjoying the baiting of a stranger from
the far distance, utterly careless of what might
happen to the victim, set up a shout, and leaving
their flock, one of them came towards the scene of
action. The shepherds' shout acted in the most
inspiriting way on the attacking forces, which at
once closed in on me, one brute flying straight at
my throat, and meeting my rifle barrel full in his
teeth, while another wilier cur, taking me in rear,
made his teeth meet in one of the tendons behind
my knee. This was more than flesh and blood could
stand, so rather than be actually worried to death,
I pulled out my revolver and let drive into two of
my assailants : the brute who had bitten me from
behind getting the first bullet. This sent the
whole pack flying for the moment ; so seizing the
opportunity before they had time to rally again, I
made for the shepherd, and being extremely savage
collared him somewhat roughly, and gave him to
understand that unless he called his brutes off and
kept them off as long as I was within rifle-shot, I
would put the next bullet into him. After a good

deal of talking and violent gesticulation, I limped off, feeling much less sure of tramping gaily home in case I did not find the horses than I did half an hour before.

But my adventure was not to end here. For some time I tried to stalk different herds along the base of the hills, and was eventually led into the hills themselves by an antelope which I imagined was wounded. In following him I must have returned to a point in the hills opposite to the scene of my skirmish with the dogs; for before I knew where I was I stumbled upon three Tartars sitting round a fire, one of whom was my shepherd friend of the morning. Seeing me they jumped up and called to me to come to them. Their fire not being in my course and my antelope still in sight, I kept on my way. The request became a command; and then seeing how the wind lay, I mentally consigned them to a more tropical climate, and looked anxiously out for the horses. As I did not come to them, two of them came running to me, while the third, from the top of the hill, sent out a signal-cry, not unlike the Australian 'cooey.' My first thought was to stand and fight, for their intentions were obviously hostile; besides I knew that I should be made to account for the damage I had done their pack in self-defence that morning. But a moment's thought was enough to show me that unless I meant to use my rifle, my chance against the four (for another appeared at once on the scene) would be extremely poor; so with a good start I took to my heels and ran. Up one hill and over its brow into the valley that separated it from another no bigger than itself,—from that to another and a third, the chase went on—the pursuers growing in numbers each time I looked back, until, when quite blown, I stopped to see whether my rifle would intimidate them, they had increased to over a dozen. A shot from my rifle did stop them for a moment or two; but before I was well at the bottom of the hill from which I fired I heard them coming on again. And here I began to feel things were really extremely serious for me. I had killed their dog—I had therefore little mercy to expect from them. I was dead beat, and my bitten leg made running all the more difficult. I had only half a dozen cartridges with me; and at the very best I could not hope to make a good fight of it, so poorly furnished with ammunition, against so many rascals with their blood up, in a place where there was no stone or bush to get behind. That they would make short work of me if they caught me I had little doubt; the quarrel would in their eyes justify any outrage, and my good rifle be an additional incentive to them to give me my quietus.

But here a double saved me. At the bottom of the little hill I was still on was a wide earth crack: into this I jumped, whilst my pursuers were still on the other side of the summit, and following the course of the chasm I doubled round the base of the hill a little way and then waited. Yelling like demons the Tartars came over the hill, and to my infinite relief, supposing me probably to have just topped the next rising ground, redoubled their exertions to overhaul me in the direction which they fancied I had taken. Once safely past me, I turned and ran back on my track for some distance, and then made for the plains. I am thankful to say that there I found my friends and the horses, and heard no more of either dogs or Tartars.

It was now getting late in the day. My friend G., disgusted with having toiled many hours and taken nothing, returned to Adolphe's. Being still keen to secure at least one head as a souvenir of Kariás, I kept my horse and the guide, to make one last effort before giving up the chase.

I had heard that by riding round and round a herd in ever-narrowing circles, a shot might sometimes be got from a nearer point than could otherwise be hoped for. Determined to leave no stone unturned to secure success, I tried this method, and after riding enough useless circles to have made both man and horse giddy, I at last got within four hundred yards of a small herd, which, standing with their heads up, were just preparing to break

away again, when, trusting rather to my aim on
foot than on horse-back, I slipped out of the saddle,
and, allowing for the distance, fired at the nearest
buck. At the report the whole herd took to flight,
the animal shot at bringing up the rear. Hardly
hoping to effect anything, I fired again at him,
and that time thought I saw him stagger as if the
bullet struck him. But he recovered and went on ;
and, after catching my horse, I rejoined my guide
and prepared to go home empty-handed.

On telling him, however, that I fancied I had
hit the last antelope I fired at, he insisted on following the herd to see if we could not run down
the wounded beast, which he thought would not
go far. And he was right : for after a ride of less
than a mile the antelope lay down, and, to my
inexpressible delight, I was able to ride back with
a fine young buck on my saddle. Both bullets
had struck him behind, but had not smashed any
large bones. In spite of my hard day and my
swollen leg, that certainly was a moment of triumph
in which I deposited my hardly-earned game in
the midst of my half-incredulous friends. But
after the way of the world, having vehemently
assured me that if I worked for a week I should
never get an antelope without dogs to help me,
now, with the buck before them, they calmly insisted that it was only the luck of a tyro, and
would be the first and last I should ever bag.

We stayed one more day at Karäis, encouraged so to do by my success on the first day, and on this second day I was again in luck, though for the time I did not know it. After a long patient stalk, by utilising the only bit of slightly rising ground between myself and the horizon, I got within two hundred and fifty yards of three antelopes feeding. One of them, a splendid white-faced old buck, with a beautiful head, stood at graze, looking towards me, and broadside on. I heard my bullet strike him as plainly almost as if it had struck a ringing bull's-eye, and at that distance I expected to see him drop in his tracks. For a moment he fell on his knees, and then recovering, came straight towards my place of ambush, passing me at a terrific pace not more than thirty yards off. I fired the other barrel at him, but though I aimed well in front, I saw the bullet cut up the steppe in a line far behind him. Had I had my horse with me I might have had a chance; but as it was, though I ran some distance on foot to see if my prize would not drop after going a few hundred yards, I had to give it up, and the last I saw of the antelope that day was as he disappeared from sight with half a dozen sheep-dogs at his heels. He was found next day pulled down and eaten by dogs or wolves; and luckily his head, which my friend Lyall obtained for me, was but little hurt. The 'express' bullet had caught him full in the centre of the shoulder blade, splitting it right and left. How any beast contrived to go as he did with such a wound I cannot understand.

Towards evening the antelopes, which had been a good deal harassed the last day or two, appeared to pack, and I once or twice came across large herds, one of which must have numbered from 150 to 300. These antelopes are, I believe, not a common variety, being found only between the Black Sea and the Caspian. The horns, which are curved back from the brow, start away from one another at the base, and curve in towards each other again at the tips. They are annulated from the base to the point at which the inward curve commences. The finest head in my possession has twenty-four rings on either horn, the horns measuring fourteen inches each. In this specimen the face is quite white from age, all the handsome black and tan markings of the younger bucks having faded out in this veteran. On my return to Tiflis I made another discovery with regard to this antelope, to wit, that of all the flesh I ever ate, its flesh is the most delicious.

Like all other game, antelope is very cheap in the bazaar; for though the Russians are far from being great sportsmen, every peasant has a gun, and dabbles in the chase for profit's sake. Amongst the Russians in the north I doubt not there are many genuine sportsmen to be found—keen men, who relish a hard day's work with a spice of danger in it, and who care very little for a large bag if it is not owing mainly to their own skill or exertions. But of the Russians whom I have met in three to four years in the Crimea and Caucasus, I cannot say so much. A Russian, though he invariably has some chaff for an Englishman on the score of tame pheasants, &c., is essentially either a pot-shot if a peasant, or a lover of battues if he be a gentleman. At Kariâs (the vice-regal preserves) all the shooting is of the battue order. At another great sporting centre in the Caucasus, where a prince preserves the shooting and wild sheep and chamois abound, even the chamois are cleverly deluded into becoming victims of a drive. Deer-stalking, as we understand it, and chamois-hunting, as the hardy Swiss follow it, is a sport unknown here, except to the Tartars of Daghestan.

Although there is a plentiful supply of antelopes near Tiflis, all those that find their way into the bazaar are run down by mounted Tartars, none being stalked by Russians.

And yet, after their own fashion, Russians are very keen about sport. They love to organise a party, and are extremely hospitable to the stranger in making him one of it ; but if that stranger be a keen sportsman, and has his mind full of visions of great game to be found and killed in their native fastnesses, the sight of the enormous supplies of

food and wine deemed necessary for a three days'
campaign will strike despair into his heart. I am
sorry to have to say it, because some Russians
have been most kind to me ; but a shooting expedition, as a rule, means an excuse for extraordinary eating and drinking, which is carried on at
such a rate that, spite of the enormous supplies,
the expedition generally has to return on the
second day, having consumed everything.

On my return from antelope-shooting at Kariâs
I had to spend four or five days at Tiflis as best I
could, waiting until my papers were all ready and
everything arranged for a start to Lenkoran.
Having left almost all my European clothing at
Kertch, I was hardly in a fit state to make much
use of my introductions, so I passed my time in
inspecting Tiflis and watching the life around me.
And my time, thus employed, did not hang very
heavily on my hands. First, there was the
Museum, where Professor Radde did the honours
in the most genial way, and added to the interest of
the collection by anecdotes of his travels on the
Amoor in the pursuit of his favourite study. The
arrangement of some of the groups of natural objects
is wonderfully artistic, the wild goats being represented in natural attitudes on their native rocks,
and the vultures gorging on a dead camel in a way
that is almost too realistic. But one of the hand-
somest things in the whole collection is a magnifi-

cent chandelier of the horns of the 'ollen' (Russian red deer) in the Professor's dining-room. The sight of this led to my being told that at Borghom, the shooting-box of the Grand Duke, the whole of the furniture throughout is made entirely of red deer's horns or other trophies of the chase.

After the Museum, the (to me) most interesting sight was the Tartar bazaar. Here it was my intention to purchase an entire native outfit in which I might travel without exciting attention, as I should have done had I worn European clothes, were it only my moleskin shooting-jacket. Our consul kindly volunteered to pilot me; but before starting on such an errand as the one in hand, certain preparations were necessary—amongst which huge boots reaching above the knee, to enable us to wade with comfort through the mud, and old clothes on our backs to blind the avaricious Armenians, were perhaps the chief. The Tartar bazaar is a network of extremely narrow streets lying near the Kûr, in which everything is sold and every race assists in the selling. Each street has its speciality: one is the bootmakers' road, another the silversmiths' or armourers'; here only vegetables and game are sold, there furs are the only commodities exposed for sale. And this system has its advantages, for you can in one glance take in all the goods of any particular kind which the bazaar contains. The whole choice of

Tiflis is before you, and if the best there is not good enough for you, you can get no better elsewhere. But, on the other hand, the rivalry of the different shopkeepers becomes first amusing, and then distracting. At one moment you appear to be in danger of being torn to pieces by contending candidates for your custom; the next, there is every prospect of a free fight among the rivals themselves. But this gradually calms down; and then sticking to one shop, you ask for what you want. An article of the kind required is produced, the worst probably in stock, and held up to your eyes tenderly and admiringly by its owner, while he pours forth its praises in the most glowing terms of the East. You don't like it, in spite of its being fit for the Prophet to wear; you don't care about wearing it yourself, you want a better. Well, heaven knows what will please the gentleman, perhaps—and then as by inspiration the merchant remembers some other specimen of the article required, and producing it pours forth its eulogy in terms ten times as glowing as those which described the qualities of the first. This goes on as long as you will stand it, and then with a sigh the rascal produces something really worth having. You decide that it will do for you, and asking its price, are promptly told that to oblige you the vendor will take double its marketable value for it. My friend taught me the next step in the proceedings; and I must admit that it is a vast improvement on the old system of haggling, which requires half an hour at least to conclude. It is simply to offer half the price asked, and being refused, turn and walk deliberately out of the shop. The tradesman will mark each yard of your retreat by a fresh abatement of price or by specious offers. Take no notice, but pursue your way in obdurate silence, and the odds are ten to one that before you are out of sight, a little boy will overhaul you and bring you back to the shop to receive your purchase at half price.

One of the peculiarities of the traders is, that they are continually wanting to shake hands with you, give you a cigarette, or otherwise scrape acquaintance with their customer. As you stand bargaining with them while they sit cross-legged in their open shop front, they stop to call your attention to one or other of the innumerable gamins who infest the narrow thoroughfares of the bazaar, begging for alms. These I believe are the children of the shopkeepers, and you are expected to toss them a copper for the pleasure of being swindled by their father. These gamins of the bazaar are an amusing race. Stunted, bright-eyed, and unboundedly quick and bitter of tongue, they have neither fear nor respect for their seniors. The lips that a moment ago were fervently kissing your hand for the copper you gave at their asking, are at the next moment going at the rate of sixty miles an hour in chaff and abuse of some grey-beard in collision with whom their owner has come. Sometimes even I have seen the gamin go the length of brickbats, but even this elicits but little remark and no punishment. Some of the Armenian youngsters were carrying on trade on their own account, one child of twelve having a shop of his own, and appearing no mean rival of the older men around him. But these Armenians begin life early and develop rapidly, passing from babyhood to manhood at a bound. Their women marry at twelve I am told, and I have frequently seen Armenian girls who looked old enough for anything at that age.

In one store kept by a Persian, I was immensely amused by the owner's admiration for the beard of a German friend who was with me. It was too droll to see the solemn red-bearded merchant in his high conical hat of black felt tenderly stroking the astonished German's beard between the palms of his hands. However, I believe my friend's beard produced such an impression, that the carpets shown us were of the best, and the prices asked not too exorbitant.

Throughout the bazaar the streets are so extremely narrow that you could in many places spring from one house to another across the street. Everywhere the mud is more than ankle deep. At

the street corners you are run over by rough carts
dragged creaking drearily along by grim-looking
buffaloes, and if you avoid this fate, a stalwart
waterman—with bare brown legs and a round skullcap of white felt, with only one garment on, and
that all open at the chest, displaying a skin of red
copper colour, with a huge jar of terra-cotta on his
shoulder filled with the precious fluid which he so
seldom uses—will jostle and knock you down. Nor
must you lose your temper; for to strike or
roughly handle one of these gentry in their own
domains would be to call down the wrath of the
whole bazaar on your devoted head. Here they
have no notion of fair play, and in a moment you
would be hustled, beaten, stoned, and all as piti-
lessly as a welsher on an English racecourse; and
if, half dead, you escaped without a knife between
your ribs, you might indeed think yourself
lucky.

The most interesting shops to me were the furriers, in which I saw an enormous number of
lynxes' skins, brought, so they said, from the Black
Sea coast; and the armourers' shops, in which with
the roughest tools they executed most elaborate
and beautiful handles in silver and black for blades
of every quality and date.

Having purchased my costume and seen as
much of the bazaar as I cared to, I returned to
Tiflis proper, and here the streets were fast filling

with the gymnasts returning from school. The difference between a Russian gymnast and an English schoolboy is as great as that between the climates in which they live. Everywhere the Russian gymnast has the same costume—a blue frockcoat with brass buttons and a quasi military-peaked cap. His whole bearing, however small he may be, is that of a little old man, half soldier, half scholar, and in all sedate and quite a man of the world. He has, as far as I have seen, no games ; bearfighting is unknown to him ; that sterner kind of fighting, which in English schooldays generally takes place behind the chapel, is equally so ; he wears gloves if he can afford it, he speaks French, and makes a poor imitation of French manners; he is nearly as much addicted to spectacles as a German student, is not the least bit shy in ladies' society, and smokes with an easy grace that many a freshman might envy. Poor fellow, his precocious social qualities are dearly bought at the sacrifice of all the merry, untamed roughness of the English schoolboy.

Everywhere the streets teem with uniforms, from that of the gymnast of eight years old to that of the general of eighty. But be not alarmed, pacific sojourner in the streets of Tiflis! Many, nay most of these warlike-looking men are at least as peaceable civilians as yourself. That gorgeous apparel which you believe must cover the manly form of a dashing cavalry officer, is but the official dress of a telegraphist or an apothecary's clerk. All those medals and orders adorn the breast, not of a veteran general, but of a well-fed, contented tailor. Why he got them he perhaps can explain to you. I have seen the phenomenon of a peaceable civilian's breast blazing with brass plates and orders at a Governor's reception, but I never could understand the cause of that phenomenon.

To atone for the warlike aspect of many of its well-fed citizens, Tiflis presents to you, in common with other towns in the Caucasus and Southern Russia, some strangely domestic specimens of the officer proper. Any day of the week you may meet on the boulevard, with sword clanking by his side and perhaps some fair dame with him, a young dragoon in full uniform, with a poultice tied round his neck, or a large white cloth bandaging his manly cheeks to cure the faceache. Such a facecloth we are accustomed to see round the scullerymaid's red face in England, but in full uniform it seems a strange appendage to heroic youth.

The Russians are a hopeless puzzle to a foreigner. They stringently prohibit the importation of the most harmless foreign newspaper, erasing whole passages in any sent to residents amongst them by post ; and yet Mr. Grenville Murray's book, ' Russians of To-day,' is allowed to be sold, and has had such a rapid sale that I could only secure a

second-hand Tauchnitz edition for love or money ;
and yet no one could lash Russian vices and foibles
with a truer or more unsparing hand than the
author of that extremely clever book. There is a
contradiction of one kind or another in every
phase of Russian life. The shopkeeper, who
speaks half-a-dozen languages well, cannot tell
what change to give you without the help of his
abacus. Bred in a wild, rough country, with splendid opportunities for field-sports, and really with
plenty of pluck and muscle to excel in them, the
Russian gentleman cares little or nothing for them.
In the south, which alone I know, few except the
military men ride much, and when they do it is
not for pleasure ; still fewer skate well, and the
best of those who skate at all are half Germans
from Riga ; there are no games to correspond to
our cricket, football, or tennis. Of indoor amuse-
ments dancing and cards are the Alpha and
Omega. Billiards, as played in Russia, resemble
skittles as much as billiards. In spite of the
gorgeous apparel of their priests, and the splendour
of their ceremonials, few educated Russians believe
in anything ; though the peasant is as truly religious as any peasant in the world. The litera-
ture most read in Russia by ladies and idle men is
that of P. de Kock, and French novelists like him.

The members of the upper middle class, if that
means men of a certain position and wealth, can

scarcely live without perfume and cosmetics ; yet in travelling, if not at home, they wash their faces much as an elephant washes his, by drawing water into their mouth and then squirting it out into their hands, whence they transfer it to their faces. Many of them despise pocket-handkerchiefs, except as a means of conveying perfume about with them. All of them will meet a male acquaintance with the bow of a courtier of Louis XV., and spit on the carpet of a lady's boudoir.

But meanwhile I have arrived at the office for the sale of ' podorojnas', or travelling tickets ; and as I am in need of one for the journey to Lenkoran, to be commenced on the morrow, I enter. At the desk are two clerks in uniform, with a counting-board before them. I state what I want ; and after ten minutes spent in referring to a book of fares, and wrangling and reckoning over the abacus, they tell me the charge is nine roubles, but suggest that perhaps I would like a return pass. 'Well, if I did, what would that come to ?' More reasoning, and a hotter dispute than ever. At last the answer is arrived at, nineteen roubles ten copecks. Now, according to all preconceived ideas, it seems absurd that a return fare should cost more than twice the single fare, so I declined, and asked for a single. Here a consultation ensues, which results in my being told with many smiling apologies that they had made a slight mistake : the single pass would cost ten roubles. 'All right,' is my answer, 'only give it me.' Here some one else's business intervenes, and the second clerk turns to have a chat and a cigarette with a friend who has wandered in, probably from some other office, in an absent way. Whilst these two shock-headed counter-jumpers are exchanging elaborate bows and grandiloquent speeches, I have to wait in sad disgust. At last, when the farewell bow has been performed, and the gentleman with the dirty white shirt-front and prison crop has had the honour of saluting his friend and wishing him good-day, clerk number one induces clerk number two to return to my 'podorojna.' Then they make a fourth calculation, going over all the old ground again, and discover with a fine smile and bow that they have made another slight mistake—the real sum should have been ten roubles fourteen copecks. To prevent further calculations I hand in a hundred-rouble note, and here follows another problem. How much change ought they to give me? Anxious to get away I solve the problem for them, and am met merely by an incredulous stare, while the beads on the abacus are rattled up and down harder than ever. At length they make it out eighty-nine roubles eighty-six copecks, and with a sigh of relief hand me ninety roubles, adding, as they turn to the small cash drawer, 'Now we owe you eighty-six copecks.' I am weak enough to set them right,

and hand them one of the five-rouble notes back.
In return for this they hand me a three-rouble note
and two singles, leaving the error as bad as ever.
Again I feel impelled by conscience to interfere in
their interests ; and apparently much against the
grain get them at last to pay me only what they
owe, or rather two copecks less, for try as I would
nothing could induce them to be absolutely
accurate.

Glad to get my pass at last, I leave the office,
meekly wondering what a pass to Lenkoran really
costs, and whether it would not be cheaper in the
end for Russia to have better-educated employés in
Government offices, even if she had to pay them a
trifle more. I took the trouble to jot down this
incident exactly as it happened at the time, because I thought I might be accused of overcolouring
my picture of Russian official imbecility.

Hugging my pass to me as the emblem of freedom from an enforced stay in a city I was already
beginning to detest, I drove round to my different
friends to say adieu, and to make my last preparations for a start, noticing as I drove the extraordinarily high-sounding names with which the Russians of Tiflis dignify their drinking dens. Two
of the lowest order, standing side by side, were
' The Rose of Paradise ' and ' The New World.'
In bidding adieu to one of my friends the conversation turned on Professor Bryce's book, he

having met the author when in Tiflis. He assured me that, in spite of all he could say, no one would credit that the Professor had really achieved the ascent of Ararat, so deep-rooted is the belief in the Caucasus that Ararat cannot be climbed, and so utterly unable are these people to judge of the value of an Englishman's word. I was struck by the remark, because Professor Bryce says in his book that none of the natives believe that Parrot or Abich ever ascended Ararat, and it seemed singular that he, too, should share their fate.

During the last day or two I had secured the services of a Pole, an ex-keeper of the Grand Duke's, who was also a kind of assistant bird-stuffer at the Tiflis Museum. Late on the evening of my last day he turned up, with a little bundle of necessaries in a pocket-handkerchief, and, having handed over to him a five-barrelled revolving rifle on the principle of Colt's revolvers, which I had bought for a mere song, he and I lay down to rest on beds for the last time for many weeks. That rifle, by the way, turned out an excellently accurate firearm, the only weapon made on the revolving principle that I ever met with of which so much could be said.

CHAPTER XI.

EN ROUTE FOR DAGHESTAN.

Start from Tiflis—My yemstchik—Travelling-carts—Caucasian road-makers—Camel caravans—On the bleak steppe—Persian hawking—Subterranean dwellings—Shooting at Kariur—Elizabetpol—An execrable journey—Hawks and starling—Banditti—Curing official corruption at Tiflis—Goktchai—A wearying day's sport—Fear of highwaymen—My guide, Allai—Arrival at Gerdaoul—Hospitable Lesghians.

ON Saturday morning, December 14, before the first team of sleepy buffaloes had dragged their load of country produce through the streets to the bazaar, before the canine concert which makes the night of Tiflis hideous had calmed down, Ivan had returned from a last farewell to his young wife, and I had put the last thing ready for a start. Early as it was, my friend Lyall and his son were up and ready to speed the parting guest they had welcomed so kindly, and before six o'clock the clattering of their horses and the rattle of my wheels were waking the echoes of the German colony. Dawn was breaking slowly as we dashed over the bridge that spans the Kur where it passes through the Tartar bazaar. The hills were standing out black and clearly defined against low, fleecy clouds, the golden colour of an English lassie's hair, while here and there a higher peak caught the bright red glow of the morning.

Our yemstchik had been taking part in a sister's wedding the day before, and, as he himself said, was devoting himself to getting rid of the headache consequent on the marriage festivities. His remedy was the old-fashioned 'hair of the dog that bit him.' But, luckily for travellers in Russia, a yemstchik never drives so well as when drunk, so our 'troika' whirled and bumped through the streets, now rapidly filling with their early-rising denizens, in grand style. In and out amongst countless high-wheeled arbas, swearing, shouting, screaming, just grazing one vehicle, slashing the sleepy or sluggish owner of another with Parthian whip, chaffing, chaffed, or cheered, we bowled along at a gallop. How we did not run over foot-passengers or smash some other conveyance I can't understand, for these yemstchiks turn the sharpest corners at full speed, and apparently reck nothing of life or limb.

Just as we were clearing the bazaar, our kind escort trying, though mounted, in vain to keep pace with us, we met a caravan of the long-eared beast the Brighton cockney loves. Our yemstchik gave a yell, the donkeys stolidly refused to budge, and then followed one of the most brilliant charges on record. The enemy, hampered by the huge packs which they bore, reeled and gave way before our chariot's furious course, and though a torrent of abuse, no doubt, followed us, the owners of the charged ones were too taken aback by the sudden onset even to make their reproaches reach our rapidly retreating ears.

Before leaving the town we met a party of musicians coming from the night's debauch which here follows every wedding. These greeted us with musical honours, and altogether our departure from Tiflis was considered full of happy omens. As for me, happy or unhappy omens were much a matter of indifference, for, longing as I did for the chase from which I had been so long debarred by trivial difficulties at Tiflis, I was only full of delight at my tardy freedom.

At the first station on the road we changed horses and drank the stirrup-cup, said good-by to our friends, and settled down to the serious business of travel. To those who have never travelled in Russia by the ordinary travelling-cart it is impossible to give an adequate idea of the miseries the shallow springless carts occasion to their occupants as they jolt over the uneven track that is here dignified by the title of post-road. The traveller's luggage probably fills the cart, and on this, with knees drawn up, he has to balance himself as well as he can, and continually exercise all the prehensile powers he possesses to retain his precarious position. Many natives never get used to this method of travelling, and suffer a species of *mal de mer* from the jolting, as well as other inconveniences. But for myself, I had done a good deal of travelling in post-carts, and except for the want of shelter in bad weather minded it very little, being even able to sleep as we drove, although how I ever retained my seat whilst so doing I could never understand.

At the first station from Tiflis we saw beside the Kûr a large congregation of vultures gathered round some carcase which the river had deposited on its banks. Amongst them was one large black vulture, a very rare bird, which I in vain endeavoured to stalk and secure.

After leaving the station of the vultures we drove day and night, sleeping in the cart whenever nature asserted her need of rest, through a plain bounded on the right by mountains, and on the left by a scanty line of trees, which marks the course of the Kûr. All along the route road repairs were going on, bringing together gangs of the most villanous-looking scoundrels the various nationalities of the Caucasus can produce. I take it, many of the highway murders and other outrages one hears of may fairly be ascribed to them. Strings of camels, with solemn tinkling bells, which seemed to stretch from us to the

distant horizon, moved mechanically onwards as we
passed them, their plumed howdah sticks nodding
in time to that slow soft stride, which from its
even regularity always impressed me with an
idea of perpetual motion. Several times, too,
towards evening we came upon large camps near
a pool of water, where some hundreds of camels
were resting, their huge forms making, as they
knelt in line, a four-sided fort, within the walls
of which were stored the bales they had brought
out of the distant East. Amongst these large
camps I noticed a few of those white dromedaries
which travellers tell us are so much prized for
their speed in the East. Save for these camel
caravans, of which we met two or three a day,
all bound for Tiflis, a few minor trains of donkeys laden with charcoal, or slow-going fourgons
filled with the carpets of Shusha and Shemakha,
our first two days' journey was most uninteresting. Dead bare steppe and barren bleak
hillside, with nothing more inspiriting than an
apparently deserted Tartar cemetery to break the
monotony, with its tall unhewn headstones of
white rock. Here and there, as the evening grew
into night, the road wound through low hills of
such a withered and blasted look that you felt
that the memorial stones, which you passed from
time to time in dark silent places, were sufficiently
suggestive of murder and evil deeds without

Ivan's ghastly narratives. Up to the large station of Akstapha, where several different routes branch off from the main road between Tiflis and Shemakha, we met or passed other travellers by tarantasse occasionally.

Once we had left Akstapha, we appeared to be the only travellers on the road. About three stations from Elizabetpol we came across the first specimen of Persian hawking which I had yet seen. The bird used was a large falcon, belled and jessed, as far as I could tell from a distance, much as an English bird might be if Englishmen still followed the pursuit of falconry. Wherever I came across a Persian dwelling between Tiflis and the Caspian, I invariably found the hawk on his perch by the doorway, and his two comrades in the chase—tall, broken-haired greyhounds—basking somewhere near him. These dogs work with the hawk, run down hares when started, and put up partridges and ' tooratsh ' (sandgrouse) for the hawk to strike. To these dwellers upon the steppe greyhounds and hawk supply the place of a fowling-piece—an instrument of destruction little used by Tartars and Persians. Each man carries a rifle, an enormously long weapon with a diminutive stock, not nearly as big round as a man's wrist, with a flint lock, and a back and fore sight, with a small hole in each through which the sportsman peers at his game. Once you can get a view of the antelope through these two sights simultaneously, you are pretty sure to hit him; but the rifle requires a great deal of manipulation (sticks arranged for a rest, &c.) before this desirable result can be attained; and in the meanwhile it is hardly fair to expect your quarry to remain motionless. Moreover, a puff of wind or a drop of moisture will ensure a missfire, and altogether the antelope is very fairly safe.

After passing the Red Bridge—a place famous for many a daring deed of highway robbery—we passed a subterranean village, or what was practically one, the roofs being almost on a level with the ground. Below these roofs are in most instances stables, in which dark and ill-ventilated dens man and horse live together. The atmosphere is worse than a London fog in the East End, and the only reason that these dwellings do not kill those who live in them is that Tartar and steed pass at least eighteen hours of the twenty-four in the pure air of the outside world. Herein lies the secret of the healthy lives and iron muscles of all Nature's happily uncivilised children. Their houses, it is true, are not such as would meet with the full approval of a sanitary inspector of the nineteenth century; but then, they look upon them as the bear looks on his den—only as a place to retire to for sleep, or to lie down in when sick or wounded. Windows are to them works of super-erogation. When they come back to their houses it is only because it is too dark to work or play outside; and never morning sun wastes his life shedding glory on windows which, with frowsy blinds, shut in sloth as they shut out daylight. It often seemed to me that if these half-civilised people only loved pure water as they love the fresh air, they might live to any length of days. But, alas, they don't. A cold tub never occurs to them, unless it comes accidentally in fording a mountain stream, or, contrary to their expectations, as a shower-bath from heaven.

At Kariur, the last station before Elizabetpol, I stayed for a little rest and sport, to break the monotony of our uneasy drive. Kariur is as bad a station as any one could wish to see—horses and men living, for the most part, together. But it looked a likely place for game; and, indeed, its looks did not belie it. Never in the best preserved parks and woodlands of old England have I seen more hares. They rose and scudded away in all directions, at every stride. Sand-grouse were plentiful, but extremely difficult to flush; although when flushed I thought them very pretty shooting, and when shot very fine for the table. The meat is the whitest of any fowl I know. Bustards we saw, and wild ducks; for the country seemed full of tiny purling streams, which should make agriculture easy and profitable, though these natural advantages are not utilised here. Antelopes were tolerably numerous; and, two or three times, large grey foxes went away in that insolently easy canter peculiar to Reynard when the hounds are not behind him. For nearly a quarter of an hour I tried in vain to stalk a flock of very large reddish birds with a decidedly game look and a shrill pipe, not altogether unlike the curlew's call. What they were I could not find out, as they were extremely shy, and I never saw any like them again. The Tartars did not know them any more than did my Tiflis gamekeeper, and I much regretted that I was unable to procure a specimen. Kariur would be a splendid place to pitch your tent near, if you wanted to thoroughly sate your appetite for fowling, and vary your experiences with the shot-gun by a day or two spent in antelope-stalking with the rifle; or, in wet weather, when the soil cakes on the flying feet of the antelope, you might join the Tartars in a capital gallop after the greyhounds, with a certainty of a venison supper at the finish.

But much shooting, especially of the antelopes, would, I saw at once, cause great jealousy and unpleasantness amongst your few neighbours; so, having had a capital day, crowned by a varied bag, and, thanks to Ivan's skill, a savoury supper, I drove off in the dark to finish my last stage to Gungha, as the natives call Elizabetpol. If any

Englishman should read what I have written, and, tempted by hope of sport, follow in my track, let him take one piece of advice from me. Never believe any one between the Black Sea and the Caspian; or, at least, never build any hopes on alluring prospects suggested to your mind by the statements of natives. To me Gungha was to be a land of perfect peace, where in a really good hotel I should lay down my weary limbs, and, after a good supper, forget, in clean sheets, the injuries inflicted on me by the merciless bumpings of my travelling-cart. I admit that the vision of clean sheets seemed far too good to be true, but when I found that the occupant of the best inn's best room could not even get a samovar until the host's family had finished with it, and no better bed than the floor and his bourka would constitute, I felt, indeed, the vanity of all human hopes.

Gungha is a much better name for the town than Elizabetpol. It has a thoroughly Asiatic sound, as the town has a thoroughly Asiatic aspect : flat-topped houses, thrown pell-mell together, without design or reason in their arrangement ; roads that are destitute of trottoirs, full of pitfalls and rocks by turns ; at one time dark wildernesses of blinding dust-storms, at another hopeless morasses, in which you sink knee-deep in mud ; open sewers by every roadside, and a sufficient quantity of trees scattered throughout to insure fever in its due season; not one decent house in the town, and nothing either of art or nature to attract the traveller, or detain him when there. There is a large bazaar, under a kind of arcade, composed of a succession of dome-like roofs; here Persian work, lambskins, and dried fruit form the staple commodities. Under one dome the boot-makers were busy; in the next your measure was taken, and a sheepskin turban of any hue or shape made for you whilst you waited. Outside, at the street corner, an itinerant barber was shaving the head of a true believer, whose tray of gaudy sweetstuff lay on the ground beside him whilst he submitted to the operation. In the square, near the hotel, a Persian, with his beard and heavy moustache ablaze with henna, was, with bell and voice, advertising the merits of a falcon which he carried on his wrist, whose broad bright eyes were hardly less wild than his own. The man and bird would have been a fine study for an artist's pencil, so wild and picturesque were they; and, as the bird huddled itself into his open shirt front, against his copper-coloured chest, or struck out with beak and claw from its perch at the incautious hand of any would-be purchaser, I felt sure that the Persian's pleasure in accepting a good round sum would not be unalloyed by pain at parting from his brave bird. But neither my man nor myself cared to stay longer at Gungha than we were obliged; and, as soon as horses could be procured, we were under way again.

The roads of the Caucasus are always execrable, but there is still a degree of evil of which that traveller knows nothing who has not travelled from Gungha to the next station. The only thing the road can be compared to is the dry bed of a mountain cataract. Huge boulders strew the path incessantly, and the arms of the miserable passenger over it are continually almost wrenched from their sockets by the leaps and bounds of the post-cart, for it is almost needless to say that nothing but a determined grasp of your seat will ensure fixity of tenure for a moment. Across the road at intervals we came upon the beds of those streams whose winter fury had so bestrewn the road with souvenirs of the mountain homes from which they sprung ; while right and left of us frequent corn-fields showed by their springing crop that the mountain stream brought good as well as evil in its train.

After the second station from our last starting-point, the view became really beautiful. The stony steppe grew narrower, and on either side high mountain ranges showed themselves, snow-capped and bright in the clear atmosphere of what was quite an autumnal morning, though we were now well into December. These distant peaks were those of Shusha and Lesghia respectively.

Every now and then the sand-grouse would tempt me to call a halt; but though the place in which they pitched was marked ever so carefully and beaten as closely as men could beat it, we found it quite impossible to flush the birds without the assistance of a dog. As the light failed, we saw phalanx after phalanx of starlings wheeling, extending, and re-massing themselves in the dusky skies; and as we drew near the reed-beds, towards which their flight tended, we became witnesses of a piece of very interesting bird-life. Near the reed-beds were several trees, say half-a-dozen, and as they were bare of leaves, we could see on every tree some two or three hawks. As the starlings swept down with rushing wings to their nightly abiding-place, the hawks would glide from their perches, and swooping amongst them, break and turn the advancing host. Quick as the marauders were, the starlings did not seem to fare half so badly as might have been expected, and at last all the wanderers were at rest in their reedy home except one small band which, arriving later than the rest, had been terribly harried by the hawks, and seemed almost to have given up all hope of getting safe home. On a tree some distance from the reeds, halfway between the ground and the highest branch, sat in silent state, or gorged apathy, a splendid specimen of the king of birds. Chivied perpetually by the hawks, and fairly scared out of their wits, the little band of starlings swept round this desert throne, and finally settled in a black throng all round the mighty bird himself. To our astonishment he took no notice, never moving a feather; and there we left them, the hawks baffled and afraid to approach the starlings' sanctuary, and the weary birds too tired to try again for their reed-bed, too scared to mind the monarch in their midst.

At one station we met a party of peasants who had been carrying soldiers' kits from one village to another, and on their return had been stopped, beaten, and robbed of their wretched little earnings by highwaymen. At another we met an Armenian merchant with a 'tchapar,' or armed courier, who was so abominably insolent to me that I was obliged to give him an excessively rough shaking, which cowed him considerably; and on the appearance of my servant, who explained to the post-master who I was, the fellow became as servile as, owing to my old coat, he had previously been insolent. Here, too, we heard of highwaymen, the post-station having been robbed of some horses, which the postmaster had been lucky enough to recover. The thieves had been caught, but I was assured that would matter little to them, as a trifling tip would set matters right with the local authorities, and they would soon be in a fair way to recoup themselves for their losses.

Later on, we met two of these gentry on the road, armed to the teeth and well mounted ; but though they honoured us with a careful scrutiny, our gleaming gun-barrels had a deterrent effect upon them, and we drove on unmolested, though our driver suffered a shock to his nervous system which quite upset his merriment for the rest of the drive. I am told that amongst these Tartar highwaymen revolvers are quite common nowadays, most of them possessing at least one of these dangerous little tools.

The conversation turning on the lawlessness of the Caucasus, elicited from my servant a strange *on dit* of Tiflis. So utterly corrupt had every branch of the civil service in the Caucasus become some three months previous to my arrival therein, that the Emperor sent down his secret agent, K——, with orders to inspect the state of affairs in disguise, with plenary powers of dismissal and punishment with regard to civil officials. He was to clean the Augean stable of Tiflis. Supported by a band of detectives brought with him from St. Petersburg, he soon became the terror of the town. Common rumour had it that three of the worst in high places died of sheer fright shortly after his advent. This may not have been the cause of their deaths, probably was not, but that they were lucky enough thus to escape punishment by natural deaths is historical. One of K——'s first acts was to try the police. Disguised as moujiks, he and his men went bullying and swaggering through the streets, apparently drunk as lords. The difficulty was to get taken up, but after some time they managed to accomplish even that, and were hauled away to the police-station. Here K—— and his men tried to get off by apologies and excuses, which were naturally vain. Then, turning to his men, he said, ' Hey brothers, suppose we give the good chief of police a rouble apiece ; he will see then that we good Christians cannot be drunk.' The roubles were paid, the liberty of the pseudo-moujiks obtained, and next day K—— came down and dismissed the chief of police and his whole staff. So through every branch of civic administration, meeting with hindrances at every step, but still steadfastly hunting down corruption wherever he suspected it. Three generals holding civic posts he forced into retirement ; then, feeling that the opposition of the military in a town still under military law was too much for him, K—— retired.

But now a bitter white mist comes creeping over the earth, wetting us to the skin in spite of our heavy wraps, and stopping all conversation by the chill discomfort it brings in its train ; so for three hours we lie down to rest at the next post-station, rising again at seven to welcome as bright a morning as any I had seen on my long drive. The country was pretty, with here and there a group of trees, and here and there a brook. The sun was bright in the heavens, the hoar frost sparkled on the ground, while every breath of the keen morning breeze brought high spirits and a hunter's appetite along with it. The country now became hilly, even close by the post-road, and every now and then we saw a covey of red-legged partridges scudding up the bare hillsides at a terrible pace. These birds seemed to have taken the place of the sand-grouse now. A drive of twenty versts from Adji Kabool brought us to Goktchai, and here my post-cart was destined to stay its joltings and bid its jangling bells be still for some little time.

Goktchai is a large village, with one broad main street, beginning at the Tiflis end in a bazaar, passing halfway some barracks, where a few soldiers are quartered, and ending in the ordinary Caucasian village. On the way through the village bazaar my eyes rested on a freshly slain tûr, or mountain sheep, as well as other game; and the sight of the noble head with its grand horns, combined with a distant view of those peaks whence it had so lately come, was too much for my powers of resistance, and I determined then and there that I too would at least try to kill a tûr in the wild mountains of Daghestan.

At the post-station I heard the most glowing accounts of the quantities of game to be met with within two days' ride of the village ; but coupled with this came the news that these mountains were so ill-famed on account of the brigands who haunted them that scarcely any of the villagers had ever been there, and none would go again for any wage I liked to offer. This I received doubtfully, and through my man made many offers, but even ten roubles a day were refused by moujiks to whom a hundred roubles would have been a fortune with which to rest content for life. However, though I began to believe in the reality of the brigands, more especially as a post-cart had during the last few days been carried off bodily in broad daylight, I determined to wait a day and see whether no one would come to accept my liberal offer.

The day of waiting was spent in shooting hares and red-legs on the nearest hills, whose steep sides were simply alive with these swift-footed birds, running like flies on the almost perpendicular faces of the cliffs, or coming like bullets overhead as my man drove them to me. The difficulty of approaching the birds—as, though continually in sight, they would never rise and never stop running—reminded me of other days over the stiff furrows of Northamptonshire; though, even with the help of a sturdy Tartar, I found the bare rocks and mud-faced crumbling hillsides worse going than the wet ridge and furrow. The hills were covered with dwarf larch and pomegranate-trees, the fruit of the latter having, alas, been all culled for this year.

Tired and thirsty, towards three o'clock we saw hanging over a steep cliff above us a large pomegranate-tree, apparently unrobbed as yet. Its bright fruit showed red and yellow through the foliage; so with renewed energy my Tartar and I struggled for a quarter of an hour to reach it. At last we succeeded, and found, to our intense disgust, that each fruit was hollow, a part of the opposite side having been broken away and all the interior taken out by the birds, who had left nothing but the delusive husks which had so cruelly disappointed us. I record this as one of many similar sells inflicted on us whilst in Daghestan.

When we started in pursuit of the red-legs we had with us a dog, but so hard was the work that in about three hours the poor beast refused to come another yard, and lay down resolutely to rest. His example was infectious, and though we kept on for some time longer, we were soon so heartily tired of the goat-like manner of progression necessary in these hills, and the perpetual motion of the partridges, that we gave up the chase and came home. There we found good news awaiting us. One of the Lesghian Tartars, who lived in the second range of mountains from Goktchai, had come in during the day to bring some game to the bazaar, and, hearing of us, volunteered to guide us to the home of the túr and the chamois for a much smaller sum than that which I had vainly offered to the Russian moujiks. Allai, as he was called, was a man about 6 feet 3 inches in height, hard and wiry in build, who unfortunately spoke no single word of any other language than his own Lesghian Tartar. The ‘starost’ (elder) warned me to beware of him, for, in spite of his gentle ways and guileless manner, Allai was suspected of knowing a great deal more of the brigands than was exactly to his credit. Still, brigand or not, it mattered very little to me, as Allai was evidently the only man who could serve my purpose, and I fancied I saw my way to securing myself and servant from any outrage which our guide could prevent. My plan was simply to arrange with him that for his and his brother’s services, together with the use of two horses for the first day, or for as far as travelling on horseback should be practicable, I was to pay him a certain sum, which sum, together with all my other valuables, having been safely deposited with a friend in the village, would only become his on my safe return from my trip. This agreement, together with the precaution of letting the Russian military authorities quartered in the village know whither I was bound, made me feel tolerably safe, even should Allai be head and chief of all the brigands from the Black Sea to the

Caspian, and so, in spite of all the evil predictions of the 'starost' and his friends, my man and I, with Allai and his brother, set our faces to the blue mountains and jogged right merrily on our way next morning.

Our first resting-place was to be the Armenian mountain village of Gerdaoul. The road was beautiful in the extreme, though it required much beauty to make amends for its roughness. The greater part of the way our course lay over the bare bed of a mountain torrent, whose tortuous windings were everywhere full of great boulders, over which no beast could move at more than a foot's pace. The hills, for the most part bare, were boldly broken and ragged in outline; at the top were frequent thickets of small firs and pomegranates, while every here and there small clumps of the same flecked the white hillsides. After surmounting this first range of hills, in which small game seemed to swarm, we came upon a table-land which separated us from the snow-capped range wherein our goal lay. On the very edge of this table-land hangs the village of Gerdaoul. The faces of the cottages composing it open out of the hillside; the roofs, mere white cones, rise out of the table-land above. Far more imposing to the eye appear numbers of haystacks, shaped like sugar-loaves, perched on high wooden scaffolds to save them from marauding buffaloes, or to give shelter to the owner's cattle in storms or at night. Here, when Allai had made known who and what we were, the village elder came out to welcome me and bid me to his house, where, near a cheery hearth, on which the huge logs glowed, cushions and carpets and slippers invited to repose. Unluckily, none of the good men of the village spoke a word of anything but Tartar, of which Ivan knew but little, and I only the words picked up during the last two days. To the hungry man and the sportsman a knowledge of the native language is not, however, an absolute necessity, though it is an immense advantage. Signs go a long way, and amongst a race who care for sport as the Lesghian Tartars do, sympathy for a brother sportsman does the rest.

It was not long before tea was brought to me, and as one after another the swarthy villagers trooped in. I soon had quite a large assembly round me. Each man as he came in gave me a courteous greeting, and then, crossing his legs or drawing them up under him, so as to squat on his heels, he took up a meditative position on the floor. Amongst themselves they were very taciturn, and never spoke to me unless I made some remark to them. When I did, instead of being amused at my mutilation of their language, they looked grave and did their best to puzzle out my meaning amongst them. In the course of time a bowl of scented water was brought me by my host, and, having washed my hands in it, he and his friends performed their own ablutions, though, their hands being all stained brown with some dye in use amongst them for the purpose, the washing had but little apparent effect. I noticed that all the Tartars and other inhabitants of Lesghia dyed their hands in this manner.

After the bowl had gone its rounds, some game I had shot, together with one of the chickens of Gerdaoul and a huge tray of boiled rice, was brought in. Everything was handed to me by the host himself, and his courtesy went so far that with his brown fingers he dexterously tore the fowl to pieces, and selecting the best, offered them to me. These people employed no table utensils except the silver bowl to wash in and the silver tray on which fowl, rice, and raisins, fried in butter, were all served *en masse*. Every one helped himself in turn from the dish with his fingers, rolling the rice into a neat ball so as to scarcely drop a grain. Gladly would I have done the same, but for the first day or two I fancy more rice went down my neck than down my throat. The meal was followed by some capital native wine, at which my Lesghian guide looked askance, although I found afterwards that his scruples were not troublesome except in public.

and his taste for strong drink only strengthened by occasional enforced abstinence.

After another ablution the meats were cleared away and pipes produced, when, to my horror, I found I had lost my tobacco pouch. However, lots of tobacco was soon forthcoming, and next morning a prettily knit purse for the fragrant weed, worked in purple and gold by the nimble fingers of one of the invisible daughters of the house, was presented to me. Anything more luxurious than a lounge on the cushion-covered carpets of Gerdaoul, with a ruddy hearth fire by your side, the good native wine to drink, and the best of tobacco to smoke, with a crowd of picturesquely wild fellows around you, and a distant view of the mountains through the open doorway, it has seldom been my lot to enjoy, and it was far into the night before I could make up my mind to leave it all for the realms of sleep.

CHAPTER XII.

THE LESGHIAN MOUNTAINS.

Gerdaoul — Shooting partridges — Native wine-vaults — Expedition among the hills—Native houses—An inhospitable village—A dangerous ride — A welcome reception — Shepherd-boys — The Lesghians—Russian love for the Czar—Unsuitable education—Mountain-climbing—Magnificent scenery—Red deer—Vegetation —A chamois—A weary descent—A happy people—Photographing the scenery—A 'baboushka'—'Developing' our photographs—A mountain châlet—The snow peaks—Wild goats and sheep—Difficult mountaineering—An alluring chase—Suspended over a precipice—A bleak night's lodging—Mountain turkeys—Black pheasants — Lammergeiers—Advice to travellers — Return to Goktchai.

THE entire population of Gerdaoul is Armenian, and the village, like most Armenian villages, is a thriving one. The Armenians are almost as good colonists as the Germans; thrifty, sober, hard-working, and astute, they are invariably better off than their neighbours, who as invariably call them thieves, and detest them heartily. In the case of the Armenians of Gerdaoul I hoped they wronged them, for I was certainly very hospitably received and honestly treated there. The women of the village kept out of our way for the most part, though we constantly caught glimpses of their figures flitting about, busy with some household work, bringing home the cattle, or carpet-making.

Before almost every house stood a large frame, constructed after the manner of the wool-work frames of English ladies, only that it was as large almost as the entire face of the hut. On these, without any copy to work from, the Armenian villagers worked those carpets, which are sold in Tiflis as Persian of a second quality, or as avowedly Armenian, from Shusha or Shemakha.

There is not unfrequently another and a smaller frame covered with canvas, on which are daubs of a brilliant colour, standing in the doorway beside the carpet frame. This is for quite another purpose, and is the property of the young men of the establishment. Armed with this gaudy shield and his old gun the Armenian fowler will procure as many red-legs as he needs for the pot. The *modus operandi* is as follows. A covey of birds having been found, the man approaches with his shield in front of him, so that from the first the birds never see their enemy. When the attention of the covey has been secured, the gunner stops, and planting his shield before him, watches the birds through a loophole in its centre. At first they probably retire before the strange thing that comes towards them, but as soon as it stops they stop too. Then perhaps the shield is gradually drawn back; as gradually, with heads craning forward, the birds follow. For some time there is a struggle between curiosity and fear; eventually curiosity gains the day, and the whole covey comes up to within some twenty yards of the snare, eagerly talking the matter over amongst themselves as they come. Suddenly the gunner gives a shrill whistle: instantly all the birds run together; and in that moment the charge of shot cuts through them, and leaves two-thirds of their number dead on the ground. Yet so foolish are they that, some of the Armenians told me, unless the gunner showed himself, the covey would keep reassembling round the snare until the last bird was killed. Thus covey after covey has been destroyed; and although the red-legged partridge is as numerous in these hills as mosquitoes in summer, still the Government has thought fit to pronounce the use of these deadly engines illegal, and to impose a heavy fine for the use of them. Of course in these hills the law is a dead letter, and the Armenians will very soon exterminate the bird that now swarms around them.

As I strolled through the village before continuing my journey, I noticed several large mounds rising abruptly in the streets, like large ant-hills. These I found on inquiry were the doors to the Armenian villagers' cellars, and beneath each of them lay buried many a huge red jar of good native wine. Easy as it would be to open these unguarded vaults and abstract the contents, the wine is perfectly safe, as the community is too small for theft to escape unnoticed. At the birth of every man child the wealthy Armenian buys and buries a large jar of wine, and this is not unearthed until the son's coming of age or marriage needs celebration. I should be glad to be present at one of these feasts, as the wine of the country only requires to be kept long enough to render it excellent.

Our own cellar on the march was all comprised in a goat's-skin, about the size when full of an ordinary pillow, with a wooden nipple at one corner. This for safety's sake I always carried on my own shoulders, and used for a pillow at night.

Having refilled this portable cellar and thanked our hosts, we resumed our ride across the table-land to the hills beyond. The day was December 18, the air brisk and fresh, with scarcely any frost in it—so mild indeed that during the ride I noticed several clouded yellow and small copper butterflies. The only life on this table-land seemed to be that of hawks and hooded crows, which were in great force. Duels between kestrels and crows recurred continually, and to my surprise the crow generally had the best of it. Once I came upon a grand specimen of the falcon, and rode as near as I could to the place where he was sitting, to get a shot at him, hoping to add him to my collection of birds. To my surprise he let me come within a dozen yards of him, and then wheeling slowly up, pitched some two hundred yards further off. I followed him: again he waited, letting me come much closer before he got up, and flying only a few yards before coming down again. This time when I approached him he had evidently turned sulky, and absolutely refused to budge until I struck at him with my whip, when he slowly moved away with a dead quail still in his talons. I could not help admiring his sullen pluck, so I left him to finish his dinner in peace.

Once out of the plain, the whole scene changed. This second range was one of genuine mountains well wooded, full of loud-voiced rushing torrents, tall columns of white mist, and hoary trees, from which the beard moss hung in grey festoons. In front of us the lords of Daghestan raised their glistening white crowns, so close as almost to seem to overshadow us. After riding some miles along the side of one of these watercourses, we came in the afternoon to a Tartar village, famous for its silk. Here on all sides were fine orchards, magnificent walnut trees, and endless rows of mulberries, on the leaves of which the silk-worms are fed. The houses were of a different character to those by the post-road and in the plain. No more mud huts, but rather châlets, the lower half of composition (mud and stone) and the top story of beam and wattle, covered by a wooden or thatched roof. As we rode through the main street, women drew up their white wrappings round their eyes, and scuttled away like rabbits as you pass through their warren. On the outskirts of the village was a large graveyard full of tall trees and grey old stones, on which the shadows fell; while through the half light a woman, in the white robe peculiar to her people, recalled a hundred and one ghost stories, which had frightened me into good behaviour as a child.

Just outside the village I shot a fine grey squirrel, the first squirrel I have seen in the Caucasus, where their skins are much prized, the furriers of Tiflis demanding as much as one rouble seventy-five copecks for such a skin as the one I secured. As the light failed, and we were beginning to feel the corners and inequalities in our saddles in a way that told us plainly how tired we were getting, another village came in sight; and here we decided to rest, though Allai did not by any means approve of the suggestion. On asking for food we were politely cursed to our faces; and when at last, in the middle of the bazaar, we found a ' duchan ' (inn), it was of so uninviting an aspect that a good appetite was necessary to tempt a traveller inside it. Under a wide awning was a room open on three sides to within some four feet of the ground, and inside this enclosure was a kind of dresser sloping gradually from the back wall of the place

to the window ledge. On this the customers sat,
whilst below them and beside them the cooking of
' sushliks ' went on. As soon as we were inside and
seated, a host of the worst-looking scoundrels I ever
saw swarmed round the place, to stare at and make
remarks upon us. Never were the lions in the Zoo
more eagerly and impertinently watched at feeding
time than were we, and certainly never by such an
ill-looking set as the owners of the shifting eyes
and high cheek-bones who surged round us. The
faces were worthy of a Chinese illustration of hell,
and I know of nothing else to which to compare
them. In their anxiety to get a good look at us,
they even broke down the wooden walls of the house.
All the time their tongues were busy, and from the
way in which they constantly spat and gesticulated,
their remarks could hardly have been favourable to
us. Unwisely I helped myself from my goatskin,
which gave great offence to the crowd, and evil
and angry were the looks cast upon us ; so that I felt
that if they could but know that it was pork that
filled out the sides of my saddle-bags, my fate
would have been an unpleasant one. My man at
this juncture lost his temper, and became abusive to
a hook-nosed individual who had for some time
past been peering down his throat. All I could do
was of no avail ; Ivan would not be pacified, and
so angry did the ever-increasing crowd become that
I was not at all surprised when a messenger arrived

from the village governor or elder, warning us that we must on no account dream of passing the night in the village, for that although he had every desire to protect us, the people were beyond his control, and we should inevitably get our throats cut. So, though the clouds were gathering black, and the evening drawing in apace, we left the 'duchan,' and went forward farther and farther into the shadows of the mountains, leaving behind an angry murmuring crowd that for one rash act would have worried us as terriers worry rats.

And now, as we trudged wearily up the pass, Allai rode up to me, and, with many ejaculations, besought me not only to ride with my gun at the ready, but the moment I caught a glimpse of a man behind either bush or boulder to fire at him first, and ask questions after. His fear was that some of the rascals of the village we had just left would get on ahead, form an ambuscade, and fire upon us as we approached. He himself was evidently determined to use his gun whenever he got a chance; and, in spite of all I could say, made us all uncomfortable by his nervousness throughout the journey; the more so, as we had opportunities of seeing that in most things Allai was as hardy as other men. All things have an end—even the windings of a mountain torrent; and at last, when our limbs were aching with fatigue, a tiny hamlet in the deepest recess of that shadowy ravine cheered us with the hope of rest and refreshment. Two more minutes spent in warding off the attacks of a clamorous host of dogs; then a door opens, a flaming brand is held up, a swarthy face peers into the equally dusky countenance of our guide, and amid many greetings, we are ushered into the one-roomed cottage of a Lesghian Tartar shepherd.

Cushions and carpets were soon arranged by the hearth, slippers being brought for me; and then the hospitable good fellows set to work to serve us with their best. In the room were but few signs of civilisation—nothing, in fact, that would have been strange in the tents of the Ishmaelites of old. The men were rough and tanned to a copper-colour by the winds and weather of their wild mountain home. Their clothes were rough and ragged, and they were all armed to the teeth, never laying their kinjals aside from sunrise to sunrise; but their eyes were broad honest eyes, that looked the stranger steadily in the face; their manner to me was deferential as to an honoured guest, but perfectly self-possessed and confident.

The women of the house had retired on our entry, and for the whole of our sojourn with these people, they remained in a kind of outbuild-ing attached to the cottage, vouchsafing us only a rare glimpse of two very pretty faces, which were lost to sight in the folds of their envious mufflers almost before they were seen. After the chicken and rice had been cleared away, two little Lesghian boys came in to have a look at their father's guests; and never in my life have I seen such sturdy, handsome youngsters as these two sunbrowned little shepherds of seven and eight respectively. Early in the morning, before the sun had risen, these two young mountaineers were astir, waked by the bell of Shaitan, the longbearded chief of their herd of goats. With crooks in hand, in rough togas of sheepskin, I watched the fine little fellows leading their hundred or more goats up steep mountain tracks, to pastures that hung far above the hamlet in the glen; and often during the day we caught glimpses of them and their charge on some precipitous pasture, or heard the distant notes of the rough flutes with which they amused themselves.

With such early training as this—taught at seven to rely on their own resources, and take charge of such wilful beasts as goats on a mountain pasture—it is small wonder that Lesghians have numbered amongst them such leaders as Schamyl and Mansur Bey. Nor is it wonderful that, passing year after year of their lives in the solitary grandeur of their own mountains, they become the priest-led, superstitious people they are. Schamyl the leader would have had but little influence had he not also been Schamyl the prophet, the divinely protected. I have frequently heard Russians say that the only reason that the Circassian war lasted as long as it did was, that it was the policy of Russia to keep the Caucasus as a training school for her young officers and raw recruits; but, though this has been often repeated by men who were in a position to know something of the matter, I would rather believe that the fiery zeal, tough sinews, and impracticable mountain homes of the Lesghians were the cause, than the calculating cruelty of their enemies. Be that as it may, the Lesghians of to-day—such at least as remain of them—are an honest race of sturdy mountaineers, who have little love for Russia, and concern themselves in no way with the outside world. Those with whom I stayed never travelled, even as far as Goktchai, more than twice a year, and, I daresay, don't know yet that the Czar Alexander II. is dead. But the evil spirit that wrought his shameful murder was never cherished in a Lesghian or Tscherkess bosom, any more than in the breasts of his own Russian moujiks. I have known the common people of Russia for three or four years, and known some of them well: for it was ever my wont to put up in peasants' huts, and share the moujik's black bread when out shooting near his village, and I have never heard anything but love and respect for the Emperor from a poor man yet. The moujik and the Tscherkess of to-day are not as tongue-tied as some would have us believe; and very few indeed are the great men of Russia whom they do not detest and abuse; but the Emperor is still to them a loving father, in whose tender mercy—if they could only get at it through the crowd of officials who fence him round, and hamper the effects of his just will—the moujik entirely confides.

If those Russians with whom I have talked on Nihilism knew anything of the subject, the Emperor's great mistake was not the freeing of the serfs—though by that he aroused the hostility of the wealthy boyar class—but the reduction of the fees of the universities to such a degree as to render a first-rate education possible to thousands who, in after life, would have to fill positions for which they were too highly educated, and in which their excessive education would only create discontent. Is it not just possible that the excessive education which we force upon the working classes of England at the present time may have a somewhat similar effect? I plead guilty to knowing very little of politics; but when I hear on all sides the complaint that domestic servants are becoming an extinct race, having grown too fine for the state of life to which (to quote the fine old catechism phrase) it has pleased God to call them; when I hear of the difficulty of obtaining agricultural labourers, or old-fashioned country servants; when every woman can play the piano, and none can cook a potato, I begin to wonder if education may not be carried too far, and whether certain classes would not be happier without it, and their work better done. There is an old adage that 'a little knowledge is a dangerous thing;' and even in England we cannot pretend to do more than give the working classes that 'little knowledge' which produces the ill effects that a perfect education might or might not cure.

But these are subjects beyond me, and I escape gladly to the mountain side. When the first pale ray of the dawn crept through the one tiny window of our 'serai,' we left our couches, and went down to lave our hands and faces in the icy waters of the mountain torrent below. During the night a slight fall of snow had made the valley white, and a sharp frost had grizzled the long beard moss on the mountain trees. We did not stay for breakfast, but just collected all our impedimenta, determining to do two hours' climbing before sitting down to eat and drink, and fasten on those abominable iron claws, without which the rest of the climb would be impracticable.

For one like myself, but little used to mountaineering, the first two hours' climb was very weary work; and when at last we stopped to rest and breakfast, the high peaks seemed further off than ever. Growing close to the boulder round which we breakfasted was a medlar-tree, whose half frozen fruit was deliciously refreshing after our toil. But Allai gave us little time to rest, so that having hurried through our meal, and spent a few minutes in watching the sun battling his way through the mountain mists, we fastened on the climbing-irons and pursued our way up steep slopes covered with forests of beeches, whose dry fallen leaves scattered from under our feet and revealed the treacherous black ice beneath.

Here we came on bear tracks, and heard the cry of the red deer in some beech woods on a neighbouring mountain side. As we peered over an abyss we caught sight of three 'marral,' as the natives call them, far out of shot on the other side. To get to them would have been a day's work ; so we could only look and long ; while the wild cry of another stag, which we could not see, reverberated through the woods, and made our hearts jump at the sound. Far down in the abyss the wooded tops of smaller mountains rose like islands from a tumbling sea of clouds like those we call woolsacks at home ; a sea that, as evening approaches, rises higher and higher, until the whole mountain top is submerged in its cold waves. But here above the clouds, out of sight of the earth which they hid, all was bright as an Italian summer, in spite of the snow and ice, until four o'clock in the afternoon. Here, beautifying the snowy forests by their presence, I found two varieties of primula : one, the commonest, a deep lilac; the other, a pure white; we also found some sweet violets, which, together with the primulas, made a handsome bouquet for Christmas time. The trees in the woods we passed through were almost entirely beech, everywhere covered with the beard moss, which gave them a quaint old-world look; amongst them were a few medlars and pears; while underfoot the blackberry briars made our upward progress difficult. Bracken and 'trichomanes' were the only representatives of the fern family which I noticed during the day.

On this our first essay on the mountain-side we only just reached the upper edge of the wooded belt, and it was here, when we had scarcely left the trees behind us, that I got my only shot during the day. Passing through a small recess in the mountain-side, where all was still dark and chill, the sun not having penetrated there since night left it, I heard a bound and a rustle, and a chamois gave me a fair running shot, of which I did not make the most, only wounding, and eventually losing him, after a day wasted in pursuit. So we turned back sore-footed and empty-handed, trudging down the mountain to the rising mist waves that crept up to meet us, and, plunging into them, felt for a time like men lost in the night, where neither the peaks of the mountains above, nor the fires of the valley beneath, were visible to us:

where trees took weird shapes, like those in Doré's pictures; where all was dank, and dark, and chill, so that a half wonder grew upon us as to whether anywhere down beneath a bright fire, cushions, and comfort could be waiting for us.

At last the house fires glimmered from below like stars through a night of fog, and hurrying on, slipping and stumbling over the wet grass, sliding off our greasy leather stockings to bump along for twenty yards or so on our aching shoulders, we reached our Lesghian house, and had soon forgotten (except when the hateful clamps caught our eye) all the petty tribulations which had interfered with our appreciation of the magnificent mountain scenery.

These Lesghians lead a happy life, though (or perhaps, because) a simple one. A flock of goats find shepherd's work for the hardy handsome boys to do. A field of corn just above the house on a little table-land keeps the family in bread. A tree which grows in the crannies of the rock, in appearance like a small sloe-bush, supplies a decoction made from its root, and leaves so like tea as to have deceived me into believing that it was what it seemed. The industry of the women strews the floor with a superfluity of carpets, cushions, and mats; makes slippers for the men, cloth for such clothes as are not made of sheepskin, and a delicious drink from the medlars that grow on the mountain. The mountain sends them down the purest of water, finds them in unlimited fuel, and provides them with a dessert as varied as that of the richest Russian in the land : medlars, beech-nuts, chestnuts, walnuts, pears, and berries of a dozen different kinds. Their religion forbids them to drink wine, so that, never having used it, they do not feel the want of it. Apples may be bought in the neighbouring village of the largest size and most luscious quality for threepence per hundred. Pheasants and red-legs abound, and are easily caught or shot (though I never heard of snares being used for them), while red deer and mountain sheep are for the bolder and stronger among the young men. Wild swine come all too close to the cornfield in autumn, and in slaying of these the Lesghian not only protects his harvest, but obtains leather of the best quality for his mocassins. Bear's fat furnishes the lamps (made after the fashion of the sepulchral lamps of Greece) with fuel ; and the rheumatic patient with an external application that beats Elliman's embrocation out of sight ; while those who suffer from colds take it internally, as English people take gruel, and, I dare say, with as good a result. From the beard moss the Lesghian makes a dye with which to stain his hands, and make them a manly brown, or 'good fast washing colour,' as the haberdashers have it : while if he be a dandy, he borrows from it a darker hue for his moustache, and for the solitary love-lock which his religion and his barber permit him to retain. Best of all virtues, the Lesghians are cleanly. In the whole of my stay amongst them, my night's rest was never broken by the antics of insect gymnasts or the attacks of burlier foes.

The Sunday we spent in the mountain hamlet, each according to his own fancy. Allai went at dawn into the higher peaks to look for traces of game. Ivan spent his morning cross-legged on the floor washing clothes; and at midday we all three met on an eminence some two hours' climb from the valley, to photograph some of the scenery with one of Rouch's patent dry-plate apparatuses. On our way we met the village hadji, who was vastly interested, and promised to come in and see more of us and our photographs in the evening.

In the valley the thermometer registered 70°, while on the higher peaks, from which we tried to take photographs, it registered 54° in the sun; meanwhile the grass below was matted with ice which showed no signs of thawing. We gathered quite a fine bouquet on our way up—primulas, violets, the white blossom of the wild strawberry, forget-me-nots, crimson clover, and a single golden buttercup. As for the photography, we chose some excellent views, and took them very carefully, going away quite satisfied that those at home would be able to share our enthusiasm for the scenery of Lesghia.

On our return we were met by an admiring crowd, amongst whom for a few minutes one woman remained, curiosity in her case overcoming the modest scruples of her race. We made the best of our opportunity, and photographed her promptly; but alas! it was only the 'baboushka.'

As the 'baboushka' is a variety of the female race to the best of my knowledge unknown in England, I may as well take this opportunity of describing her. She is quite an institution in Russia, no household being complete without her. Generally she is the mother of the paterfamilias, sometimes only his mother-in-law, at others merely an aged female relative who wants a home and is willing to undertake the housekeeping in return for one. Whatever she is, wherever she comes from, there she is, the motive managing power of every moujik's home : in manner quiet, giving precedence to the wife, making no complaint when the husband gets drunk, no stirrer-up of strife, no busybody, but just a quiet old crone, with an eye on the children, an immense capacity for drudgery, and sufficient experience to help the wife in all her little troubles. Her corner is on the top of the 'petchka' (oven), whither she retires early in the evening, emerging thence to get the samovar ready long before daylight. Her weaknesses are volka and the papiros, and her greatest happiness a village wedding, at which she generally assists as one of a kind of chorus which I have described before. It is needless to add, perhaps, that in appearance she is sufficiently gruesome to hold the youngest child in awe of her.

Having photographed the 'babonshka,' we went in to our evening meal, during and after which guests dropped in rapidly, until we had quite a crowded reception. Photography was evidently the attraction; and as soon as our pipes were lit the aged hadji moved that the photographs be exhibited. To comply with this request it became necessary to 'develop.' Now to stand behind a tripod with a black rag over your head, and direct the machine as required, Ivan and myself had found fairly easy; but when with chemicals and other diablerie we had to make manifest the results of our mumming on the hillside, we began to grow nervous. Still we put as good a face upon it as we could, and made at least a show of understanding what we were about. The fireplace was covered over with a bourka, the lamp extinguished, and the wondering guests seated in a circle, with strict injunctions not to shout above a whisper or stir save at their peril. Then a candle was prevailed upon to remain on an inverted dish within the threefold walls of a yellow baize screen, whence it shed a ghastly light upon all the inmates of the hut. Seated cross-legged, with a solemn face like an owl by daylight, sat the chief photographer, and Ivan served him with a due gravity. Bowls of water, and bottles of various baleful drugs, lent an air of devilment to the whole scene, which, with the wild faces round, was suggestive rather of witchcraft than photography. The first plate produced having been carefully washed, was subjected to the developing fluid. Thrice and four times was the dark liquid washed backwards and forwards over the pure surface. Interest in our guests rose to excitement; diffidence in ourselves to panic. To and fro, to and fro went the black water, but no sign of any sublime peak or picturesque village was slowly shadowed forth upon the glass.

Horrid suspicions began to take possession of us. Surely no mistake could have happened this time. True, we remembered that on the only other occasion on which we attempted photography we certainly did make a group of Tartars miserably quiet for a quarter of an hour, in all sorts of picturesque (and uncomfortable) attitudes in the main street of Kertch; that we also kept ourselves and our friends' servants at work for two weary hours in preparations for developing, after which we opened the slides and found that no plates had ever been inserted. But this time there was no mistake about the plates. One after another we opened the slides and poured the developing fluid over their contents ; but alas! none of that 'flashing' appearance of which Mr. Rouch so emphatically speaks resulted therefrom. On the contrary, the surface of the plates maintained an exasperating sameness in appearance.

At last, however, when almost all the plates had been laid by in disgust, something dark which would not wash out, and so small that even Allai could not quite manage to put his thumb exactly on it at the first attempt, did appear. What applause it met with ; what speculations as to what it might represent. We distinctly remembered to have photographed certain majestic snow-peaks, to do which we had almost broken our hearts with up-hill toil ; we knew we had photographed a village from a bend in a mountain torrent at the cost of wet feet ; but what was this ? Could it be Allai's hat ? Might it be a back view of the stooping Ivan ? Could it possibly be a fancy portrait of the photographer himself as he appeared under his robe of mystery ?

Whatever it was, we explained to the credulous Lesghians that, after undergoing a magnifying process at home, it would no doubt convey a correct idea of the scenery of Daghestan to English minds. With this explanation we were thankful to see they were content, and silently resolved to give away our photographic apparatus at the first opportunity.

The next entry in the rough log I kept at this

time is made after my return from Daghestan. On December 23, Ivan, Allai, two other Lesghians, and myself started for the higher peaks, in which the tûr, or mountain sheep, are said to dwell. After a day of hard climbing we reached a ruined bothy used by mountain shepherds in the height of summer, which marks the highest point to which any of the neighbouring flocks attain even then. When we reached it, the roof had been partly blown off, and the walls broken in; snow surrounded us as far as the eye could see; snow had formed a drift inside the hut on the side opposite the breach in the wall; snow in a broken wooden trencher was being melted with difficulty over a wood fire in the middle of the hut by one of our men for tea; while, without, the hard profiles of the snow peaks surrounded us on all sides.

We had started that morning at five, and when we reached the bothy the starlight was glimmering on the snow. Once during the day I had had a glimpse of a flock of wild goats, in colour black, with fine horns and tremendous beards. They were within 150 yards, and I might easily have secured one, but unluckily was persuaded by my man to let them come a little closer, so as to make assurance doubly sure. For a moment they disappeared round a large boulder, and I waited for the leading goat to appear on my side of the mass, determined to fire as soon as he did so. But my hopes were doomed to disappointment. The next I saw of those goats they were going like mad things down the mountain-side a quarter of a mile off. Several times we saw tracks of bears, and once I heard one scrambling away, within shot of me probably, but I could not catch sight of him in time amongst the fir-trees. Another time we came upon a steep ascent, from the top of which a shower of small stones apprised us of the flight of three tûr; but though my men caught a glimpse of them, they were too far off even had I seen them, which I did not. My man Ivan had a long shot at a chamois and missed him, so that, after a hard day's climbing, we reached the bothy empty-handed.

Once fairly amongst the snow and ice on the bare rocks, cutting steps for our ascent, and climbing rather with our hands than with our feet, I did not so much mind it; though running across a rattling moraine as it shifted from under us was a new and startling experience to me. The almost perpendicular grass slopes which we had to cross before getting clear of the forest were the greatest trials we had. Under the guidance of Adolphe Follignet, of Chamounix, I have since tried mountaineering in Switzerland, after the tourists have all returned, and a few chamois may be seen not further from Chamounix than the Aiguille Dru; but though he does not choose the easiest tracks when in pursuit of his favourite game, or stop too often to help his less goat-like followers, I never crossed with him such difficult places as these Lesghian grass-slopes. Too hard to give you any hold for your alpenstock, the short fine grass slips from under the iron claws of your clamps; the butt of the rifle slung across your shoulders comes in collision with the steep bank and almost hurls you into space; the claws of the clamp catch in your other boot as you cautiously pass one foot over another, and at every step it seems a toss-up whether you go or stay.

It required, then, no small inducement to tempt me to continue my toil when the end of the day's journey had been reached. But the inducement was there. As we stood for a moment at the door of the hut to take in some of the grandeur of the scenery which surrounded us, seven glorious red deer came tossing their heads as they followed one another round the boulder of a neighbouring crag. Between us and them was a great gulf fixed, which could only be crossed by a difficult and tedious climb; but the stag's magnificent head was a prize worth trying for; so, tired though I was, I took one of the Tartars with me, and as soon as the herd had passed behind a ridge, started on their track. Following close in their steps, we had to cross a sheet of frozen snow hanging like a pentice over the edge of a bottomless abyss. My guide went first, scooping hollows with the butt of his rifle in which to put his feet, and in his steps I followed with comparative ease, though it required a good head to look down from our perilous pathway.

Still the excitement of the chase kept me up; and once across this long stretch of snow the going was easy enough, until we came to a small chasm which had to be crossed by jumping. Had we not looked too long at it the jump would not have appalled us, as it was easily within the powers of the most third-rate athlete. As it was, it was not without a good deal of screwing up that I got myself to the sticking-point, and gave my guide a lead across. After this I went on by myself, my Lesghian going back, in despair of ever getting nearer to the deer. For nearly an hour I continued to follow up the track, expecting every time I peered over a ridge to find the herd in range just on the other side; and so alluring was the chase that even now, looking back, I cannot help feeling that if I had only gone on to that next bluff I should have had my reward.

But the human frame won't go on moving for ever, however much the will may desire it to, and my unlucky limbs kept reminding me by certain aches and stumbles that they had almost reached the limit of their powers of endurance. So all unwilling I gave in and turned back. And now my difficulties began. The climb back, like all such climbs, seemed twice as long as it had appeared in coming. My eyes were getting heavy and feet like lead. There was no game ahead to allure me forward, no guide by my side to advise or direct my steps. I began to regret my persistent pursuit of the red deer. Still, in spite of my fatigue, all went well until I began to cross the roof-like sheet of snow between myself and the hut. Here the light seemed worse than it had been in coming, and the footholds hard to distinguish. When halfway across I very nearly concluded my travels, not only for that night but for ever. One of my feet slipped out of the hole in which I had placed it, and brought me on my face on the snow. Instinctively I fell inwards, driving my rifle-barrels with all my strength into the snow, and there, for the worst minute of my life, I hung, one foot still in one of the steps and the other leg hanging loose on the smooth surface, not daring to lift myself, for fear lest any extra pressure should break my remaining foothold or loosen the grip of my rifle in the snow, and so send me tobogganing down the slope, over the edge of which I should infallibly shoot into eternity. However, it was Christmas Eve, and some good angel buoyed me up; and when in fear and trembling I slowly made the effort, I did with difficulty regain the upright position, and in a few more minutes got off that treacherous snow-slope, with a feeling of relief that almost compensated for the trouble it had cost me.

In the hut the scene was anything but suggestive of Christmas cheer. Thawed snow and a little stale bread was our only fare ; our only music a bitter wind, until now unnoticed, that whistled through the gaps in our walls. Even the Lesghians could not sleep, though they lay almost in the embers of the fire, the pungent smoke from which effectually blinded us for the time. All night long we moved about like wild beasts in a cage, in a vain endeavour to keep warm. Now and then one of us would sip the few drops of thawed snow from the half-burnt fragment of the wooden bowl on the fire. Once or twice a few minutes' sleep came to us, but they were soon ended with a start and a shiver that effectually brought us back from dreamland.

I don't think any one slept that night : the stars were almost as bright as ever when we left the hut to warm ourselves by exercise, and make believe that a new day had begun. For some few minutes before we left our bleak night's lodging shrill whistlings on all sides had made me believe that other human beings besides ourselves were astir. As our eyes got accustomed to the light the true source of the noise was revealed. All round us groups of that great grey bird the

Lesghians call the mountain turkey were busily feeding, and vigorously whistling as they fed. Tame as they were, I found that shooting them in that dim light with an 'express' rifle was no easy work, and the only one I killed fell in a crevasse, in which we were obliged, hungry though we were, to leave him. Had I tried when I first left the hut I might have easily killed several, as they would let me approach within a dozen yards of them, so tame were they. But at that early hour we had hopes that along some one of the well-beaten tracks near the hut we might see tûr or wild goat descending to the pastures below; and with this possibility in view we let the turkeys alone until the coming dawn had made them comparatively wild.

Before dawn we saw some birds which the mountaineers call black pheasants—birds with a flight and shape in every way justifying their name. These, as well as the turkeys, disappeared as if by magic at dawn. The peaks, which had been loud with their calls and alive with their bustling forms half an hour ago, were now still as if they had never known them, and but for their tracks upon the snow, one might have fancied they were mere nightmares which the daylight had dispersed. The cause of their sudden disappearance Allai pointed out to me in the forms of two broad-winged lammergeiers that came with the first glow of morning, sailing on steady pinions round the mountain top.

Later on in the day, when, owing to lack of supplies and disaffection amongst my men, I was retracing my steps to the valley, I saw more of these mountain kings. We had stretched ourselves on a ledge of rock on which the sun shone rather warmly, and, weary of climbing, were resting in his cheering beams, when a shadow came between us and him, and looking up, we saw the form of one of these bearded robbers hovering over us. A bullet from my 'express' cut out a handful of his pinions ; for a moment the great bird staggered as if he was coming down, but, to my chagrin, righted himself and sailed on, steady and calm as ever, to finish his circuit round a neighbouring mountain top, and, crowning insolence, to repass us exactly as he had passed before, except that this time the bullet did not fly so near its mark.

My time was now getting short ; so that though I had to leave my mountain home empty-handed, I decided to pocket my failure, and return at once to the post-road, to continue my journey to the Caspian. Had I had a good guide, who was also a keen sportsman, a good stalking glass, and had I come a month earlier, I am sure the result of my visit from a sporting point of view might have been widely different. It is easy to see that game is extremely plentiful, and I still look forward to a good time coming, when, knowing my ground and my men better, I may profit by my past experiences, and make a bag that any sportsman might be proud of. It is, I believe, always very long odds against a man making a large bag in a country utterly strange to him without efficient guides.

My farewell to my Lesghian hosts had in it more of regret than characterised my leave-takings generally in the Caucasus ; and my presentiments did not deceive me, for it was long before I met with such a cleanly, hospitable home again. Christmas Day I spent at Gerdaoul, where we had a deer drive among the mountains on a pouring wet day, which made our style of sport peculiarly unpleasant. Unluckily, Ivan shot a doe early in the day, and over the carcass of this the whole band of Armenians—who were to us both beaters and hosts—fought like dogs over a bone. Seeing there was no chance of more sport that day, I left them to stab one another for a half pound more or less of venison if they liked ; and feeling a twinge or two of rheumatism, trudged on towards Goktchai, leaving Allai to follow with the horses.

At one of the villages on my way back I was met by a deputation, asking me to sanction the release of a wretched Tartar, who had applied some abusive language to me on my journey to the Lesghian hamlet, of which, in my ignorance of the dialect, I had been utterly unconscious. It seems Allai had found time to send over to the elder of the village, representing me as a prince under the protection of the Russian Government, and on his representations the poor devil had been confined in a miserable dark hut ever since. Of course I gave the necessary sanction, though I felt that it might be as well not to correct Allai's mistaken notion of my position until I was safe again in Goktchai. I may here mention that, though we luckily escaped without molestation, we were continually advised to take an escort ; and even Allai secured one at his own expense to see his brother and horses safe back to the post-road when he left us with the Lesghians. The Lesghians themselves never leave their houses without one well-armed man to protect their goods from the pilfering Tartars, who abound in these little-visited regions. I am thus particular in mentioning these things, in order that no one who may be led to follow in my steps may come to grief through a want of proper caution, induced by my good luck. On our way back to Goktchai I saw one of the beautiful Dalmatian creepers which sometimes occur here, though Allai assured me they are by no means common.

CHAPTER XIII.

FROM GOKTCHAI TO LENKORAN.

Rough travelling—Shooting by the way—Shemakha and Aksu—
Tarantasses and post-roads—A wretched station—Mud volcanoes
and naphtha springs—Bustards—On the road to Salian—Swarms
of wild-fowl—A rascally official—Disappointed hopes—A good
Samaritan—Rival hosts—Asiatic fever—The Mooghan steppe—
Pelicans and myriads of other birds—Tartar orgies—Banished
sectaries: the Molochans and Skoptsi—Arrival at Lenkoran—A
Persian gunsmith—Fellow-sportsmen.

THE day after our return to the post-road, we
found on waking that the change in the weather
predicted by our mountain guides had already set
in. There was no longer that crisp raciness in the
air which carried us through the day's work with
comparative ease and pleasure, but a steady cold
rain, with occasional snowstorms, blinded the sun
and changed the roads into morasses. The hills
were already snow-clad in that one night, and had
we not left Gerdaoul when we did, we might have
remained for the winter. As it was, the prospect
of our journey to Lenkoran was not a bright one.
Every rill that crossed the road was fast swelling to a torrent, and the fifty-seven versts which
formed our day's allotted work, and terminated at

Aksu, were versts of misery and discomfort hard
to bear.

At Aksu the postmaster refused to give us
horses, alleging that, in the present state of the
weather, to attempt the range of hills between his
station and Shemakha would only result in the
destruction of the post-cart, loss of horses, and
broken limbs for the fares, especially now that the
mists and darkness of night were rendering what
road there was invisible.

On the road, before reaching Aksu, we came
across three of the brigands of whom we have
heard so much, in charge of a band of 'tchapars'
(mounted policemen), who seemed a vast deal more
like the highwaymen of romance than their sorry-
looking captives did. On the morning of December 28 we left Aksu for Shemakha, a distance of
forty versts, over hills whose sides were like wet
ploughed fields. Here the post-cart was unable to
proceed as fast as we could walk, so that we
solaced ourselves by shooting *en route*, and derived
some consolation from the abundance of game which
we found on these hillsides. Red-legs, hares, and
pheasants swarmed ; and what with these, the owls,
and other birds of prey with which the hills
teemed, we had a very lively time. Wolves, too,
have their haunts here, as witness a deserted post-
cart, on the horses attached to which a traveller
and his yemstchik had escaped during the preced-

ing week, leaving their cart with the baggage to take care of itself.

I used to believe, before I saw Aksu, that nowhere in the world did magpies more abound than in Galway round Loughrea, or in some favoured parts of France; but here in Aksu I counted seventeen of these poaching rascals all together like a flock of sparrows. In the hills halfway between Aksu and Shemakha I saw quite a mob of eagles and hawks, busy, I presume, with the half-frozen smaller birds and hares. Two or three lammer-geiers tempted me to a prolonged chase; but though I hit two of them, my number four shot would not bring them down, and I confess to being unable to touch them with my rifle, in spite of their slow wheeling flight.

Shemakha is not a town to detain a weary traveller long. The only inn I could find was an underground 'duchan,' to which access was obtained by a flight of stone steps leading from the road above to a kind of vault, in which puddles stood on the floor, drained off from the mud above; and here the cooking and liquor were as infamous as the accommodation. Shemakha is mainly composed of flat-topped Asiatic houses and a few smart new ones of the common Russian stamp, with white plastered sides and green roofs that looked bitterly cold and out of place in their setting of snow and winter storm.

The roads of this town are, without exception, the worst for a town I ever saw; nothing but the bed of a mountain torrent could be worse. The town bore traces of damage done by that volcanic action from which it is a too frequent sufferer. The principal residents are, I believe, Armenian; the principal industry the manufacture of carpets. Shemakha is, I am told, an extremely old town, and was, in days gone by, the capital of a 'gubernia,' though before the Russian rule, in the early Persian days, the great town was Aksu, the post-station at the foot of the hills, and not Shemakha. Now Aksu has declined to a very insignificant position; and even should the contemplated railway from Tiflis to Baku ever become a reality, the volcanic spasms from which it so frequently suffers will probably prevent Shemakha ever attaining to any real importance.

After leaving Shemakha the main post-road runs on to Baku, the principal port on this side the Caspian. As, however, my object was to get into Persia, or, at least, so near to Persia as to run a chance of finding tigers, I left the main road at Shemakha, and bore away to the south-east for Lenkoran. The road between Shemakha and Lenkoran being extremely little used, I was destined to see, before I reached the Caspian, the lowest depths of the discomforts of Russian post-travelling. Hitherto there had been at least three 'troikas' (teams) kept at each station; now no station had more than two. One of these teams being always retained for emergencies (such as the needs of a special courier), there remained one team to do all the work. Luckily for me, I appeared to be the only traveller; had it been otherwise. I might still be stranded at some post-house on the borders of the Mooghan steppe.

As Shemakha held out no great inducements to me to remain. my man and I were not long in resuming our journey. After a stage of twenty versts through rough hilly country, we put up for the night at a station which I have recorded by name, that I may make it infamous as the very worst post-station in the Russian empire, and, therefore, probably in the world. It seems a great deal for one to say who, after all, has seen only one side of the mighty empire of Russia; but it must be remembered that in speaking thus I am simply relying on the Russians themselves, who assure me that the Russian post-roads in the Caucasus are the worst in the empire, and of these I have had some experience. Though I have carefully examined my map. I cannot find the name of the station of which I am now writing upon it; but then I have had considerable difficulty in recognising many other well-known places, owing to differences in the spelling of the names, and even in the names themselves,

since it is no uncommon thing to meet with a
village boasting of nearly as many names as
inhabitants. Tchaillee is as near the phonetic
spelling of the name of this villanous collection
of hovels as I can make it.

When we arrived, night had set in, and with
it foul weather. We were tired, wet, and hungry.
No horses could have been had even if we would
have continued our journey that night; so we
decided to remain, and asked our way to the
traveller's room. The station is placed on very
high ground, and in an exposed position. At
the most exposed corner is the room in which
we were to pass the night. The floor was literally
more wet and filthy than the road without; you
could not stand out of a puddle unless you stood
on the only piece of furniture in the room—a solitary bench, extremely rickety with old age, and
not large enough to hold one man in a recum-
bent position. The hearth was in ruins, the
window blown in, the door off its hinges, the
ceiling had partially fallen, and even the coloured
print of the Emperor, with which no post-house
or public office can ever dispense, hung in
wet fragments flapping against the mouldy
walls.

We tried to bale the water from the floor, but
it was labour wasted; it returned as fast as we
expelled it. Do what we would to block out the

wind, our barricades were useless against its fury, owing to the many breaches it had already made. We asked for wood or coal—the people had none. We asked for food—they had none. We tried the stables, thinking we might find shelter there. Standing over their fetlocks in filthy slush, in an atmosphere that would stifle an English horse in three minutes, were the few wretched-looking beasts whose lot it was to live and labour at Tchaillee. And yet, in spite of adverse circumstances such as these, in spite of short allowance and no grooming, these hardy brutes, though they look mere bags of bones, do more work than our well-cared-for English horses, never seem to suffer from coughs, colds, mud fever, or any of the hundred and one ailments to which an unnatural amount of coddling makes our animals subject. There is this to be said for the Russian, if he does not provide his beast with good food and comfortable stabling, at least he leaves him the coat that nature gave him.

After trying in vain to find a resting-place elsewhere, Ivan and myself bribed the chief yemstchik (who was also the post-master) to let us share his one-roomed hovel for the night. The man was a Molochan, and lived with his parents and his children, in a state of slovenly misery, in this one room. The poor wife made the night hideous with a deep racking cough that led one to hope that she would not have to drag out a miserable existence at Tehaillee much longer. The children were dirty, listless skeletons, too lifeless even to quarrel or play. The man seemed to do his work as driver in the apathetic way in which a horse might work in a mill, taking no interest in his task, and feeling no desire to better his condition. The apathy of the Russian moujik is the truly wonderful part of his nature. Here was a man not more than thirty-five, with half his days idle, with his wife and children dying before his eyes for the want of a little comfort, which a week's work would have given them, and yet he never seemed to dream of mending the windows or roof, of draining the water from the floor, or of doing anything to prevent the stifling inroads of the smoke, any more than his wife dreamt of cleaning or rendering comfortable the inside of her dwelling. And yet these people were Molochans, a religious sect, professing to lead a pure life according to the light of their own reason, disbelieving in fasting as practised by orthodox Russians, and, as a rule, more sturdy, cleanly, and useful than the average Russian moujik. The Russian peasant settlers in the Caucasus struck me everywhere as deteriorating rather than improving with their change of country. Far into the night my man and myself lay unable to sleep, tired though we were, in this miserable den, passing the time by knocking over with our kinjals as many as possible out of the droves of mice who made a playground of our prostrate forms.

After leaving Tchaillee we got down again into the plains, where the weather was much milder, and travelling more interesting to a sportsman, since wild-fowl began to abound by the roadside, owing probably to the proximity of the Kûr. Between the third and fourth station from Shemakha, the names of which were apparently of such a crack-jaw nature as to render all reproduction in English hopeless, we crossed a tract of land covered with mud volcanoes, some of which were as much as fifteen feet in height. Here, too, we saw naphtha welling up from the ground and running across the post-road in large quantities. The yemstchik told me that the whole country for miles round was full of it, but very little was utilised, as the difficulties of transport rendered the working of the oil unprofitable. Should a line of rail ever be opened to Baku from Tiflis, I should imagine that these naphtha springs will become valuable property.

Whilst staying at the next station after the mud volcanoes, I was lucky enough to witness a passage of the strepita or lesser bustard (*otis tetrax*). These magnificent birds were in millions all over the steppe. The ground was grey with them: the air full of their cries, the sky alive with the movement of their wings. With them were a few small flocks of another bird, which I thought I recognised as the golden plover, but of this I am by no means sure. So much struck was I by the strange sight which this enormous passage presented, that I stayed the greater part of the day to watch it ; and when at last I left, the almost inconceivable flood of winged creatures was still rolling on over the steppe from west to east in undiminished numbers. The Russian powder which I bought at Tiflis had turned out so badly, that at this time I had almost given up using it for anything larger than teal, and even then it was necessary to be at very close quarters to bring the bird to bag, so miserably weak was it. Thanks, however, to the dense masses in which the bustards stood and flew, I was enabled to secure sufficient to supply my man and myself with a welcome change of diet, by the expenditure of only two of my treasured 'express' cartridges. Judging by what I killed, I should say the birds were only just starting from their summer haunts in the Crimea and Caucasus for their winter quarters in the East. Had it not been so, they would hardly have been as deliciously plump as we found them.

But whilst watching the bustards we had let the day slip through our hands, and to our intense disgust we found we could not reach Salian that night ; so we had to content ourselves with the last post-station on the road thither, where we slept. In the early morning I went down to the river, glad to see the Kur again, if it was only for the sake of its abundance of clear water, offering a bath without stint to the dirty wayfarer, and the promise of caviare almost without cost to the hungry epicure.

Thank heaven, a Russian yemstchik's toilet does not take long to make. A shake, a yawn, a cigarette, and, if times are good, a glass of neat vodka, and he is ready to face anything, from his sweetheart to a north-easter. Would that his horses' gear was as speedily arranged as his own; unluckily it is not. Still, in spite of the scores of breakages in the harness of rotten rope and still more rotten thong, our impatient desire to be off was gratified at last, and with glowing visions of at least a clean hut and heaps of good fish and 'ikra' at Salian, we bumped all breakfastless along our last stage to the land of promise. All along our route wild-fowl swarmed, and through the low covert we saw numbers of foxes threading their way. All the way from Adji Kabool, a station at the foot of the hills in which Shemakha lies, and of which I can find no trace in my map, any more than I can of the large lake near it, to Salian and thence to Lenkoran, the country is full of ponds, estuaries, and lakelets, which teem with wild-fowl. I stopped the cart once to kill some pochards for dinner, and a couple of beautiful white egrets for preserving.

And now the river came in sight, a broad,

imposing stream, with the post-house on this side,
that is to say, on the eastern bank. To our disgust, hungry as we were, we were detained at the
post-house for an hour, by the rascally Asiatic who
presided there, under the pretence that our papers
must be first examined by the authorities on the
other side before we were allowed to cross. So
well did the fellow impose on us, that though both
my man and myself were as puzzled as we were
angry, we submitted, until a Russian coming upon
the scene, informed us that the fellow was only
trying to extort black-mail from us for his supposed
services in getting our papers in order ; and our
new acquaintance, having a fellow-feeling for his
countryman my servant, took the Asiatic by his
beard, spat in his face, and with many abusive
epithets ordered him to see to our immediate
transport to the other side, unless he wished to be
placed in charge of the police. Our courtesy and
civil speeches the brute had answered with all
possible rudeness, attributing our politeness, as all
these people do, to a sense of our own weakness ;
but to the greater brutality of the Russian the
weaker nature of the Asiatic yielded at once, and in
a few minutes we were waving adieux to our timely
helper from the other side the Kúr.

Our first business was to inquire where the
hotel was, and our next where caviare might be
bought, resolving mentally to purchase sufficient

to feed us all the way to Lenkoran. Of course I
might have expected the answers to my questions,
after all I had seen of Russian promises and their
fulfilment. Of course there was no hotel. There
were but six Russian families of any kind in Salian,
all the rest were Tartars. Whatever you wanted
you might buy from Tartars in the open bazaar,
who would not serve you if they could help it ; if
you wanted to eat, you might eat standing there
or in the doorway of the merchant who sold vodka.
There was no caviare at Salian to be had for love or
money. It was not the right season for fresh ' ikra,'
and ' pressed ikra ' (*i.e.* caviare) could not be bought
nearer than Bosghi Promysl, the great fishery,
fifteen miles off, where it cost rather more than it
does in the Crimea. Even had I been at Salian
at the right season, I could only have purchased
this luxury, for which it is famous, by stealth, as
the whole produce of the fishery is bought up by
merchants at a distance, to whom it is sent direct,
it being specially provided by contract that they
should have an entire monopoly. Thus, though
Salian and Bosghi Promysl are the places whence
the greater part of the caviare sold in Russia
comes, they are the two most difficult places at
which to buy it.

Standing moodily in the wine-merchant's doorway, munching a lump of dry bread, the meagre
realisation of all our dreams of luxury and rest,

our wayworn looks arrested the attention of a
good-natured Russian custom-house officer, one of
the few Europeans in Salian. This good Samaritan, when he heard the story of our blighted hopes,
took us home to his own house to dinner, and
whilst waiting for it a curious thing happened. A
messenger arrived from another Russian official,
of whom I had never heard, also asking me to
dine. Of course, I sent back the most polite
answer possible, pleading my previous engagement,
and promising to come and thank him for his
civility before I left Salian. To my astonishment,
the messenger came back in a few minutes to say
that I was not to heed Mr. So-and-so—he was
only a poor devil of a custom-house officer—but
was to come and dine at once with the great man,
his master. My host seemed by no means surprised at the message, or even annoyed, though it
was delivered, to my intense chagrin, in his presence. There was but one thing to say in answer
to this second message of my would-be host; and
having said it, I sat down to dine with my first
friend, meditating much on the manners and cus-
toms of the East. But my astonishment increased
when, after dinner, my host entreated me to go
with him to his rival's, that that rival might hear
from my own lips that it was no fault of my host
that I had dined at his house in preference to that
of the greater man. Of course I yielded, and both

he and I met with a very favourable reception at the hands of the great man, who produced in my honour, on hearing that I was an Englishman, two bottles labelled beer. These bottles of beer had been the good man's pride for many a day, and I verily believe it gave him more pleasure to be able to see a real Englishman drinking his beer than it did that Englishman to humour his whim.

In every house in Salian the Asiatic fever seemed to rage ; half the inmates of either house in which I was entertained were down with it, and this, too, at the time of year when it is least virulent.

There being no inducement to remain in the place, we walked through it, and having found it destitute of all objects of interest, ordered a fresh team of horses to proceed on our journey to the Caspian. For once the story that there were no horses was found to be a true one, and, unable to find lodging in the town, as we were unwilling to burden either of our hosts with our presence, especially since the fever had deranged both their households, we made energetic endeavours to obtain some conveyance to the next station, which was reported weather-proof, and a capital station for wild-fowling. Whilst thus engaged we came across a Tartar selling foxskins, and were much struck by the enormous quantity, all recently killed, which he had for sale. They were skins of the common fox, shot in the neighbourhood, and were being sold at from 30 to 50 copecks apiece.

Never had we such difficulty in procuring horses as we had now. None of the Tartars or other peasants would take us, late as it was, across this first strip of the Mooghan desert to the next post-station. It seemed that all the steppe was covered by nomad Tartars, who descend every year from the hills and winter in the Mooghan. These men bear (probably with justice) an extremely bad reputation, and, although we at last persuaded a young Tartar of Salian to convey us in his 'arba,' it was only after we had spent all our persuasive powers upon him, showing him how well armed we were, and promising that we would keep ourselves out of sight, in order not to excite the cupidity of any of the wandering gentry we might meet; in addition to which he stipulated that a place should be provided for himself and 'arba' within the protection of the walls of the post-station until next morning.

Under these conditions we stowed ourselves away in the bottom of his cart, which resembled nothing so much as a huge oblong wicker-basket on solid wooden wheels, some eight feet high. This edifice was drawn by one horse, through rather than over eighteen versts of villanous road, the consequence being that we proceeded at a foot's pace for the whole distance. Far and near in

every direction were the fires of the Tartar en-
campments. Several times, much to our driver's
disgust, we had to pass within a few hundred
yards of their wretched tents, which consist of four
sticks stuck in the ground, and a piece of black felt
stretched over the top. Under this they rest, the
four sides open to every gust of wind, while a large
fire close by warms them where they lie, and with
its flickering flames lends additional wildness to the
scene, as well as to the grim figures passing and
repassing before it, and strangely magnifying the
group of animals tethered hard by. These nomads
must be more than mere gipsies, from the number
of horses and cattle which I saw in their encamp-
ments. They are a great bore to the sportsman,
for, though the Mooghan is alive with antelopes
in the summer, these sensible little beasts leave it
as soon as the Tartar hordes make their appearance.

As we left Salian the evening was closing in
fast, and the whole sky was a vivid stormy crimson, which, being caught by the endless level plain,
had a very grand effect. A vast flight of pelicans
in marching order, line upon line, came slowly
winging their way from the fishery at Bosghi
Promysl to their night's rest in some reed-bed on
the Kúr. The solemn even flight of these great
birds, their countless numbers, great size, and
quaint grave aspect were in wondrous keeping

with the scene, and formed with it a *tout-ensemble* not easily forgotten. Once or twice *en route* a wild-looking fellow on horseback rode up and inspected us, but, though our driver's nerves were much upset by these visits of inspection, no evil came of them, our visitors probably thinking one such wretched horse as ours was hardly worth the stealing.

From Salian to Lenkoran would have been an excessively uninteresting drive had it not been for the teeming bird-life on all sides. The nearer we got to the Caspian, the more the fowl increased. At one place we shot splendid Numidian cranes, whose stately forms might frequently be seen. At another flamingoes, white and rosy, tempted us from our tarantasse. In the mist of early morning an eagle, alit by the roadside, almost frightened us by his apparently gigantic proportions ; and even when he flew away, unharmed and but little alarmed by our bullets—when, too, we had made all allowance for the exaggerating properties of the mist—we could scarcely believe that he belonged to any known species, so gigantic did he appear.

In those parts of the journey where the post-road ran through sand-hills near the sea, the noise of the fowl was simply deafening. In the Crimea the varieties of wild ducks are extremely numerous, but here it seemed almost as if there were as

many different species as there are ducks anywhere else. The most striking, after the flamingoes, swans, and pelicans, were perhaps the bright
red duck, called here 'gagar,' and the beautiful
mandarin duck, which I only saw once at close
quarters. But amongst the countless flights there
were scores of different plumages, to whose wearers
I could give no name; and I feel sure that any
ornithologist who is at the present moment looking
for some new ground over which to follow up his
favourite study, would find ample reward for the
journey in a visit to the swamps round Lenkoran
in the winter months.

Travelling by night over the steppe, we passed
a Tartar village at some little distance, from which
came an unwonted glow of red light, and cries as
of pandemonium let loose. On asking Ivan what
it meant, I was told that it was the Tartar
Bairam, or rather the preparation for it. Anxious
to see what was doing, I, contrary to my driver's
advice, slipped out of the tarantasse and stole
unobserved upon the scene—a scene wilder than
the witches' meeting in Macbeth. Among the
huts and hayricks on the wet steppe, a mob of
half naked Tartars had erected a post, and on this
post had fixed a monster firebrand. From this
the light glowed and flickered on the brown limbs
and wild faces of an excited band of dancers, who,
in perfect time, kept advancing and retreating

around it, singing in time to their steps the while. Now and again another band, which formed a chorus to the principal performers, broke in with a chant, of which I could only catch two constantly-repeated words, seeming to my ears to be best represented thus, 'Shaksay, Maksay.' The dance, though extremely rude and simple, was effective from the surroundings and the great accuracy with which each performer executed his part; and this was the more remarkable since every male from four to eighty in the village seemed to be taking part. The women only were idle spectators.

After watching them for some time the dance came to an end, and the people began to scatter, a signal for me to get back to my cart before any one caught me intruding. Ivan, my man, told me that in another fortnight they would begin still wilder rites, hacking and mutilating themselves with knives, after the manner of the priests of Baal.

The Russian peasants tell you that the Tartars do this in memory of a certain Lutra, queen and Amazon, erst of Erivan, whom Russian soldiers slew. She, dying, bade the Tartars thus maltreat themselves once a year in memory of her, the which if they did, she on her part would in thirty years' time rise again, to lead and rule over them in great glory. Many a thirty years has passed since then, and Lutra the queen has not kept her word: through which some of the Tartars have of their own accord ceased to observe these rites; others have yielded to the power of Russian law, which forbids these savage orgies under penalty of very heavy punishment; while still a few practise their rites in the darkness of midnight and in the desolate wild places of the steppeland.

For at least thirty versts of our journey the road was impassable, owing to the overflow of the river; and this necessitated a long circuit extremely unwelcome to us. In the villages that we passed through towards the end of our drive, the people were for the most part Molochans, clean, hard-working peasants compared to those around them, but very objectionable from at least one point of view, as nothing would induce them to cook our game for us for fear of defiling themselves—fifty per cent. of the birds we shot being unclean in their eyes. These Molochans, near Lenkoran, are probably some of the descendants of the 1,500 or 2,000 that the Emperor Nicholas drove out of Russia into the Caucasus.

The country near Lenkoran is in places good meadow land, covered even now with rich young grass; here and there it has been broken up for cultivation, and in such places the soil appears extremely rich.

At last a long line of sordid huts announced

themselves as the suburbs of Lenkoran, and the homes of another sect, which the Emperor Nicholas, with greater reason perhaps, expelled from Russia. These are the Skoptsi (eunuchs), or White Doves as they prefer to call themselves. Besides mutilating themselves, these people drink no strong drink, and eat very little of anything beyond bread and oil. The people of Lenkoran say they live a quiet, harmless life. Those I saw of this sect were big bloated men, with faces as devoid of expression as the lives they lead.

Though Lenkoran was of course not the paradise it had been represented to be at Tiflis, it was, however, less disappointing than many of the places I had seen. There were really a few Europeans in the town; there was a fair bazaar where food could be bought; there was a room attached to the establishment which grandiloquently styles itself the Lenkoran Club, in which we could sleep on a wooden floor in comfort; there was a post-office, and (although it took a long time to find him, and when found, he had nothing but a single pair of shears for apparatus) there was a barber. For the rest Lenkoran is at this time of year a sea of mud; in the summer it must be a cloud of dust. The streets are in places paved, though badly; there are no shops outside the bazaar, which is held in an open space without the town, and where most of the traders are Persian or Tartar; the houses are ill-built; and from the dismal, sickly-coloured sea, which lies motionless by the walls of the town, comes an offensive odour which must be unbearable in summer. The officials of the place are almost all Armenian.

Soon after my arrival, I went down to the bazaar to look for a gunsmith, and finding an old Persian cross-legged in a booth hung with ancient arms and dangerous-looking guns, submitted my fowling-piece to him for repairs. The injury he had to set right was a bad dent in one of the barrels, got by a fall from the tarantasse on our road here. The last I saw of him he had the end of something like a poker down the muzzle and was belabouring my luckless gun with a sledge-hammer. I think this must have nearly roused me; but it evidently did not quite, for my next recollection is of waking suddenly in the booth beside the old armourer, who had long ago finished my gun's repairs, and was now gravely amused at Ivan's face of surprise at the odd position in which, after half a day's search, he at last found me. Be it said to the honour of that Persian, when I left the bazaar my gun was fairly mended, and there was nothing missing from my pocket.

During that first day at Lenkoran I had much to do, especially as my man was told by the employés of the local forester that we should not be allowed to shoot without a licence. An interview

with the forester himself soon set this right, and
in his house I saw the skin of a recently killed
leopard, which gave me greater hope of success than
I had dared hitherto to indulge in. On the day
after my arrival I was lucky enough to make the
acquaintance of a German gentleman named Müller,
who from the moment he discovered my nationality
took me under his especial care. We met first at
the house of one of the sportsmen of Lenkoran,
who, having heard of my arrival, had arranged a
banquet in my honour. Here, after dinner, whilst
discussing the chance of seeing a tiger—a chance
which grew more and more remote the more I
pursued it—one of the guests proposed that I should
make a house of his in the neighbouring forest my
head centre during my stay. This hut he called
the 'Shabby Shanty,' and the chance of resting under
the roof of a house with an Irish name and an
English-speaking master, with capital sport all
round, was too good to be refused ; so as usual I
decided on the spur of the moment to entrust myself to my new friend's care.

It is only fair to say that wherever I went in
Russia, I invariably met with ready hospitality, so
much so that my whole journey was little more
than a series of expeditions begun, if not finished,
under the auspices and at the suggestion of some
new-found friend.

CHAPTER XIV.

SHORES OF THE CASPIAN.—RETURN TO TIFLIS.

Lenkoran—Abundance of game—Eryvool forest—Native fowlers—A
hunting lodge—Swarming coverts—Wild boar—A paradise for
sportsmen—Pigs at bay—'Old Shirka' and his quarry—A dying
eagle—Caspian woodpeckers—Festive nights—Watching for a
tiger—Forest life by night—The eagle-owl and his prey—End of
a long vigil—The rainy season—The streets of Lenkoran—The
return journey to Tiflis — Adventure at Adji Kabool—Experiences of post-travel—Bullying a station-master—Armenian Pro-
testants—Russian telegraph service—In miserable plight—A spill
over a precipice — Refitting our tarantasse — *Argumentum ad
hominem* — An awkward predicament — Chasing a yemstchik—
Renewed life at Tiflis—Great snow-fall—Running down antelope
—The 'black death.'

LENKORAN is almost surrounded by marshes, in
which snipe and woodcock, with all manner of
long-legged, long-necked strangers to a British
eye, together with hundreds of the falcon tribe,
disport themselves daily. Here my man and myself spent a day or two shooting specimens of the
birds least known to us; but on the third day we
took horse and rode to a larger lake, on which we
embarked with our friend the German, intending to
cross over to the woods which fringed the further
side, somewhere in the depths of which the 'Shabby
Shanty' lay. On this lake were simply myriads of

water-hens. The whole surface seemed dark with them, the reeds alive with their ceaseless cries. The sale of these birds is quite a feature in the street life of Lenkoran. The bazaar is full of their carcasses ; at every street corner you meet men hawking them for sale ; every other peasant you see is carrying two or three home for the pot.

On the lake are many flat-bottomed boats in which the fowlers pole themselves through the mazy waterways in the reed-beds, until at a sudden turn a closely packed bevy of water-hens offers them a remunerative shot. So cheap are the birds in the bazaar, that to kill them singly with the gun would entail absolute loss on the gunner. But besides these wild-fowlers, who are after all but occasionally employed in their pursuit, there are the regular enemies of the poor little fowl, men who have decoys, and nets drawn across certain straits, down which they drive the birds, until in diving to escape they are caught by scores in the submerged net. There are naturally quantities of other fowl on these lakes, but the water-hen seems to thrive and abound most, and is so much more easily taken than the others that it is the staple food of a large number of the inhabitants of Lenkoran.

On our voyage we overhauled one of the regular fowlers, a Tartar, with whom we had a rather hot dispute. As he drew up his net full of struggling or already drowned birds, we were horrified to see

that instead of killing outright those which were
not yet dead, he took the trouble to break their
legs and wings, and so cast them a living, helpless
mass of pain and fear into the bottom of his boat,
there to live for hours in horrible anguish. We
explained to the fellow how much simpler for him,
and how much kinder to the birds it would be,
to wring their necks outright; but we might have
spared ourselves the trouble. The Tartar intellect
could not comprehend the beauty of mercy, and all
we could get was a grin and the assurance that if
he did not break their legs or wings they would
escape him; and as he might be out a day or two, if
he killed them at once they would not be fresh
when taken to market. It was no good arguing
any more; so merely insisting on putting all he had
so far taken out of their misery with our own
hands, we left him, feeling that were we to give
way to our own impulses he would have spent the
next few hours with four broken limbs in the
bottom of his own boat. The water-hens are sold
at about fivepence, wild duck at about sixpence a
brace.

On the far side of the lake a troop of villagers
were waiting to carry our baggage through the
swampy forest, where neither horse nor cart
could now conveniently travel, to our host's log
hut.

The chief objects of cultivation here were rice

and mulberry-trees ; and though the wild boars played the deuce with the rice-fields, the mulberry-trees and their devourers the silkworms throve amazingly. Mr. Müller, our host, had not knocked about in all the odd corners of the earth for nothing, so that when we reached his Shanty, though at a couple of dozen paces or so you might meet with impenetrable jungle, we found it the most comfortable well-built house we had seen since we left Tiflis. In the night wild boars had dug up the small patch of garden by the door ; on a little lawn not far off, a badger had turned up all the turf in his nocturnal gambols; while right and left as we approached snipe and cock went off like crackers from under our feet.

During the first three days of our stay at Eryvool, we did nothing but shoot cock and pheasant, or, with a pack of fine dogs, the pride of Mr. Müller's heart, hunt the wild swine that abounded in the thick places of the forest : while east and west, and south and north, our messengers went forth offering large rewards for tidings of any tiger or leopard within three days' march.

To those who have not seen the wild-fowl shooting of the Caspian, any account of the swarms of cock and snipe (chiefly jack) at Eryvool in the beginning of the year 1879 would seem overdrawn. We were sick of shooting before the three days were over, though it took more than one day of ceaseless firing to get used to the snap-shooting, which is alone practicable in these dense coverts. Wherever the forest was at all dry—and this was for the most part in fairly open places—the rush and glitter of a pheasant's noisy wings broke the monotony of cock-shooting. Once, as I snapped at one of the ghost-like little birds flipping over the top of the thick bush with silent wing, that had kept me engaged all the morning, the bushes at my feet were parted with a crash. With an indignant snort, and tail curling crisply over his retreating quarters, the black form of an old boar afforded an excellent mark for my second barrel. Luckily for me he did not charge, or a rent in my waistcoat might have rewarded me for foolishly assaulting so formidable a foe with No. 6.

Everywhere the forest was carpeted with flowers, though the crocuses, of which my English correspondent Mr. Maw was so anxious to obtain specimens, had not unluckily shown their heads as yet. The commonest flower of all was the crimson cyclamen, and next to it its white congener.

Day by day the story was the same. Cock-shooting in the morning, a run with the dogs in the evening, a merry night with Mr. Müller in the Shanty, but still no tidings of a feline foe. Let the history of one day stand for that of many. An hour's plodding through mud and slush on a bright spring day, with every now and then a snap-shot at a brown flash of light that glides through the trees before us, has at last brought us to that thick covert in which we expect to find the great wild boar. All the dreamy spirit of the young year is abroad; and as we lazily drag our legs over the clinging morass, every briar that winds itself round us almost tempts us to give in and roll over on the soft black mud, rather than resist any longer the sleepy influence of the season and the perpetual assaults of bog and briar. The weight of our rifles has doubled; never before were our coats so thick, never before did an old mossy trunk look so irresistibly tempting; and take it all in all, we begin to think a cigarette and castle-building, with the buzz of the woodland life in our ears and the languor of spring in our blood, would be infinitely better than this ceaseless toil for a boar who as little cares probably to be roused from his deep dreams as we care to rouse him.

Luckily at this moment, when we were all but yielding to the temptations of the sunshine, the deep voice of old Shirka sounded a *réveillée*: in a second dreaminess had gone, the briars ceased to hold, and if the young wood did swing back and nearly switch our eyes out or break the bridge of that too prominent nose, we heeded it not. For before us, with gruntings and with snortings loud enough to wake the whole drowsy woodland, a great black sow is crashing through the covert, the sable imps, who call her mother, pressing close behind, while the deep voices of Shirka and his mates urge them on to still more desperate endeavour. Each gunner, who up till now has been but half animate, plunges recklessly through the rending thorns to gain some point at which to turn the chase or make that shot which shall render him the after-dinner hero of the day. And now from the deep baying and the cessation of the crashing amongst the scrub, we judge that Shirka and his friends have collared the quarry in the thick thorn yonder ; so thick that the light can barely penetrate, and so viciously tenacious and spiteful as to give the invading sportsman an idea of personal malice. From a point of vantage we at last get a glimpse of the fray. There are seven small pigs, and on the flanks of each a dog is hanging, while the great yellow dog Shirka and another are struggling silently with the old sow in the middle of a small pond of black mud and water. But she is too strong for them : we dare not, however, help with our rifles, and cannot get to close quarters in time with our knives ; so one by one the little squeakers wriggle themselves away, and the old mother and her litter, after another rapid burst, get clean off, and leave us all lamenting. Had the pigs been of larger growth the dogs would in all probability have concentrated their attentions more upon one object, and so our chase might have had a happier issue.

As it was we pursued our way in crestfallen

silence, until Shirka makes a point at a small thorn-bush by our side. ‘Nonsense, old dog, come away; we can see through it.’ Hardly were the words out of our mouth than with more activity than you would give a pig credit for, a huge old boar springs from the very heart of the thicket, and the brave yellow Shirka plunges recklessly at him. The veteran hound is one great record of a thousand fights, his tawny hide seamed and knotted with the marks of many a tusk, but he is as reckless now as he was when a puppy; and dearly as his master loves his old hound’s pluck, he would give a great deal to see a little of that discretion mixed with it which might save his favourite from an untimely end. As the hound closes the boar turns, and in the turning offers a fair mark for the rifle on the other side of the thicket; so once more old Shirka is saved from those gnashing ivory bayonets which he has so often rashly challenged.

After this there is a lull. The hounds’ loud voices have proclaimed to every living thing that death is abroad in the forest, and boar and roe have moved off to some deeper recess, where in shadowy silence they can spend the spring noontide unmolested. One bird the rifle’s reverberating voice has not scared, and as the great eagle comes wheeling over the forest path, he throws quite a shadow on his enemies below. But the voice that stilled the wild boar can still yours, too, poor forest king, and though you come down but slowly, you must rest awhile on that old gnarled oak before your pinions are strong enough to bear you away again, to die in peace. Yet though the blood drops slowly from your beak, you cling fiercely to the tough old oak with iron claws worthy of their perch, and look in silent, wondering rage at the foe scarce thirty feet beneath. Then with one supreme effort you launch yourself on your last voyage : again the leaden hail strikes upward under the now failing pinions, and the great lord of air furls his sails and with a dull thud comes down, eyes still unclosed, talons still drawn back to strike, and the curved beak eager for other blood than the red stream that dyes it now. Peace be with you, brave bird ; like many another, when the shot had been fired, I would have given the last rouble in my pocket not to have fired it. Still as a hunter you lived, and, by a just retribution, by a hunter's hand you died.

After this the handsome form of the great black woodpecker attracted our covetous eyes, and for nearly a couple of hours his delusive whistle lured Ivan and myself from tree to tree, always near us yet never in sight. All things come to those who wait, and at last his crimson crest was added to the scalps of those already slain. During this day, too, we were lucky enough to shoot that rare bird the *picus St. John*, a woodpecker much resembling our common spotted woodpecker. *A propos* of woodpeckers, my friend Mr. Müller, who was a keen observer of natural history, assured me that he had frequently observed near his house during the last two years an extremely small woodpecker, in shape like all its congeners, in size if anything slightly less than a sparrow, and in colour brilliant emerald green. Being a zealous preserver of rare birds, he had never attempted to molest the pair, which he assured me built every year near his hut ; and I fear that it was my keenness to see the bird and his suspicions of my evil intentions with regard to them, which prevented his ever pointing out to me these specimens of a woodpecker as yet unknown I believe to British ornithologists.

Towards evening, tired with the chase, we would light our cigarettes and make our way home by some well-known track, shooting as we went sufficient cock and pheasants to secure us against the possibility of scarcity during the next few days. Not uncommonly, as we drew near the house, the dogs that for the last quarter of an hour had been wearily following at our heels, with drooping tails, stopping from time to time to lick a lacerated paw, would suddenly erect their hackles, and fresh as ever charge furiously into the home enclosure, where, after the manner of more fashionable beings, the wild swine family had been paying us a visit, having first carefully ascertained that we were sure not to be at home.

The nights sped by blithely enough. The New Year's festivities, if not of any very formidable pretensions at Eryvool, were at least lovingly protracted, and every night our great-limbed German friend might be seen mixing his loved lint wine for our delectation and his own.

But one night the lint wine was not brewed, not more than ten 'papiroses' were smoked, the talk was no longer of Australian gold-diggings or American prairies—for had not the natives brought tidings of the game we had come so far to seek? At some distance from our dwelling two nights before a reiving tiger had struck down a Persian's cow at a little settlement on the edge of the forest; there was the cow lying still, plain for all eyes to see, and the tiger's track clearly marked on the sand-bank of the little rivulet hard by. The next night saw an eager trio of sportsmen on the spot. Round the copse where the tiger had been, and to which we hoped he might return, Mr. Müller, Ivan and myself posted ourselves, each perched in a tree, and pledged solemnly to one another to wait there in silence through the livelong night. Their perches I did not see, but my own I have cause to remember. A tall tree-stump, perhaps twenty feet high, had been roughly hewn or broken at the top, the ragged edges of which were terribly apt to break, and pierce the too confiding being who placed his weight upon them. Round this rough throne some small branches made a fairly dense screen; and as some compensation for the deficiencies of my seat, I discovered two deep cavities, into which my long jack-boots fitted admirably. Perched here, I heard the last soft scrunch of my companions' retreating tread; and then taking a preliminary look at my watch, I fairly settled down to my night's vigil.

For a time, of course, we could expect nothing. Our passage through the woods was sufficient to have precluded all hope of seeing any game for an hour to come. How still it all seemed. Even the sea is a noisy babbler compared to the depths of a forest at night. What a glorious moon that was that gleamed down through the network of creepers and wild vine above, throwing long shadows on the grassy opening below. But how slowly the moments pass! Is it possible I have only been here a quarter of an hour? I move restlessly, though silently, on my perch, and then the intense cold which is numbing my right leg calls for attention. On withdrawing the suffering limb from its hiding-place the mystery is solved—that comfortable hole, which fitted the foot so excellently, is a natural well, in which the offerings of many forest showers have been carefully stored. No wonder that, as the water soaked through during that frosty night, the unlucky leg grew numb. The change of

posture necessitated by this discovery is decidedly
a change for the worse, and stronger and stronger
grows the conviction in my mind that a fair set-to
with Mr. Stripes for a quarter of an hour by broad
daylight would be far better than this silent night-
watch on a painfully acute tree-stump.

Gradually the inmates of the woods seem to
regain confidence. That sharp querulous bark
came from a jackal, who is ' loafing around ' as the
Yankees say, just within the shadow of the
thicket opposite us. Then there is a whish, whish
of whirling wings, and we hear phantom flights of
duck come sweeping over the tree-tops close to us,
but invisible to our eyes in spite of the bright
moonlight. The silence is one moment intense;
then, before you have time to blink, the rush
of wings is upon you and past you, and the birds
are rattling and plopping down into the dark little
forest pools, in the soft mossy places, or, best of all,
amongst the young wheat of the luckless Persian.
What a merry chuckling they make as every fresh
flight comes in from its day-dreams and play on
the sea. Each batch of new comers takes at least
ten minutes to publish its budget of news and
arrange for its places at supper.

Again a sudden silence falls on them. Too-
whoo-op! too-whoo-op! Ah! you may well crouch
trembling under covert now. But as soon as the
shadow of the great night-fiend has passed on, the

ducks are as merry and noisy as ever. It is well for them that they have no human minds, or the horror of his presence would have stilled their innocent merriment for the night. A more terrible foe than the eagle-owl to all that are too weak to resist him it is hard to conceive. The huge spread of utterly silent wings, the lugubrious cry, the enormous talons, sharper and more tenacious than those of an eagle, and those great fierce eyes, luminous with yellow fire, all contribute to make a *tout-ensemble* of which a Hindoo devil might be proud. Ghostlike, he glides by close to the earth, a silent cloud in the moonlight, on wings that never seem to stir. Woe to the crouching hare whose ears, quick though they are, have told her nothing of the approach of her mortal foe.

If the Tartars and moujiks of the steppes where the eagle-owl is found are to be believed, once the great bird seizes its prey, it has not itself the power of relaxing its grip immediately. Knowing this, and dreading lest the old grey hare, gaining fresh strength from terror, should in her mad career under thorn-bush and briar tear her unwilling rider to fragments, the owl clutches the ground or some other object with one talon, while with the other she strikes the prey. And now it becomes a tug of war for life and death. If the owl's muscles are strong enough to hold the prey, well for the owl; but if not, the moujiks tell strange stories of having found half one of these grim birds, one talon still clutching the ground, and the other, with the remainder of the bird's body, still firmly fixed to the back of its escaped victim.

By-and-by, without even a rustle to announce his approach, a large uncouth beast, like a small bear with extremely bandy legs, is performing strange gambols on the moonlit turf beneath our hiding-place. After watching him long enough to recognise in him a large badger, he catches a glimpse probably of my rifle-barrels, and noiselessly as he came, so noiselessly he melts as it were out of the moonlight into the mysterious shadows beyond. And so, with here and there a glimpse of the private life of its denizens, the long night in the forest passes away, growing colder and colder till near the dawn.

At last there is a sound that startles the whole neighbourhood, and the rustling of retreating feet tells plainly that, though we saw them not, every shadow had its tenant. A crashing of boughs, and a firm, soft tread comes direct to my hiding-place; and with straining eyes I watch, until the outline of the great beast shall slowly emerge from the shadow.

'Hulloh! are you asleep up there? Come down, and have a pull at my flask. No more chance of a tiger to-night.'

And so the vigil ends. The great beast was our friend M. The night had worn to morning, and, slowly unbending my stiffened limbs, I let myself down to *terra firma*, glad that the watch was over, even though it ended in nothing better than a nip of *eau-de-vie*.

Once more after this I watched the stars brighten and fade in the cold grey of morning, waiting alone for a tiger which never came; then, fearful lest the wet season should set in, and prevent our return to Tiflis, I bade adieu to my friends, and on January 11 we started on the return journey to Tiflis.

As soon as our cart came round the sky grew gradually blacker, and with the first jingle of the horses' bells the patter of the first instalment of the rainy season was mingled. From the time we turned our faces to Tiflis until the moment when Ivan left me in the baths of that city, waiting till he should bring clean clothes in which to attire me for my reappearance in a partially civilised world, the weather went steadily from bad to worse, and discomfort grew to actual misery.

I will not weary my readers with more than a few glimpses of the return journey, of which the first shall be the suburbs of Lenkoran. As we approached them the road became so bad that our horses could barely proceed at a walk; and, looking ahead, we found the street a morass, bridged with planks, through which we could by no means pass. At the sides of the road, where the trottoirs had been, women, with their scanty clothing tucked up round their waists, were taking a mud bath and walking exercise simultaneously, with this trifling drawback, that, should they miss the trottoir, they would probably disappear in the dark profound beyond. This was, of course, an exceptionally bad state of things, and we were told only happened during the first day or two of the rainy season, after which the streets got better, the filth accumulated during the summer having been washed away by the rains.

Wishing the 'white doves' a merry time of it, we with great difficulty got our vehicle out of the road on to the steppe; and here, though progress was slow, it was at least better than it had been. Two days spent in alternately being dragged over morasses by our horses, and dragging them and the cart out of the same, did not sweeten our tempers, I presume; and it was perhaps for this that a luckless Persian suffered at Adji Kabool. Here in the early morning I was sitting huddled up in my bourka amongst my luggage in the extremely narrow space allotted to one of two passengers in a Russian post-cart, when a 'tchapar' calmly pushed me to one side, and seated himself comfortably beside me, without ceremony or apology. On inquiring what he meant, and explaining that the post-cart was hired by me, paid for by me, and intended only to be tenanted by me and mine the intruder just deigned to tell me that he was a ' tchapar,' had a right to travel in any cart he chose, and meant to travel in mine, whether I liked it or not. Now, if this were true, it would not be an additional attraction in Russian post-travelling; but I fancy it was not: so I requested my would-be fellow-traveller to make himself scarce at once, and as he persisted in refusing, I hoisted him into the mud by the wheels. As soon as he recovered an upright position he clapped his old flint-lock rifle to his shoulder, and putting the muzzle almost into my face, deliberately pulled the trigger. Luckily for me, in his fall all the powder which should have formed the train to the charge had been spilt. Moreover, his barrel was choked with good holding clay, so that, taken all together, had the piece not missed fire, the danger would have been greater to him than to me. After this display of rage and impotence, he turned to the people of the station, and so worked upon them by his arguments that, had I not taken the reins out of my yemstchik's hands and driven off, whether they would or not, I am persuaded I should have been detained perhaps for days at Adji Kabool, until I could communicate with Tiflis or Lenkoran.

To travel by post-road in this part of the Caucasus, and indeed all over Russia I believe, a man should be as voluble, as loud-tongued, and as profane as the proverbial Billingsgate fisherwoman or a certain English M. F. H. I wot of. The only kind of language a Russian servant, most of all a Russian car-boy, can understand, is loud swearing. From his childhood he has been accustomed to it. His mother's term of endearment to him as she dandled him on her knees was probably 'ach te sukin sin' (ah, you son of a she-dog), about equivalent in English to 'you little monkey.' His master's name for him when good-tempered was 'rosbolnik' or 'mashanik' (thief or scoundrel), and he himself, in addressing his horses, of which he is often extremely fond, and to which he seldom applies the lash, heaps on them epithets of the fondest endearment and foulest abuse at one and the same time.

Our experiences of post-travel on our return to Tiflis were of the very worst. At Aksu in midday we were refused horses on the old plea that there were none—an excuse utterly untrue, as a glance at the interior of the stables assured us. Reiterated demands were met by sulky refusals, and on following the station-master to his own private room I was reminded that the guests' chamber was my place, whither he would come if sent for. On sending my man he found the door barred, and all further interview denied. This little trick was more than I could stand, so crossing the yard to the fellow's room I demanded the horses or the complaint-book—a book in which travellers have a right at all times to enter their grievances, which is kept affixed by a seal to the table in the guest-room, and which is the sole check upon the absolute power of a station-master. To remove this or to refuse to produce it, is the greatest crime the station-master can commit, and would, if reported, ensure his eviction from his post. But in this case the man remained firm, being deep in a drinking bout with his yemstchiks, and refused point blank to produce either horses or book, or to let me in. Feeling convinced that I had Russian law on my side, and that the fellow, for his own sake, dare not make any report, I kicked his door down, and taking him by the arm brought him across to the guests' room, where a couple of Armenian merchants in the same plight as myself were kicking their heels and cursing the cause of their needless delay. Having got my enemy into the room, I had the doors shut, showed him some letters of introduction I had with me, and then telling him I knew to what he was liable if I reported his refusal to produce the complaint-book, I began to solemnly roll up the cuffs of my Tscherkess costume, preparatory, as I informed him, to administering to him severe corporal punishment. The letters, my knowledge of Russian post-road rules, and perhaps a certain air of meaning what I said, had their effect, and in a minute the other side of the Asiatic character was revealed, the insolent brutality giving way to disgusting, fawning complaisance as if by magic. But I knew my man too well to let him go, so that, having made him order two troikas, one for ourselves and one for the Armenians, I kept him a close prisoner until the carts were actually at the door, when, with many thanks from my fellow-travellers, I left Aksu rejoicing.

These fellow-travellers claimed my help again at the next station, alleging that they were co-religionists of mine, being members of the Protestant Church at Shemakha. It seems that forty years ago their sect was founded at Shusha, my informants said, by English missionaries, but the names they gave them, 'Larambe' and 'Fanther,' sounded very un-English in my ears. Shortly after the founding of the Protestant Church at Shusha, the non-Protestant Armenians rose against their newly-converted brethren, and induced the Czar to have them expelled from Shusha, whence they migrated to Shemakha, and there founded a church, in which they now celebrate five services a week, and number 500 of the richest inhabitants of Shemakha amongst their congregation.

From Shemakha I sent a telegram on to Capt. Lyall or Mr. G——, I forget which, friends of mine at Tiflis, to announce my return, and to prevent my letters being sent on to Lenkoran. To give some idea of the Russian telegraph service

between Tiflis and the Caspian I may here mention
that, though I took many long days to get from
Shemakha to Tiflis, that telegram only arrived
simultaneously with me, whilst one sent from
Baku, three weeks before, arrived two days after
me ; and though I travelled by the post-road,
and spent some days shooting *en route*, a letter
posted by me in Lenkoran just before I started
arrived long after me.   So much for internal com-
munication on this side the Caucasus.

Day after day we plodded on, getting dirtier,
more starved and ill every day ; travelling often
as much as sixteen hours in an open cart at a
stretch, the best travelling we ever accomplished
being 132 versts in that time.   At Shemakha we
stopped to shoot antelopes, as much for the sake of
the pot as for the sport.   A day's rest and a good
dinner had become absolutely necessary ; and though
the accommodation at Shemakha was so bad as to
make the rest impossible, we obtained the dinner.
Thus refreshed, we turned our faces on Friday
morning towards Tiflis, with a fixed resolve to
make no further stoppage in the thirty-six hours'
travelling which remained between ourselves and
the good things of that place.

For the last ten days my leading idea, my favourite day-dream, the *ultima Thule* of my ambition, had
been a hot tub.   To sit and boil in a hot bath of
sulphur water and get out a clean man into a clean

shirt, had been the one luxury in life to look forward to; and now that it was within thirty-six hours' travel of me, I felt almost content as I curled myself up in my cart, though snow and rain soaked in through my ragged old clothes, through which the wind cut almost to my backbone, and the red mud splashed up, plastering eyes and mouth, until we had passed beyond all semblance of humanity. But there were to be more trials yet. As we neared Akstapha the night had fallen, and, weary with perpetual motion, I had cowered down under my bourka in a vain endeavour to hide myself from the cold and doze away the tedious hours. The weather was abominably raw; an icy night fog, blown by a cutting breeze that met us in the teeth, wetted and chilled us to the bone. The hour was between nine and ten, the moon had not yet risen, and the night was starless. The road was through the hills, and needless to say heavy and hard to find in the darkness.

Suddenly I was roused by my man's voice calling me to get out at once. Peeping, half-asleep, from under my rugs, I could see very little of anything except that my man and the yemstchik had both got down and the cart had stopped. 'What is the matter?' I asked, feeling for my revolver, and expecting the oft-promised highwaymen. 'One of the horses has fallen down,' came the answer. Cross at being disturbed for so little, and not wanting to get my stockinged feet wet in the mud, I was curling myself up again with a sulky injunction to the men to let the horse get up and be hanged to him, when, to my horror, I felt the cart tilting over in a way that threatened soon to reverse our relative positions. In a moment I was wide awake. The cart was already so far over that I was obliged to jump the way it was falling, and my next sensation was that of travelling through space, such as one sometimes experiences in a dream. This came to an end with a jerk, and my next recollection is of being dug out of the mud at the bottom of a considerable precipice from among the *débris* of boxes, broken cart and horses, which had accompanied me in my fall. By the greatest good luck nothing had struck me, though the heavy built cart had fallen so close as to pin down the corner of my bourka, which was still on my shoulders. Luckily, too, only one of the horses was so far damaged as to be unable to proceed. There was no village within reach. To walk on to Akstapha in the then state of the roads and weather would have been a wearisome trudge, even if we could have persuaded the driver to leave his horses and guide us, or ourselves to leave our belongings in his charge, which we could not do.

Here, then, I had a splendid opportunity of witnessing the really wonderful handiness of Russian peasants in extremities. Thanks to our love of tobacco we had with us a box of brimstone matches; grovelling about by the light of which we retrieved all that was not utterly destroyed of our luggage, and by means of old ropes, pocket-handkerchiefs, and what not, so tied and spliced together the broken harness, that after two hours' work in that bitter winter night we managed to extricate our cart and make yet another start for Tiflis.

Beyond Akstapha, snow had evidently been falling for some time past, and still continued to fall until we reached Tiflis. Every verst showed us deeper drifts, and at the last station from Tiflis the drivers, in defiance of their master's orders, refused to get out of their warm corners to drive us through the wintry night to the end of our journey. After many threats and much persuasion one was prevailed on to mount the box, and though we only proceeded at a snail's pace, we consoled ourselves with the thought that every minute brought us nearer our bourne. At last, when we had got some three versts on the way, the horses were brought to a standstill by their driver, who calmly announced his intention of returning.

We were already half-frozen and irritable from constant mishaps, so that his announcement was not very cheerfully received, and every effort was made to urge him on. Everything else failing, in an evil moment Ivan persuaded me to use the common Russian argument, and, if he would not take copecks, give him stick. He took a very fair thumping as stolidly as an ox, and then utterly nonplussed me by quietly handing me the reins, and decamping into the darkness before I had time to think.

Never in my life did I feel in a more awkward predicament. The roads were deep with snow; the night dark as pitch; the way unknown, over a succession of hills down the sides of any of which one false step might at any time hurl us. It would never do to let the rascal go. As quickly as we could Iván and I dragged our team round and, risking everything, galloped hard in the direction of our runaway into the darkness behind, until, as luck would have it, we nearly ran over him. Having found him, all manner of bribes were devised, every fearful threat conjured up that our imaginations could furnish us with, and by the joint pressure of hope of reward and fear of punishment we at last got the sulky brute on to his seat, and at about six in the morning drove into Tiflis.

True to my resolution, I made the cart set me down at the baths; large subterranean places, in which, in an extremely hot atmosphere, you may bathe yourself in little baths of natural hot water, strongly impregnated with sulphur, after which a swarthy little Tartar, nearly naked, comes and, kneeling on your chest, kneads your body with his clenched hands, thumps and smacks you, pulls out your different joints and replaces them, making your fingers crack in a marvellous manner, and finally dries and leaves you, feeling as if you had just had the gloves on with the celebrated Professor Bat Mullins, of Panton Street renown. Meanwhile, my servant had taken away every rag I possessed, and in a state of happy, cleanly nudity I sat awaiting that greatest of boons to a weary wayfarer, a clean shirt and an invitation to breakfast. Both arrived in due time, and feeling once more that I was a few steps removed from a Tartar beggar in appearance as well as in feelings, I betook myself to an Englishman's house, vowing that, if I could help it, my experiences of Russian post-travelling should never go beyond my last stoppage at the sulphur baths.

The snowfall that now enveloped Tiflis was—so the inhabitants told me—the heaviest they could ever remember, and certainly never could Tiflis have looked better than it did under the white pall that hid all its foulness and lent such *éclat* to whatever beauty it possesses. For me, too, the snowfall had its advantages, in affording me an opportunity of witnessing the pursuit of the antelope on horseback as practised by the Tartars of Kariás. About two score well-mounted men, all carrying rifles on their shoulders and a powerful greyhound on their horse in front of the saddle, started at an early hour for the steppe. Having found a herd of antelope, they proceeded to surround and break it up, so that the quarry might separate. Then each man chose his own prey, and for the first part of the day followed it slowly from place to place, never pressing it hard enough to make it gallop any distance, yet never losing sight of it. In this way travelling slowly over the unfrozen snow, which 'balled' fearfully on its pointed feet, the antelope became weary and harassed, the continual slow pace tiring it far more than a smart gallop, during which the snow would not have so much chance of clinging to the flying feet. When the poor little beast is sufficiently exhausted, the hunter begins to close in, and even should the antelope make a dash at the last it is ten to one it gets headed by one of the hunter's comrades. If, however, it lets the Tartar get tolerably near, he drops his hound from its place beside him for the first time, and cheering him on with voice and example, speedily runs down the already exhausted prey.

What puzzled me most was how the Tartars induced their dogs to retain their equestrian position, but I presume early training will teach the dog as much as it does the man.

Whilst staying in Tiflis, I first heard the report of the 'black death' or black small-pox, as the Russians called the plague which was devastating Astrachan; and fearing lest the story should be true that it was spreading with rapid strides towards Russia, or at least, that having come from the coasts of the Caspian I should be put in quarantine, I determined to make my way to the Black Sea, have one more turn at the bears of Golovinsky, and then get back to England before the fever became prevalent. The Tiflis authorities made very little difficulty, only taking my larger impedimenta under their care, for the purpose of disinfecting them before sending them on to England; so that in another day or two I found myself once more at Poti, with my faithful Ivan the Pole still with me.

CHAPTER XV.

THE RAINS.

WE left Tiflis in a snow-shroud, which had, after
three days' continual fall, frozen hard. We found
Poti in her spring dress, bright with violets and
cyclamen. Here we were detained two days
waiting for the steamer, and it may give some idea
of the place, when I say that the second day was
passed in hunting wild boar within a verst of our
hotel, which is the centre of the town; and so suc-
cessfully, that after plunging about in pools waist-
deep from dawn to mid-day, we carried back a fine
porker in triumph for our dinner. To help us in
the hunt we had some sixteen dogs and all the
able-bodied roughs of Poti, one of whom was armed

with the only specimen of an ancient blunderbuss which I ever saw in actual use.

The neighbourhood of Poti must at no very distant date have been one of the most favourite habitats of the red-deer in the whole world. The Mingrelian nobles were all staunch preservers of game, and it was not until Russian greed of territory had angered them, that they in revenge for their wrongs, real or fancied, at the hands of their somewhile ally, and to deprive that ally of his favourite recreation, taken with or without their consent, slew all the tall stags and graceful roebucks in their land, whenever they could find them, by foul means or fair. So it came to pass that within the last ten years speculators have bought cartloads of stags' horns in the neighbouring 'aouls' for a few roubles the load, and even to within the last three years it was still possible to find in out-of-the-way places ladders used to reach from the peasants' ground-floor to his loft, composed entirely of the branching glory of the forest king. These things are now of the past, for the Mingrel has discovered that stags' horns are marketable commodities: native middlemen have ferreted out every pair of antlers in the province, and established a regular trade in these and in boars' tusks, the majority of which articles were sent to France to be made up into the hundred and one knicknacks with which people adorn their libraries. Still the red-deer is by no means extinct even now; in proof of which a gentleman working at Poti, in the capacity of a civil engineer, told me that a few months before my arrival he had been invited to a large shooting party on the domains of one of the neighbouring princes, on which occasion not less than one hundred shots were fired at red-deer during the day, although, owing to bad shooting, very few were bagged.

From Poti we steamed to Sotcha, where I was entertained by the agent of a German gentleman, Mons. G., who stayed on the estate to protect it throughout the late war. The danger to the property, he informed me, was to be apprehended not from the Turks but from the Russians, more especially the Cossacks, against whose evil doings he inveighed very bitterly. According to my authority, wherever the Turks camped during the war, private property was respected, and crops only mulcted of as much as was necessary for the immediate use of the troops. On the contrary, wherever the Cossacks were, there too was wanton destruction. Their only excuse if remonstrated with was, 'if we don't do it the Turks will;' and their officers refused to interfere. At a small place in the immediate neighbourhood of Sotcha, for example—Adler or Pol Salian—the Turks never showed their noses, and yet the place is in ruins. No compensation was granted to any of the sufferers from Cossack wantonness after the war by the Government.

In Sotcha roses were in bloom when I arrived, as well as strawberries; and my host told me that a few days before my arrival he gathered half a dozen ripe strawberries in his garden, which had ripened out of doors, and this in the beginning of February. Up to the time of which I write there had been no frost at Sotcha. The chief produce of the neighbouring gardens are grapes, of which several varieties grow in great luxuriance on the slopes just above the town—if town you can call the few houses that surround the landing-place. But if the Governor has not been misinformed and is not too sanguine, Sotcha has a future, and may at no distant date develop into a second Yalta. A little table-land on the Poti side of the town has already been laid out in sites for villas, to be erected as summer residences for a number of old military officers and their families. Better still, all the sites are bought and paid for.

During the day which I lost at Sotcha waiting for horses—for of course I lost one, as every impatient traveller in this land of delays must be invariably content to do—I heard again of the fearless depredations of the lynx. During the night the dogs of Sotcha—an extremely large and influential body—were heard raising their voices in a manner altogether unusual even with them; and

on inspection it was found that one large beast of
half sheep-dog, half setter breed, had been killed on
his chain by a lynx in the very middle of the town,
and partially eaten where he lay.

It has been said that there is very little game
in the Caucasus, and it was partly to correct that
mistake that this book was written. To show
how far from true the assertion is, Mons. G., with
whom I was staying at Sotcha, told me that before
the Tscherkesses left the Caucasus it was their
custom to make an annual expedition to the main
chain of the mountains along the Black Sea coast,
between, say, Anapa and Sukhoum, to obtain game
to salt for winter use. On one of these expeditions
my informant accompanied seven Circassians, a
few years before their evacuation of their native
wilds; and, during a fortnight, of which at least
a week was spent in coming and going, the eight
guns made an enormous, though by no means
unusually large bag, of which one single item
was forty-two chamois. There were also bears,
ibex, moufflon, and red-deer among the slain ; and
though on this occasion they saw no aurochs,
Mons. G. assured me that he has seen some even
more recently than that.

On the second day at Sotcha, after a row with
the chief of the Cossacks, I managed to get horses
for my now formidable party, composed, with the
exception of myself and servant Ivan, of volun-

teers from the little town we were leaving. Some
of these volunteers, however, when they had it
finally explained to them that my little bell-tent
would really only hold two, and those two would
certainly be my friend Mr. Digby Lyall and myself, made up their minds wisely to stay behind;
so that in the end the party only consisted of Mr.
L. and myself, my servant Ivan, a guide Niko, an
Imeritine—whose services, had I only been lucky
enough to obtain them on my first visit, would
have been invaluable—Ivan Kotoff, a Russian
moujik or peasant proprietor, and a Cossack with
the horses named Kalivan; while at Golovinsky
I added my old ally Stepan to the motley crew.
This was by far the largest party I had ever had
with me in the Caucasus; and by their aid, and
the aid of Stepan's dogs, I expected to do great
things with the bears and boars of Golovinsky.

As soon, however, as we arrived at the place,
I found times had changed. Stepan had now
some work to do; and a gruff German telegraphist
was in possession of the hut in which I had formerly
taken shelter. However, by the help of his chief's
letter of introduction to all telegraphists at the
various Caucasian stations, and thanks to my bell-
tent, I was soon fairly comfortable; but the next
morning revealed a very sad state of things. Where
in early autumn the bears' tracks had been as thick
as leaves in Vallombrosa, there was not now a

single broad footprint to be seen. All the family of Bruin was either hybernating, or had moved off to winter quarters in some more favoured spot. Boars, however, were as plentiful as before, and the first day's sport gave me as fine a run with the dogs after a wounded sow as I ever wish to have. Crouching in a narrow track, which her kindred had worn by frequent use through the dense covert of blackberry bushes, I first saw her come pounding down upon me in an opposite direction to that in which I was going, and for a moment expected to be run over by her if no worse. She saw me luckily in time to pull up, and before she could turn I gave her a bullet from my smooth-bore, which lodged somewhere near her spine. After this the dogs got round her, and snapping and snapped at she carried the whole pack headlong down the precipitous wooded banks at a pace that rendered human pursuit all but hopeless. For all that, ten minutes break-neck work, with many a crashing fall and all too rapid slide, brought me to a point from which I caught a glimpse of the old black beast brushing through a thicket, with the dogs all over her; and hardly thinking of the risk the pack ran, I took a snap-shot, and, as good fortune would have it, turned her there and then into pork.

Leaving her suspended in slings of wild-vine tendrils beyond the reach of prowling wolves or marauding jackals, we kept along the edge of the cliffs until we came to the fairest site for a sportsman's grave that the mind of man could conceive. Here, on the very summit of a gracefully rounded hill-top, was some three acres of greensward, almost as fine and even as an English lawn. Up to its very edge rose the dense forest-trees, through and over the tops of which came glimpses of the opalescent sea far down beneath. Here, in the morning, the soft sea-breezes shook music out of the rustling leaves, and in the evening the lengthening shadows wove strange traceries on the grass. Here the wild cherry-blossoms whitened the sward in the spring-time, and in autumn the drooping vines hung heavy clusters over the dead chief's tomb, in recognition of the tender care his ancestors had bestowed upon the parent vine in days gone by. What a difference between this breezy sunlit hill-top and the terrible regions of brick and mortar in which, after their narrow life in town, the dead of London lie pent ! One could almost echo the sentiment of a veteran fox-hunter speaking of his favourite grass country as compared to another, ' It would be better to be buried here than live there.'

But in the midst of our day-dreaming a distraction of a sufficiently startling nature called us back to the present. In admiring the view we had strolled from our first post of observation into a thicket of already budding yellow azaleas, from which, as soon as we put foot in it, went forth the most extraordinary noises, while we found ourselves the centre of what appeared to be an enormous black shell in the very act of exploding. A second glance revealed the true nature of the black objects that rushed frantically about on every side of us. Unwittingly we had disturbed the rest, nay, stepped right into the middle of the resting-place of a big black sow and her litter of lively black imps. Such a hunt after sucking pigs as followed it would be difficult to describe. The dogs had been sent home; so all the work had to be done by ourselves; and from the small size of our prey and the thickness of the covert, it was almost as easy to catch as to shoot the succulent morsels. Most of them escaped us, but we got enough to satisfy us; so, tired and fairly content, we retraced our steps.

During the rest of our stay at Golovinsky we had excellent sport with the wild swine, killing one boar whose head an English naturalist declared to be the largest he had ever seen in England. But all boar and nothing else grew monotonous; and after a week of this sport we struck our tents and moved away to Yakorski, where, with hills and woods all round us, a clear purling brook by our side and the sea at our feet, we had good sport till the weather changed. The only drawback was that the tent which was meant to hold two had to hold four, and owing to accidents and oversights, our gear was of the most primitive nature. We had one enormous caldron, in which we boiled our pig-soup or our tea, as the case might be, and from this, when its contents had somewhat cooled, we, sitting in a circle round it, had to bale our dinner with spoons constructed by some genius from the bark of the willow. The process was rather slower, owing to the incommodious shape of the spoons, than lapping would have been, but it was the only way. Amongst the many things for which I have to be grateful to the Indo-European Company is the one teacup which did service for the four. This was neither more nor less than a broken insulator which some one found, with a piece of wood inserted in the hole at the bottom to prevent leakage.

Living in this primitive fashion, we passed several days, and enjoyed fair sport; the large supply of meat which we had hung on the beech-tree nearest our tent, attracting nightly bands of jackals, who formed a cordon round us and kept our dogs in a state of excitement the whole twenty-four hours. Apart from the sport, my man Niko was almost sufficient amusement in himself. A wilder, less tutored fellow could not be found, unless it were among savages; full of superstition and stories of the chase, he always kept us amused by the camp-fire. Amongst other things in which he firmly believed, as do most of his people, was the 'evil eye.' He had a gun with him, with which he told us that last year he had wounded eighteen wild boars in succession without bringing any to bag. Alarmed by this bad luck, he went to the 'wise man' of his village, and by him was reminded that the gun had been lent for some time to a friend. This friend possessed an 'evil eye.' The only remedy was to secure a gun belonging to his friend and spoil it, after which his own gun would return to its natural good behaviour. Niko took the 'wise man's' advice, and I presume paid him for it, surreptitiously spoilt his friend's gun, and from that time his shooting improved rapidly, until he was again the Niko that he used to be. Nothing I could say would convince him of the folly of his story; and so much did he believe in it that he even tried to persuade me, when one of my guns went wrong through an overcharge of powder, that the 'evil eye' had been at work on my own weapons also.

But after a few days the clouds began to gather blacker and blacker amongst the mountains, and the rainy season, which we believed we had left behind us by the Caspian, was upon us with a rush. On Friday, February 15, the rain swept over us in torrents; but, though the hills were all hidden, and the creaking and groaning of the trees almost frightened us, whilst the ground underfoot became a morass, the bell-tent kept us fairly dry. A temporary lull in the storm on Friday afternoon tempted us out of our shelter; and, though the woods were dripping and full of the music of a hundred newborn rivulets, we essayed a farewell hunt. The rain seemed to have aroused all the dormant energies of the porcine race; and, at one time, the noise they made amongst the fresh pools as we came on them unawares was rather suggestive of a morning in a cattle-market than one spent in a mountain forest.

It is difficult to believe how wild swine swarm in some parts of this coast, warrening the bushes with their runs, and covering every marshy place with their bathing-holes. Once we were fairly in the forest the heavens opened their sluices again, and before long our clothes were so sodden as to be almost too heavy to carry, our boots parting like wet blotting-paper; and when, weary and drenched, we got back to camp, we found the camp-fire submerged, and our bell-tent merely an awning over a pond about a foot deep. The men had neglected to entrench our position, and we were fairly washed out. Luckily my aversion to beetles had induced me to have my bed raised some two feet from the ground, and, cowering on this, we spent our time until Sunday morning. To make a fire was impossible. There was not a dry spot of earth within a square mile from our tent

on which to lay it ; and, even had we found a dry
spot, the blinding sheets of rain would have washed
it away as soon as laid. No fire meant very little
food, as none of us could eat raw wild swine's
flesh, and we had very little else.

In the night a lot of wolves descended from
the mountains, and, attracted by the smell of our
beech-tree larder, came right into the camp, their
weird howlings, as they answered one another from
point to point, sounding very eerie in the storm.
Worse than that, Niko, who had been hunted by
wolves only a year before, within a mile or two of
this spot, got extremely nervous, and, worse still,
made the other men so. This, they said, was the
month in which wolves were most to be dreaded ;
and, in a pack, with no fire to scare them, there
was no certainty that they might not invade our
tent during the night-watches.

To get back to the telegraphist's hut was our
first idea ; though, remembering its fragile nature,
I had my doubts whether there was much better
accommodation there than with us. This, however, was rendered impossible. During the night
the mountain streams had risen, and a man who had
attempted to cross them in the evening was all but
drowned before he could get back to shore. At
the outset of the storm our Cossack, with the
horses, had deserted and left us to our fate, so that
there was nothing for it but to sit perched like

owls on our little platform in the bell-tent, and smoke away the time until the rain should cease. My wretched men had no change of garments, so that for the two days they had to sit and sleep in their sodden clothes, and nothing but constant application to their beloved vodka-bottle could have saved the poor devils from fever. During that last night the rage of the storm increased, and, though our tent was in a wonderfully sheltered place, it rocked and tugged at its moorings in an alarming manner, whilst at last it ceased to be waterproof, and our roof resembled nothing so much as the rose of an immense watering-pot. I think on Saturday night I must have gone to sleep in spite of the streams from above and the howling wolves outside, for in the morning I was quite startled by a gleam of sunshine, and, roused, I fancy, by the cessation of that perpetual pattering of rain-drops which had lulled me to sleep. As I moved my stiff limbs my clothes cracked with the frost that had followed the rain, and our tent itself was hard frozen, while outside the sun was shining through a heavy snow-storm going on in the second range of mountains behind and giving but a very cheerless light to the miserable scene around. Still, it was sunshine, and as such stirred us to fresh endeavour, as nothing but sunshine can stir a human being. By dint of drainage and a few sticks we had kept moderately dry, we managed to light a fire, although, except for the few feet drained for the fire-place, there was still no dry spot for the sole of a man's foot. But the crushing blow was to come. The rain had done worse than wet us— it had washed down the meat from our larder. The watchful wolves had been rewarded for their patience, and we were left breakfastless !

Very miserable wretches must we have appeared when rescue came in the form of our returning Cossack, late that afternoon, with some strong horses to carry us safely through the rapidly-subsiding torrents ; and a bare-legged ride on bare-backed Cossack horses, through streams which wetted, and nipping north-easters that froze, our half-starved bodies, was no pleasant finale to our adventure. It was hardly to be wondered at that when we did get to shelter my men told me they had had enough sport for some time to come, and meant to return to Dnapsé as soon as possible. I myself was no longer as keen as I had been, and it was agreed that we should gradually make our way to Dnapsé, stopping for one last hunt, if only to supply us with food, at the ruins of Heiman's Datch.

On February 19 we bade adieu to Golovinsky for the last time, and since then its bay of wooded hills, with the three tall blasted trees marking the spot where my first bear fell, has been only a memory to tempt me back. I should like to see it once more, with its glorious cone-shaped tulip-tree in full blossom ; its jungles of rose-bushes, whose enormous berries testified to the size of its perished blooms, in the perfect beauty of summer ; its great forests of chestnut decked with spires of flowers ; and its long stretches of rhododendron and azalea in their summer dress. It must indeed be lovely then ; and if the fever were only a possible and not an absolutely certain consequence of the enjoyment of its wonderful beauty, the pleasure would be worth the risk.

But the wintry scene around us now was very different. Above, the ragged clouds hung black and threatening. Out at sea, the waves were for some distance yellow with the influx of turbid mountain torrents. Trees were hanging their heavy dripping heads, broken and mutilated by the three days' storm. The sea, too, had been at wild work during the night ; and when the Black Sea does wake to mischief it is a demon in its gusty rage. The shore was strewn everywhere with driftwood, and over the carcass of an unhappy stranded porpoise eagles were poising and soaring. Two of my little party had a touch of the fever, and my own throat was sore and swollen, so that the tonsils seemed almost to choke me if I made any unwonted exertion. It was evidently time to get home. At Heiman's Datch a forest fire had recently raged, and no game could be obtained for the larder, so that we were almost without provisions.

Taking all these things into consideration, we determined next morning to go straight on to Duapsè, and give up any further hope of shooting. Thus resolving, we built up a fire of drift-wood under the old flooring, and lying round it dreamed of home, dry clothes, and good dinners. Alas! that good resolutions should always be formed too late. When morning came, like a nightmare came upon us that creaking and groaning of the trees we had learned to know so well; that rush and babble of waters that meant imprisonment for a starved-out garrison. The tiny rill below the ruin, which the day before had been nowhere ankle-deep, was now boiling and foaming with a rage perfectly ludicrous in such a baby river, and with a force that made it almost unfordable. Not a moment was to be lost, and in spite of the pitiless storm we determined to push on foot along the shore to the next Cossack station for horses before we were hopelessly hemmed in by the mountain-streams.

It was already doubtful if we were not too late; so leaving Ivan the Pole at the ruin to guard our effects, my young friend L., Ivan Kotoff, and myself, shouldered our small kits and trudged away breakfastless over the wet shingle. It was heavy going over the yielding beach, laden as we were with bourkas and what not in that blinding rain, and I was thankful when I saw my friend L.. safely at the end of it. Young as he was, I am bound to say he made less trouble of it than our burly Russian fisherman, whose red beard kept wagging the whole time, and whose complaints were the harshest sound even in that stormy scene.

At Selenik's Datch we found the stream that there empties itself into the sea swollen beyond recognition, and divided into two, forming two small cataracts, which hurtled along the big boulders in a way that was a marvel to those who had only seen it in its days of restful calm. Kotoff at once pronounced it unfordable, and, being our guide, the others unluckily would not listen to my arguments, though at considerable risk I backed them by fording the first stream, which was more than waist deep, by myself. Naturally, though I was several times all but washed off my feet, and to lose my footing would in all probability have been to lose my life, it would have been simple enough to have crossed had we all linked ourselves one with the other, and together breasted the torrent. But the Russians were white-livered, and would not come, so that I had to wade back again ; and wet through, disgusted and hungry, with my throat as I knew in a dangerous state, I felt very like throwing up the sponge.

After a weary tramp through the long wet

covert, Kotoff found us a dismantled cowshed on the Selenik property. Here we kindled a poor fire, and tried in vain to dry the clothes which the rain, driven through the broken roof, soaked as fast as we dried them.

Our only supplies were three or four handsful of rice, and we had a two days' appetite to appease. Hunting about in the cowshed, we found an old paint-pot, and having cleansed it by burning, patched its leaks with clay, and boiled in it the rice and the few bunches of sorrel which we found growing near, we made our first meal since noon of the preceding day. What with the unpleasant taste which the pot possessed and imparted to what was put in it, together with the naturally disagreeable flavour of the coarse sorrel, it was all we could do to eat the mess when made, in spite of hunger, and the root of horse-radish which we boiled with our greens to give them a flavour. After this we brewed our last pinch of tea in the same pot, and immediately regretted the waste, as the horse-radish flavour so far predominated that the addition of tea to the water was useless.

In all our distress we had one consolation. I had by great good luck saved a box of really first-rate cigars which I picked up in Tiflis ; and with these to comfort us, young L. and myself huddled together in a corner where there was more wall and fewer crannies than elsewhere, and prepared to make a night of it, while the men lay huddled in their bourkas. Nothing save the voices of the storm and the spluttering of the fire, which the rain soon extinguished, broke the sullen stillness of the night.

It was not a cheerful end to my shooting expedition ; and again the truth of the Russian proverb, which the men sometimes muttered, appeared a possibility, ' the chase is worse than slavery.'

During the night one of the men sang us some wild Cossack songs, one of which I had often heard the women crooning parts of before. Whether it was that the wild forms and scenes that were round me lent them a beauty the words do not really possess, or whether there is in fact some charm in this cradle-song of a warlike race, in some things not unlike our borderers of two centuries ago, it seemed at the time very impressive. I will therefore try to help my readers to judge for themselves, from a translation of Poushkin's verses, which, if it does not convey all the spirit of the original, is at least a close transcript of the words and metre.

COSSACK CRADLE-SONG.

Sleep, my darling boy, serenely,
  Bai-oosh kie-baiou.
While the still moon, calm and queenly,
  Gleams thy cradle through.
I will rise and tell thee legends,
  Chaunting rhymes thereto ;
Ah, thine heavy eyes are closing,
  Bai-oosh-kie-baiou.

'Neath the rocks grim waves are sweeping—
  O'er them glides the Turk ;
Comes the vengeful Tscherkess creeping,
  Whets an hungry dirk.
Peace ! thy father, battle-hardened,
  Keeps watch keen and true.
Sleep then, darling, sleep securely,
  Bai-oosh-kie-baiou.

Know thou, too, that days are nearing,
  Loud with war's alarms.
Thou shalt spring to horse unfearing,
  Bearing warrior's arms.
I'll weave charms upon thy saddle
  With a silken clue :
Sleep, my baby, sleep, my heart's blood,
  Bai-oosh-kie-baiou.

Cossack to the core I read thee,
  Hero-like thou'lt stand :
To the field myself I'll lead thee—
  Child ! dost press my hand ?
Ah, the bitter tears in secret,
  Tender mothers rue ;
Sleep, my angel, stilly, sweetly,
  Bai-oosh-kie-baiou.

Ah, the bitter grief, the sorrow,
  Comfortless to wait !
Each morn praying for the morrow,
  All night guess thy fate.
I shall dream thy days are wasted,
  Pining fond and true—
Sleep—cares all as yet untasted—
  Bai-oosh-kie-baiou.

Round thy neck, my boy, I'll fasten,
  Ere thy path be trod,
Relics rare thy life to chasten,
  And to lead to God.

> Tender heart, grow strong for peril,
>   Be to mem'ry true !
> Now, sleep on—wild days are coming
>   Bai-oosh-kie-baiou !

The words ' bai-oosh-kie-baiou ' are merely the refrain of the song, and as untranslatable as our ' lullaby,' so that I have left them in the original.

From scraps of songs which I have from time to time heard crooned in the Crimea and elsewhere, I should almost imagine that Poushkin's words here translated are only a remodelled and completed form of some popular cradle-song in use in his time among the Cossacks.

I am sadly afraid the Cossacks are no longer the romantic personages they were when the poet wrote of them. ' Richard's occupation's gone ' may be said of them. There is no one left for them to fight, and their existence as Cossacks would lack an object were it not for their duties as postmen. They are as rough as ever, but not, I should say, as ready with their weapons. Their love of cattle-lifting can no longer be legitimately gratified, and I fear I have cause to add that it has degenerated to the level of petty pilfering.

Singing and smoking we passed the night, trying in vain to still the voices of our unappeased appetites with the dull narcotic which refused to numb our pain. The rain had partially ceased at dawn, and with that wonderful rapidity which characterises their fall as well as their rise, the mountain torrents, which had been our gaolers the night before, had now sunk to such a degree that arm in arm we just managed to struggle through.

Once free from our prison, with the prospect of breakfast and horses at the next plantation, even Ivan pulled himself together, and before midday we were all lying rolled up in borrowed rugs, while our clothes were dried, and our appetites appeased by a meal of black bread. This was all we could get, for, like ourselves, Koylor's Datch had been in a state of siege, and if the rain continued was likely to remain so.

These Russian plantations in the Caucasus are terribly unremunerative I am told, in spite of the richness of the soil. I think the reason is chiefly that they are very much neglected by their owners, no capital being expended on them; in addition to which there is no market for their produce within reach, and no reasonable roads anywhere. Moreover, fever demoralises the workmen, and the wild swine devastate the crops.

Whilst refreshing ourselves at Koylor's Datch, we sent for horses, intending to make all speed for Duapsé; and to our great joy the weather cleared a little in the afternoon, so that when the horses and the Cossack guide arrived we were able to swing ourselves into dry saddles and proceed forthwith.

Between our starting point that afternoon and

the Cossack station, at which we hoped to pass the night, a mountain stream larger than most of its fellows emptied itself into the sea, and it was of this stream that we were most afraid. The Cossack who brought the horses reported it extremely high, but in one place still fordable, so that it was with eyes fixed anxiously on the sky that we hurried on. My young friend L. had become so far knocked up that he thought it wiser to stay at Koylor's Datch, from whence I was glad to hear that he eventually got safe back to Sotcha, and thence to Tiflis.

For the first verst or so of the sixteen we had to travel before nightfall, the weather kept clear and bright, after which it grew suddenly murky and overcast. The sea, muddy and discoloured near the shore by the unwonted access of turbid fresh water, spread itself out in broad streaks of vivid green and Oxford blue in the distance. The waves rose apace, and came washing right under our horses' feet till they touched the cliff that walled us in beyond. Thunder began to mutter, and the whole under-sky seemed to grow into waving plumes of dark purple smoke. Then the rain came again, with sheet lightning, near thunder, and little drifts of snow, which seemed strangely out of place with the vivid lightning. By this time the cold had grown so intense that I was glad to fasten my rapidly stiffening bourka round my neck and bury myself in its voluminous folds. Suddenly the snow and the thunder ceased, and for ten minutes there was a respite, the sky growing more wild and eerie every moment. What with the fury of sky and sea, the horses became so panic-stricken as to be almost beyond our control. Then the sun, after being long hidden, showed himself low down on the waves—for it was already five o'clock, and owing to the storm nearly as dark as night. In shining out now he only added to the horrors of the scene the most ghastly purple face ever sun put on. And no wonder, for he was peering through a hailstorm, which soon reached us, whitening the waves with its volleys of ice-bullets as it advanced.

Never before or since have I seen such a hail-storm. The stones gave us positive pain as they struck our faces and hands, and were as large on the average as the bullets of my 'express.' Meanwhile the thunderstorm had commenced anew, and, while the lightning flashed with extreme brilliancy so near us as to be dangerous, the voice of the thunder almost drowned all other sounds. Alas! in the intervals between the thunderclaps we now began to hear another voice—the voice of gurgling, fighting waters, and of the heavy stones and tree-trunks whirled along by them in their fierce career seaward.

When at last the stream came in sight, its appearance was no more inviting than its voice; but from its great breadth for a mountain stream, I judged it was not so deep as its turbid appearance led one to believe. Deep or shallow, it had to be crossed. The Cossack said he knew the ford, and offered to lead the way; and, after all, its wild foamings were little worse than the hailstorm that raged around. So, when he plunged in, leading the packhorse behind him, I followed close on his heels, entirely trusting to his local knowledge for a safe passage. Luckily for him, the Cossack was only a featherweight, while the horse he bestrode was one of the largest and most powerful I had seen during my travels: so that, though the packhorse with his burden was immediately upset and washed away, the man, clinging to his horse, which made a gallant swim for it, got safe to shore a long way down stream. I was less lucky than the Cossack, whose fate I had not seen; for, while half blinded by a vivid flash of lightning, my wretched little screw toppled over into the deep water, and was immediately carried after its comrade, leaving me to swim for my life in a stream like a mill-race, with my long wet bourka round my neck, hampering my limbs and drowning me with its heavy folds, and a ten-pound 'express' rifle on my shoulders. It was well for me then that swimming had been one of my favourite forms of athletic exercise in my boyhood, or I should never have managed to extricate my hands from the bourka and make a fight of it with the stream.

Something, a stone or some drift-wood I suppose, gave me a severe blow on the kneecap in crossing, but this I only discovered subsequently, and when at last I struggled somewhere safe to shore amid the shouts of my men, I think, as I stood spent and dripping in the hailstorm after my icy bath, I fully realised the pleasures of travelling in the Caucasus in the rainy season.

To go for the Cossack who had led me into the scrape by his ignorance of the ford, to deprive him of his horse, and, having seen my men cross by the true shallow higher up, to gallop madly for the Cossack station, were my first acts on recovering myself a little; and between my bath and the station I never drew bridle until I tumbled off breathless at the door, whence, regardless of questions, I made my way to the room where a dozen Cossacks lay loafing in every stage of dirt and idleness. Casting all squeamish scruples to the winds, I stripped off my icy clothes where I stood, borrowed a shirt from one dirty rascal and an unutterable sheepskin from another, got a wandering telegraphist, who happened to be at the station, to give me about half a pint of neat spirit and as much hot tea as I could drink, and turned in with my back against the stove, trusting to the heat within and without to restore my circulation— which the ride had failed to do—and so save me from the consequences of my immersion.

In the course of the evening my men arrived, having saved most of the baggage, which had got loose from the unfortunate packhorse, and when I woke in the morning I found myself quite a hero for my swim, and, better than that, a hero with some moderately clean dry clothes to get into. In the night, nevertheless, the gallant Cossacks' chivalry and respect had not prevented their stealing my watch and what remained of my sodden cigars. Having dried these in the oven, they had converted them into fine-cut tobacco, which, when I woke, had provided every loafer amongst them with a little store of cigarettes. But my throat warned me that it was no time to make a trouble of trifles, and that it was imperatively necessary to get back to Duapsè at once, catch the boat thence on the morrow, and get to Kertch in time for medical advice if I needed it.

In the night the sea had come up to the foot of the cliffs, thus barring the usual road to Duapsè, and obliging us to ride some forty versts, by precipitous and rugged bridle-roads, over the cliffs, during which ride the horses' vile pace, the infernal machine called a Tartar saddle, and the ruggedness of the roads combined to inflict on my already aching frame unspeakable tortures. Worse than all, when the last jolt had been suffered, and the last writhing submitted to in fording the stream that separated us from Duapsè, we found that, owing to the bad state of the weather, the Odessa steamer would not touch there for a week, so that for seven days we might kick our heels and be miserable in that charming watering-place.

That week was too dark an era in my travels to say much about it. I prefer, if possible, to remember the Caucasus without Dnapsé. Despondency took hold of my faithful Ivan, as soon as he had got his pay: like a true Russian, he took to drink, and all through my illness left me to my fate, in a drunken peasant's cottage, while he wept and sang by turns in the only 'duchan' in the place. Day by day my throat became worse. The telegraphists were kind to me; but neither they nor the doctor (veterinary, I believe he was) knew what was the matter with me; and every night the steam that rose from the damp mud floor of my room only added to my illness.

Once the Governor came to see me; and as he, too, was a doctor, gave me some advice; but I doubt whether his prescriptions, had he left any, could have been made up in his government. However, he brightened half an hour for me with his chat, and that, doubtless, did as much good as any medicine would have done. He told me of some wolves which had gone mad, and were keeping a couple of villages in a state of panic by their attacks, having already bitten a man and several cattle, all of which had since died from hydrophobia. This madness of the wolves is not by any means unfrequent, I was told, and, strangely enough, generally takes place during the coldest part of the year. I had intended to have gone to the villages in the morning to see what I could do for the peasants with my 'express,' but was unluckily tempted into a wrestling match with a celebrated native wrestler; and the exertion of winning one fall out of three against him was the last straw that broke the camel-like back of my constitution. The fellow was a capital wrestler and extremely strong; he had acquired some of his best throws, oddly enough, in England; so that, though he threw me handsomely twice, I could console myself with the reflection that he had learnt to do it in my own country.

That night there was a wedding in Duapsé, and every one naturally got drunk; and whilst I was tossing in high fever on my bed a score of drunken moujiks in enormous boots were dancing and shouting in the next room. Two nights this lasted; at the end of the second, when I was very nearly beyond any further enduring power, Providence willed it that the steamer should arrive; and as the doctor insisted that I had nothing more than a bad sore-throat the matter with me, I was taken on board and landed at Kertch, in a critical stage of a violent attack of diphtheria.

So ended my shooting adventures in the Caucasus, and I may well be thankful that in the person of M. Bulberg, of the Russian telegraph service, I found a kind friend and attentive nurse, as I did also in my old friend the English Consul. After a fortnight's careful nursing at M. Bulberg's rooms by a clever German doctor—whose name I am ungrateful enough to have forgotten, though I am not the less grateful for his services—I tided over my illness. As soon as I was pronounced in a safe state to travel, both as regarded myself and others, I started for England, still wearing some of the rough gear in which I had travelled, and arrived at the station of the town in which I dwelt such a deteriorated specimen of the English race, that what with my rags and my beard, the first people I met on alighting—who were the ladies of my own family—cut me dead, and for quite a couple of minutes refused to recognise me.

THE END.

LONDON : PRINTED BY
SPOTTISWOODE AND CO., NEW-STREET SQUARE
AND PARLIAMENT STREET

STANDARD WORKS

STANDARD WORKS